the Larder

THE GUIDE TO SCOTLAND'S FOOD & DRINK

THE LIST GUIDES SCOTLAND

EDITED BY DONALD REID

the Larder

THE GUIDE TO SCOTLAND'S FOOD & DRINK

First published in Great Britain in 2009 by The List Limited, 14 High Street, Edinburgh EH1 1TE

Copyright © 2009 The List Ltd.

A CIP catalogue record for this book is available from the British Library.

ISBN 978 0 9557513 1 8

Printed by Acorn Web Offset Ltd, Normanton, West Yorkshire

Editor Donald Reid

Assistant Editor Claire Ritchie

Contributors & Researchers Josie Butchart, Mary Contini, Gordon Davidson, Catharina Day, Darren Deakin, Anna Docherty, Jo Ewart Mackenzie, Nicki Holmyard, Malcolm MacGarvin, Anna Millar, Nell Nelson, Benjamin Newall, Frank Park, David Pollock, Carine Seitz, Barry Shelby, Mike Small, Christopher Trotter, Jo Whittingham, Jane Wright

Production Manager Simon Armin

Art Director Krista Robertson

Senior Designer Lucy Munro

Sales & Sponsorship Brigid Kennedy, Sheri Friers, Jenny Dryden, Juliet Tweedie, Adam Coulson, Andrea Krudde, Brendan Miles

Digital Simon Dessain, Andy Carmichael, Bruce Combe, Iain McCusker

Accounts Georgette Renwick, Tasmin Campbell

Publisher Robin Hodge

Project Director SFQC/SOPA Peter Brown (www.sfqc.co.uk)

Project Manager SFQC/SOPA Owen Freeman

With thanks to
Martha Bryce at VisitScotland, Margaret Stewart and Laurent Vernet at QMS, Iain and Karen Mellis, Andrea Pearson of Fan Hitter PR, Martin Wishart, John Sinclair at Craigies, Bruce Bennet at Pillars of Hercules, Jim Cowie, Frank Park, Audrey Cassels and David Forsyth of Benchmark PR, Tim Bailey at SFQC

Cover image Getty Images

contents

foreword

SOPA is the largest organic certifier in Scotland and is passionate about thoughtfully produced, tasty food and drink. We are delighted to be sponsoring the partnership between *The List* and SFQC, making *The Larder* possible. *The List* is a well known, informed, independent voice of people with a real interest in Scottish food culture while SFQC is a respected food and drink certification business, deeply involved in checking and validating claims made by Scottish farms and food companies.

We care passionately about the way that food is produced in Scotland and believe it is time to provide more, properly researched, interesting information about Scottish food and drink to help inform consumer decision making. Research indicates in these challenging times consumers are increasingly buying direct from local food producers. Why is that? Shoppers believe they can get real value for money by buying direct – and at the same time help local farmers produce traceable food with a low carbon footprint. Many farmers who sell locally tend to be smaller, less intensive businesses and they have intimate knowledge about the products they sell. Whether it be the full history of the animal that will be your Sunday roast or the list of all the ingredients in their special recipe – local producers know all about their produce and are more than happy to tell you all about it! Buying local will spice up the way you eat Scottish food.

The Larder is for people who enjoy thinking and talking about food as well as buying and eating it, which is probably most of us, be we shoppers, chefs, locals or visitors. We hope you enjoy *The Larder* but, more importantly, enjoy great Scottish food and drink.

John Hamilton
SOPA Chairman

introduction

The simple fact that we are what we eat has never been more relevant. The effects of our diet on our physical and emotional well-being are increasingly highlighted by medical and social science. The implications for our future of the fragility of a natural environment we have so long taken for granted are now a major political issue. The recent realisation that once seemingly impregnable economic structures can suddenly collapse has raised questions over the viability of the supply chain. These many factors have all combined in a growing awareness of the need for sustainable systems of sourcing and producing nutritious food.

Alongside these developments, there is stronger recognition that the way we eat and drink is at the heart of our culture. How food is produced and prepared forms an integral part of the history and heritage of a people. Eating together is fundamental to family and social life.

The Larder aims to be something that has not been possible until recently: a wide-ranging, independent and detailed guide to Scottish food and drink published both in print and online. Our starting point was not the many excellent, high-profile restaurants, nor the well-known stories of whisky and prime beef – although these are both featured. Instead we go back to the sources of our produce, tracing the links up the food chain – from the oats and grains used to bake bread to the milk that makes cheese and the apples that grow in our back gardens.

The Larder is a celebration of Scottish food and drink – where it comes from, how it is grown, harvested, prepared and served. But this is just part of the picture. We also focus on where and how to find it: in markets, delicatessens, shops and restaurants across the land. That we found so much to cover, particularly in the realm of small, local and artisan food producers, is clear evidence of the vitality of Scottish food today. The only problem has been one of space, as we know there are many more excellent foods, interesting stories, engaging characters, specialist retailers and places to eat than there has been space to include.

Because there is so much more out there, and because it is an ever-changing picture, we are accompanying this printed edition with a website (www.thelarder.net) which will include an even bigger and broader range of producers, wholesalers, distributors and retailers of food in Scotland. These listings are fully searchable both by produce and geographical location to provide useful details and inspiration about the food and drink scene in Scotland.

Here at *The List* we are very grateful to SOPA for helping us to realise a project that had been imagined for many years. We would also like to thank the many organisations, businesses and people who have backed the idea in different ways. Everyone involved has supported the publication because they too believe in the quality of Scottish food – and that more people should have the chance to share it.

What's in The Larder?

There's a whole feast of delights packed into the next 150 pages. Here are a few of the highlights.

Bonny Bread

The best of Scotland's bakers can be found alongside our guides to oats and barley, toffee and tablet, famous regional cakes and some remote chocolatiers. *See page 49.*

Choice Cheese

The Iain Mellis team pick out their top ten Scottish cheeses. *See page 62.*

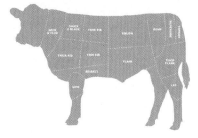

Cuts of Beef

Master butcher Jonathan Honeyman helps sort out a rib from a rump. *See page 34.*

Fife Fare

Mike Small spends a year eating local food on the Fife Diet. *See page 12.*

Smoking Allowed

Sort out your haddies from your smokies with the help of Martin Wishart and dive into the stories behind some of Scotland's most interesting fish and shellfish. *See page 78.*

Where to Buy

Each chapter of The Larder contains useful lists of the best places around Scotland to get hold of local produce. *See page 18.*

Where to Eat

We include a selection of over 100 places to eat around the country. *See page 126.*

Grubbing Around

From salads grown from seaweed in Arran to the fertile school yards of Inverness, we dig out some of the best of our home-grown fruit and veg. *See page 91.*

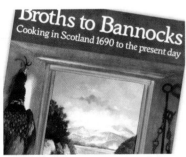

Books by Cooks

Chef Christopher Trotter picks out his top ten Scottish food books. *See page 144.*

Farming Today

We round up of all Scotland's farmers' markets in a handy table. *See page 150.*

School Meals

Our taste trail leads to all of Scotland's main cook schools. *See page 142.*

Liquidity

The Larder is a guide to drink as well as food, so Scotland's range of liquid assets, from spring water to old whisky, features inside. *See page 109.*

Mr Mussel

Winklepickers at the ready for our handy guide to cooking shellfish. *See page 82.*

THE FOOD OF SCOTLAND

Why food from Scotland means something

Is eating Scottish food a bit like supporting the national football team – done out of patriotic instinct rather than an appreciation of quality? Donald Reid opens up *The Larder* with the search for a Scottish food culture.

Food is one of those dualities that the Scots do so well. We're dour Presbyterians but also spirited Gaels, we helped explore darkest Africa but seem to prefer midge-infested glens, we've produced great practical engineers and logical philosophers yet get misty-eyed about half-baked schemes from the Jacobite Uprising to Argentina '78. The larder of Scotland, stocked full of grass-fed Aberdeen Angus, succulent lobster, rich game and golden whisky, if not quite

without equal (as some hyperbole would have it), is genuinely admired around the culinary world. The diet of Scotland – what we actually eat as a nation, on the other hand, tends to draw furrowed brows and a bit of a free-for-all on the subject of deep-fried Mars bars.

Battered confectionary doesn't, in truth, figure in the daily diet of many Scots but then neither do locally grown apples or mutton chops – both of which would cost less. There's a danger that

we regard our larder as we do historic castles and wearing the kilt: something to be vaguely proud of but hardly the concern of day-to-day life. To any other generation in the history of mankind such a disconnection between the food-providing fields and seas around us and the food on our tables wouldn't just be counter-intuitive but downright perverse. However, the modern ways of trade, food distribution and shopping have allowed the production of food and the eating of it to drift far apart.

Where this disconnection exists, it's hard to make a case for a distinct, vibrant or even coherent food culture.

Scotland isn't the only place where this is happening but we have a fairly acute case. Yet all those who eat here needn't abandon hope. For a start, the quality is not mythical but out there and available – Michelin-starred chefs in Paris and surprised but impressed visitors will vouch for the world-class standards it can reach. Secondly, there are not dozens or hundreds, but many thousands of farmers and fishermen, gardeners, cooks, bakers and shopkeepers around Scotland who aspire to work with real food and manage to make a living doing so. Thirdly, the promise of locally sourced food must strike an instinctive chord with us somewhere, for why else would supermarkets plaster Saltires on their packaging or restaurants, cafés and even pubs be at such pains to highlight their local food credentials – even if their claims can be a little sketchy? Local food does mean something to most of us.

When the growing and eating of food draws closer together, the possibility of a discernible food culture appears. Make no mistake, Scotland is a wonderful place to grow and source certain types of food. Grass grows green and lush in our damp, warm summers, not just in fenced fields but all over moorland and hills, providing ample fine grazing for livestock and game. Cold, remote and relatively unpolluted waters are excellent for fish and shellfish. The long summer days allow berries to ripen slowly but surely to full sweetness. Barley grows better than wheat and once whisky is made from it, the climate is temperate enough for it to remain in barrels for ten years without evaporating away to nothing.

Some of these natural advantages

have shaped our diet over centuries – we've eaten game and smoked fish and oats for long enough. Such traditions offer a depth of heritage to the Scottish food culture, even if a number of other elements in the celebrated larder – langoustine, for example, or bottled water, or lamb (as opposed to mutton) – have limited historic resonance. That doesn't mean that the relatively new innovations, responding to changing markets, tastes and technology, don't have a place in the Scottish food culture. If something grows well here, or is being produced with skill and imagination, whether it be asparagus, salad leaves, cheese or cured meat, we can and should value them. These products may not be unique to Scotland, but brought to market at sufficiently high standard (as many are), they begin to establish a distinctiveness endowed by where and how they are made. Perhaps the most encouraging thing about the current Scottish food culture is that it is still discovering itself – it is being defined as we speak, rather than being shackled to a comparatively limited culinary past.

Scotland has been able to show that quality helps establish identity. We can

do it with whisky – why not food as well? Identity also encourages quality. When something is good, a greater analysis takes place of the factors that make it good. Regionality – the distinctiveness small climatic or cultural differences can make – is appreciated more acutely. In the context of quality, the importance of history and heritage becomes apparent, whether it's the thriftiness that made haggis popular or the hospitality that honed so many baking skills. When food becomes attached to a place, greater value seems to accrue to both the product and the place. When we eat 'food with a view', both the food and the views – spectacular enough in Scotland already – are enhanced.

Crucially, by far the most important components of Scotland's developing food culture are small-scale, local and artisan food producers. They are not given attention out of quaintness or charity. It is the small, local and artisan food producers who provide the diversity which creates richness, the knowledge and dedication which establishes quality, the humanity which reinforces character and the drive which underwrites innovation and progress. Large systems of food production, manufacturing, distribution and retailing may still dominate what we buy and eat, but such systems cannot create or nurture a food culture.

The equation is completed by a simple truth. The primary market for most small producers in Scotland is a local one; in other words, they are dependent on us eating their food. We have to know where to find it and be prepared to buy it, but awareness and appreciation tend to go hand in hand. This interdependence means that local food is a reality in Scotland, and it lies right at the heart of the Scottish food culture.

Food fit for a kingdom

Is it really possible to live off food from our own fields, farmyards and harbours? Mike Small, pioneer of the Fife Diet, reflects on his year of eating local food.

I n the mad world we live in, an idea such as eating food from near where you come from is groundbreaking and extraordinary. Bizarrely, it was regarded as a big news story. I was one of hundreds of people who chose to eat this way for a year and have decided to continue doing so, mostly out of a real sense that climate change and peak oil were converging along with all of the other multiple dysfunctionalities of our food system. Many of us feel that eating locally is a change that will be coming anyway. As the saying goes: 'If you want things to stay the way they are, things will have to change.'

With the Fife Diet, the idea was never to try and eat 100 per cent regionally. That would be very hard

and I'm not quite sure what it would represent. The idea was to get to know your food region (what the French call the *terroir*) to celebrate what already grows and is reared and landed there, and explore what your place *could* produce.

So, what did we eat and what did we miss?

We ate seasonally and we ate what could be easily produced here without great artificial heating and for the most part without pesticides. At the end of the year we polled participants for a summary of their year. Sam from Rosyth ate 'potatoes, carrots, onions, pork, beef, venison, beans, lettuce, spinach, tomatoes, pumpkin, ice cream, butter, oats'. Wendy from Dunshelt wrote: 'We found meat the easiest with Fletcher's venison,

Jamesfield beef and pork from a small holding near Kinghorn, also pheasant and rabbit when available. Vegetables from Bellfield supplemented by the Pillars [of Hercules] and what we grew ourselves. Fruit locally when in season and often foraged. Eggs from our own chickens.' Another participant wrote of eating: 'Meat: beef, buffalo, chicken, lamb, pork, venison from the farmers' market. Fish: various fresh from Inverkeithing, and St Monans kippers. Veg from the veg box. Fruit from the farmers' market. Also eggs, honey, cheese.'

Inevitably it was traditional dishes we cooked: pies, soups, casseroles, stews.

So it's a diet that is made up of unprocessed foods – with few exceptions. We ate probably double

the recommended five a day of fruit and veg, though admittedly fruit of a more limited range than the standard supermarket shopper has available. We ate a low (but high quality) meat diet, sourced from farms we knew well and trusted.

What did we miss? The ease of ripping open the pizza and ten minutes later chowing down on some rubbery hydrogenated tomato product was something we yearned for. But the 'convenience' of food is predicated on a lifestyle lashed to the job and the hectic whirlwind of the treadmill. Fast foods can be replaced: omelettes and frittata appeared instead of pizza. We allowed ourselves coffee and tea and sugar and debated about vegetable oils. It was easy enough to source the vast bulk of our food from the region of Fife. Beer from Clackmannanshire and fruit wine from Perthshire

constituted welcome 'contraband' goods.

Fife is blessed, but not super-blessed. Lots of people I've spoken to said a variation on 'Of course you can do this in Fife but you couldn't do this where I live'. It's a bit of a cop-out. Of course Argyll and the Highlands and the North-East has fishing that Fife would be jealous of. Many cities have better bakeries than we could dream of and surrounding regions that could easily provide wheat. Ayrshire boasts better dairy produce than Fife and Perthshire has some of the best soft fruit in Europe.

We've conned ourselves that we're the poor man of Europe when we have a fantastic range of food here in Scotland. We've told (and taken) too many gags about deep-fried Mars bars, and it's probably time we owned up to some of the food we have around. It's funny that some of the best of it gets exported (seafood particularly) directly to our Celtic neighbours in France, Spain and Portugal.

We just need to learn our regions and what they can produce, re-learn how to cook and grow together, how to pickle and bottle, then how to exchange the things we long for, but can't grow here – for some of our own delicacies. The truth is we can't achieve a low or zero carbon society by transporting food about the world as if nature, the changing seasons, or 'place' doesn't exist at all.

The idea is not self-sufficiency, but sufficiency. Living within limits is liberating. Try it.

Below: tempting local food from the Wee Restaurant in North Queensferry, Fife

> LOCAL RESOURCES

Inspired by local eating projects such as Vancouver's 100-mile diet, Mike and Karen Small initiated the Fife Diet in 2007. By the end of their first year in November 2008, over 600 people were involved in the project. These are some of the local food outlets Mike Small turned to (and has stayed with) while eating his Fife Diet:

'Some of the best suppliers of fresh food in Fife include **Pillars of Hercules** (organic veg box delivery), **Puddledub Pork at Auchtertool**, **Ardross Farm Shop** (by Elie) and, not forgetting the need for ice cream and beer, **Lucky Ales** (by Cupar) and **GG Ice Cream** (Leven).

'**Fife Farmers Markets** were important, and if you want to combine international solidarity with your local food why not support **Zapatista Coffee** (www.edinchiapas.org.uk/merchandise/coffee) or the **Zaytoun Palestinian Olive Oil Producers** (www.zaytoun.org)?

■ *Further details on these local outlets are listed elsewhere in The Larder and at www.thelarder.net. For more on the Fife Diet see fifediet.wordpress.com/about*

Why eat local?

The Larder offers a case for local food from A to Z.

Artisan – someone who does skilled work with their hands. Around Scotland there are many cheesemakers, bakers, brewers and other food producers who can be described as artisan, most of them working on a small scale and aiming to produce a high quality, individual product.

Baking – the Scottish tradition of baking is a strong one, with baps, bannocks, butteries, bridies, oatcakes, pies, tarts and cakes regarded as a distinctive but very homely aspect of our historic food culture. While most of our bread is produced in 'plant' or 'industrial' bakeries, small, artisan craft bakers are returning to our cities and villages too – a good sign of a healthy attitude to real food.

Cooking – this isn't just the domain of celebrity chefs, but a crucial – and creative – partner to eating and living well. Simple, practical, day-to-day cooking has few better starting points than fresh, tasty, interesting local food.

Distribution – the efficiency with which food moves from where it's produced to where it's bought is a critical factor in how and what we eat. However, distribution needn't always be about large articulated lorries moving between different hubs: farmers' markets are a form of distribution, as are veg box delivery schemes, and the Royal Mail.

Environment – local food is intimately connected to the environment. This is especially the case in a place such as Scotland where natural purity is an important element of our food and drink production. From farming practices to food miles there's a need for environmental awareness throughout the food chain, not least in the realisation that a re-localisation of food may soon become a necessity rather than simply a choice.

Fishing – a fundamental part of Scotland's food heritage and current economic make-up. The many different forms of fishing in Scotland, including deep-sea trawling, inshore creeling and aquaculture, are increasingly wrapped up in debates and initiatives concerning the sustainability of stocks and the appropriateness of fish farming systems.

Globalisation – around three quarters of the global food and drink industry is controlled by just 200 companies. None of these are Scottish owned. However, being part of a globalised food economy doesn't necessarily mean Scotland has to be subjugated by it.

Home-grown – like hand-made, this is a tag indicating care and craft rather than industrial efficiency. But they have no legal definition; you have to trust the person using the term.

Information – getting to know about a food product isn't simply a case of reading the label. Direct contact with a food producer, or through a close intermediary such as a shopkeeper, is a great way to discover information, as is a visit to the place where the food is produced. Useful information can come from other sources too – cooking tips from a book or a friend can help you to get to know a product.

Journeys – except for exotic foods such as spices, coffee, chocolate and some fruits, it seems a bit of an anathema for food to spend long periods in transit. In the case of livestock sent to slaughter, long journeys can cause distress to the detriment of animal welfare and the taste of the meat.

PHOTO: SCOTTISH VIEWPOINT

CLAIRE MACDONALD ON LOCAL FOOD

It is now so many years ago that I cannot remember exactly when that the Skye and Lochalsh Horticultural Association invited all hoteliers and restaurateurs in the region to their AGM and I was the only one to accept. But that was the start of our contact at Kinloch with local growers and producers. In those days 'local' still could mean a three to four-hour round trip to collect foodstuffs. These days we have a Food Link Van, initiated and funded by the LEC (Local Enterprise Company) but now self supporting. We have a plethora of salad leaves and fresh herbs, berries in season, vegetables, garlic, cultivated wild mushrooms, as well as mussels, fish and shellfish, and smoked fish. We are all hoping to get our abattoir re-instated, but it is possible to buy local venison, lamb and beef.

Scotland has the richest larder of any country in the world, both natural and cultivated. It is thrilling work indeed when doing cooking demonstrations around the UK (and in other countries around the world) to be able to tell people about our wonderful foods. It – the food – is the single most appealing aspect of Scotland. Many other mainland European countries have the same wealth of beauty and history as we do. But we have, I most firmly believe, the best foodstuffs by far, in sheer quality. We should be so proud – I most certainly am.

■ *Claire Macdonald runs the hotel and cookschool at Kinloch Lodge, Sleat, Isle of Skye, 01471 833333, www.kinloch-lodge.co.uk, www.claire-macdonald.com For more on food from Skye and Lochalsh, and the Food Link van, see www.skyefood.co.uk*

Kitchens – whether domestic or professional, these are key places in the journey from field to fork. Here simple produce is converted into dishes and meals that nourish us and – ideally – are enjoyable too. Good produce is the bedrock of good eating, but it's cooking that really entrenches our relationship with good food.

Local – what does it actually mean? On the one hand, many of us regard food from Scotland as local. But if you live in Edinburgh, Stilton cheese (made near Nottingham) is about as locally produced as Grimbister (in Orkney). Localness is partially bound up in identity – recognising where something has come from, and partially in practicality – why should we need to look further to obtain certain products.

Markets – farmers' markets are one of the principal points of contact for genuinely local food produced by small-scale farms and businesses. Although they're regarded as a recent phenomenon (they began in Scotland as farmers sought a way to recover from the foot-and-mouth epidemic of 2001), the simple fact is that they're a return to a very obvious economic reality: food grown locally being sold to the closest available customers.

Natural – food has much to offer in its natural state. After all, the miracles of nature create much of our food, and plenty of it at that. A good deal of Scotland's best food benefits from its close connections to nature, a purity and wildness that isn't much found in other parts of Europe.

Organic – a system of farming that aims to work with natural systems rather than dominate them by encouraging natural biological cycles in soil, plants and animals and avoiding the use of agro-chemical inputs. Other key principles include

animal welfare, the avoidance of pollution, the protection and encouragement of the natural environment including wildlife and a consideration for the wider social and ecological impact of farming.

Procurement – public food procurement – food bought using government funds for schools, hospitals, prisons and other institutions – is worth £85 billion in Scotland each year, so has a massive influence on the country's food and drink economics. Should public procurement always seek best 'value' (the lowest prices) or be seen as a means of supporting local food production?

Quality – a word commonly used in food production, retail and marketing. Local food, or organic food, or food from small producers, is not necessarily better quality than mass produced food, but on the whole small, local and artisan producers will strive for a higher quality than mass-produced equivalents.

Regionality – while we tend to talk about Scottish food under a single identity, the truth is that most well-developed food cultures still nurture regionality as a key aspect of diversity, tradition and distinctiveness. Different growing conditions, soils, vegetation and climate exist in different regions of Scotland, which inevitably creates difference in food produced in these areas. Other places describe it as terroir. A greater awareness and respect for these different identities is a sign of a maturing food culture.

Seasons – the annual cycle of different local foods coming in and out of season before our eyes would have been fundamental to everyone who lived on this planet up until the last quarter of a century. It remains engrained in many of our traditions and feasts, yet the surfeits, delights and desire-inducing droughts created by the seasonality of food have been clouded by the remarkable availability of all foods 12 months of the year. Seasonal eating is very much a part of local eating, and of being tuned into the rhythms and bounty of the world around us.

Transition – the transition to less fossil fuel dependency, as championed by the 'Transition Towns' movement. In the future we will be obliged (by the price of fuel, and by shifting government policy) to refocus on what's local to us. If we can grow food locally, why do we need to get it from further afield? At the moment the answer to that is cost and convenience. The cost equation will change, however, not just as fuel becomes more expensive, but if local production is stepped up then the supply and demand equation will allow local prices to become more competitive.

Uniqueness – Scotland is unique in many ways: in its culture, history, geography and people, most obviously. What about its food? Certain aspects of Scottish food are unique, but Scotland's food culture as a whole has yet to impose its mark on the nation's identity.

Value – too often 'good value' is seen as synonymous with cheapness. Value, however, considers quality alongside relative cost. Local food often doesn't carry the same transportation costs and overheads as imported food, so a higher percentage of the cost of the food can be allocated to the item itself. Also, value isn't just a monetary thing: there are also cultural, environmental and human values to consider in the food we buy.

Welfare – whether for animals, human or communities, an important consideration in local food production. Many standards of animal welfare apply, including organic systems, free-range and specific schemes relating to different farming practices.

X(E)Xcess – food waste at most stages of the food chain, from entire crops being rejected by grocery buyers to mouldy carrots in the fridge, is a standard feature of the way we handle food today. It is argued that smaller-scale food systems produce less unrecycled waste and in

households too, food bought more thoughtfully from a local supplier is more likely to be used up with care.

Youth – children today grow up in a very different food culture to that of their grandparents. There's more food around, but less awareness of where it comes from and fewer cooking and food handling skills.

Zeitgeist – 'the spirit of the age'. We are moving from a time when small and local was thought of as meaning insignificant and inferior. In this age small and local can be key pointers towards quality and distinctiveness.

> SCOTTISH OR SCOTCH?

Read the label carefully if you want to scotch the myths about where your food and drink comes from.

Is that food Scottish? Well, if it was grown, or manufactured, or perhaps landed (in the case of fish) in Scotland, it would seem obvious. Yet in the complex world of food labelling, things aren't always so clear. Note the difference between smoked Scottish salmon and Scottish smoked salmon. It's possible that the wording of the latter has been deliberately used to cover the fact that the salmon has been smoked in Scotland, but not necessarily sourced from Scotland.

In fact only a few products have a legal framework governing their definition as Scottish. If you see the label 'Scotch Beef' or 'Scotch Lamb' then you know that the product has been subject to the strict guidelines of Quality Meat Scotland and has been born, reared and slaughtered in Scotland. Meat described as 'Scottish' or 'from Scotland' isn't necessarily inaccurate, but it doesn't fall under a legally enforced definition.

Likewise, the term 'Scottish Salmon' can only be used for salmon that has been reared and caught in Scotland and is kept in check by the Scottish Salmon Producers Organisation.

'Scotch' Whisky is protected by the Scotch Whisky Association and a strict legal definition regarding the way it is made has been in place for many years – central to it is that the whisky must have been made in a distillery in Scotland and matured in oak casks in Scotland for at least three years.

And beyond these definitions? Well, it's essentially a matter of trust between consumer and producer. Local shops, farm stalls and farmers' markets offer opportunities to get closer to those who make food in this country and increasingly you can visit the farms, distilleries and factories to see exactly where they're made and – just as importantly – how.

WHERE TO BUY

Delis and general food shops listed regionally then organised alphabetically.

EDINBURGH & LOTHIANS

■ Damhead Organic Foods

32a Damhead, Old Pentland Road, Lothianburn
See Fruit & Veg Specialists

■ Dobbies

Melville Nursery, Lasswade, Midlothian
0131 663 6778, www.dobbies.com
Mon–Sun 9am–6pm; Thu 9am–8pm.
Café.
Dobbies' passion for horticulture doesn't stop at helping you grow fresh produce – it extends to selling it in its farm food halls. Choose from a good selection of locally sourced fruit and vegetables, fresh baked goods including bread and cakes, as well as honeys, jams and preserves. Well stocked meat and cheese counters groan with an impressive array of goods from Scotland and further afield, many of which are organic. Treat yourself to a bottle of champagne, a luxury pudding or some Scottish hand-made chocolates.

■ Earthy

33–41 Ratcliffe Terrace, Edinburgh
0131 667 2967, www.earthy.co.uk
Mon–Fri 8.30am–7.30pm; Sat 8.30am–6pm; Sun 10am–5pm.
Earthy is a local food market, online store and home delivery service selling a wide range of fairly traded, local, seasonal and organic produce in and around Edinburgh. Choose from a wide range of fresh fruit and vegetables, meat, fish and dairy produce from passionate growers and producers, as well as breads, pastries, biscuits and cakes, pulses, pastas and grains, teas, coffees, beers, wines and a whole lot more. Tastings of local, Scottish and UK regional produce take place regularly and there are producers' days when you can meet some of the people who make the food.

■ Fenton Barns Farm Shop

Fenton Barns Farm, Near Drem, North Berwick
01620 850 294
www.fentonbarnsfarmshop.com
Mon–Sun 10am–5pm.
Café.
As well as a supply of chutneys, smoked fish, sausages, cheeses and local fresh fruit and vegetables, Fenton Barns Farm Shop fills its shelves with

items made on site, such as casseroles, pies and home-made stock, not to mention frozen meats and ice creams. A deli counter offers tarts, pâtés and game pies to take away, as well as sweet treats and cakes. The owners' idea was to make the space almost a general store – albeit a fairly luxurious one – so it also sells pasta, milk, butter, spices and other basic items. The award-winning café sells simple but tasty home-produced sandwiches, stovies, tarts and special dishes of the day. Truly a farm shop with a difference.

■ The Fisherman's Kitchen

96 High Street, North Berwick, East Lothian
01620 890245
www.fishermans-kitchen.com
Mon–Sat 9am–5pm. Closed Sun.
Rod Bunney's fish and food shop in North Berwick is a quality seafood delicatessen with an emphasis on fresh, seasonal and local produce. As well as fresh and smoked seafood, it has an impressive selection of additional products, including fine wines, home-made soups, salads and quiches, fruit, vegetables and bread. The shop also offers a line in speciality gift baskets guaranteed to please the most prolific foodie. The friendly staff will offer helpful advice and provide recipe sheets for those looking for guidance on how to cook something in particular.

■ Gosford Bothy Farm Shop

Gosford Estate, Aberlady, East Lothian
See Beef, Lamb and Other Meat

■ Harvey Nichols Foodmarket

30–34 St Andrew Square, Edinburgh
0131 524 8322, www.harveynichols.com
Mon–Wed 10am–6pm; Thu 10am–8pm;
Fri/Sat 10am–7pm; Sun noon–6pm.
Café, Web/mail order.
Billed as 'the most fashionable food destination for die-hard foodies and fashionistas alike', Harvey Nichols Foodmarket is the place to be and be seen for the stylish Edinburgh food fan. At 3000sq ft, the Foodmarket has an impressive selection of fresh foods with a strong emphasis on local sourcing and grocery products from around the world, as well as its extensive, and always stylish, own-label range. A deli counter offers an array of high quality cheeses and charcuterie, as well as antipasti and patisserie. In addition, the adjoining wine shop stocks a wide variety of interesting spirits and over 300 hand-picked wines and champagnes.

REAL FOODS With over 30 years' trading experience and a product range of over 10,000 natural, organic, health and wholefood lines, Real Foods is the largest Scottish retailer of organic, Fairtrade, vegetarian and special diet foods. It introduced the concept of buying natural foods loose and in bulk, and both branches carry a vast array of dried fruits, nuts, pulses and cereals, dozens of different teas, a variety of Asian and ethnic foods and a selection of organic fruit and vegetables. A wide selection of health and vitamin supplements is available and knowledgeable staff can advise on your purchase. See page 20.

■ Henderson's

92 Hanover Street, Edinburgh
0131 225 6694
www.hendersonsofedinburgh.co.uk
Mon–Fri 8am–7pm; Sat 9am–6pm.
Closed Sun.
Café.
Founded by Janet Henderson in 1962, Henderson's is an Edinburgh institution. Committed to selling wholesome, natural food at reasonable prices, the deli makes up one part of the business, with the salad bar located beneath, the bistro alongside, and most recently an art gallery one floor up. Bread and cakes come from Henderson's wholemeal bakehouse – now located on the same premises. An array of vegetarian and vegan specialities are available, along with locally grown fruit and vegetables (organic where possible). Salads, soups, sandwiches, ready-made meals and fresh juices are available to take away.

■ Herbie of Edinburgh

• 66 Raeburn Place, Edinburgh
0131 552 3048
Mon–Fri 9.30am–7pm; Sat 9am–6pm.
Closed Sun.
• 1 North West Circus Place, Edinburgh
0131 226 7212
www.herbieofedinburgh.co.uk

Mon–Fri 8.30am–6pm; Sat 9am–6pm.
Closed Sun.
Café.
Stockbridge has a reputation as one of Edinburgh's best neighbourhoods for good food and small specialist shops. Right at the heart of that reputation are the two Herbie stores. The original, with barely room for three customers beside the fridges and bread displays, has retained its popularity despite the arrival of a bigger sister up the hill towards town. Here, a long cheese and salami display shows off Herbie's real depth of quality in these departments, though there's also room for wine (South African is a speciality) and a few tightly packed tables and chairs with an excellent little café menu offering dishes prepared in the kitchen downstairs.

■ Mel's Bells

13 Randolph Place, Edinburgh
0131 220 2300
Mon–Fri 10am–7pm; Sat 10am–5.30pm;
Closed Sun.
Melanie Jones' speciality food shop is located in Edinburgh's west end, tucked in behind Charlotte Square. With its straightforward layout and old dressers and tables it has the feel of an old-fashioned grocer, though the range of food stocked is certainly tuned in to

interesting foods, including chocolates from Coco of Bruntsfield, Tea Pigs teas, fresh East Lothian vegetables and Linda Dick chickens. A house speciality is ready-to-cook grab bags: these contain a recipe along with all the ingredients required to cook yourself a delicious meal at home. Regular tastings also take place.

■ Peckham's

• 49 South Clerk Street, Edinburgh
0141 445 4555, www.peckhams.co.uk
Mon–Sat 8am–midnight; Sun
9am–midnight.
Café.
• 155–159 Bruntsfield Place, Edinburgh
0131 229 7054
Mon–Sat 8am–midnight; Sun
9am–midnight.
Café.
• 48 Raeburn Place, Edinburgh
0131 332 8844
Mon–Sat 8am–midnight; Sun 8am–11pm
Café.
Established in Glasgow in 1982, Peckham's now has ten branches, three of which are in Edinburgh. Open until midnight, these delis are well respected and well used in their distinctive neighbourhoods. One of Peckham's strengths has always been its range of produce, including continental meats,

HEART BUCHANAN Fi Buchanan set up her little shop over seven years ago and it has flourished to become one of the finest delis in Glasgow. The award-winning Heart Buchanan is a Mecca for lovers of food, with shelves crammed full of goodies and well chosen wines. The on-site chef prepares a variety of dishes using the best local and seasonal produce every day for hungry customers to take home. Examples of the type of food on offer are a salad of confit Scottish salmon with fennel, winter citrus and tarragon; stuffed tomatoes with basil risotto; and mushroom, bacon and spinach salad. If you take along your own dish they'll even prepare your dinner in it for you. See page 22.

smoked salmon, cheeses and pates, freshly baked bread from its own bakery, patisserie and chocolates as well as sandwiches, salads and hot soups to take away. A strong range of wines, whiskies and beers is also available. The Bruntsfield Place restaurant has a restaurant in the basement, while the other two venues have coffee bars.

■ Real Foods
• 8 Brougham Street, Edinburgh
0131 228 1201, www.realfoods.co.uk
Mon–Fri 9am–6.30pm; Sat 9am–6pm; Sun 10am–5pm.
• 37 Broughton Street, Edinburgh
0131 557 1911, www.realfoods.co.uk
Mon–Wed & Fri 9am–7pm; Thu 9am–8pm; Sat 9am–6.30pm; Sun 10am–6pm.
See photo entry on page 18.

■ Relish
6 Commercial Street, Edinburgh
0131 476 1920
Mon–Sat 8.30am–8pm; Sun 10am–8pm.
Café.

Leith seems to have Michelin-starred chefs to spare these days, but rather fewer places to buy good local food. Callum Morrison has been holding up that side of the market almost singlehandedly in recent years with his uncomplicated but reliable deli Relish. It's the kind of place you can stop in for a lump of cheese, a loaf or a handful of veggies, though there's a range of dried products available and some nice bottles of wine by the back of the shop. Coffee, soup and sandwiches can be taken away or eaten in at the tightly fitting tables. A few blocks away, Morrison has recently opened Rocksalt on Constitution Street: he calls it a café-deli but essentially it is a daytime and early evening eating spot.

■ The Store
13 Comely Bank Road, Stockbridge, Edinburgh
0131 315 0030
www.thestorecompany.co.uk
Mon–Thu 10am–6.30pm; Fri/Sat 9am–6pm; Sun 11am–5pm.

Established in 2000, the family-run award-winning Store has an outlet in Edinburgh's Stockbridge as well as a shop on its farm in Foveran, Aberdeenshire. Specialising in produce raised on the farm – from sheep and Aberdeen Angus beef raised in small numbers in open fields before being traditionally hung, to vegetables grown without artificial fertilisers and pesticides – the Store strives to promote high quality, regional food with passion. It sells a selection of chef prepared meals, produced using its own meat and no added preservatives or colours.

■ Valvona & Crolla
19 Elm Row, Edinburgh
0131 556 6066, www.valvonacrolla.com
Mon–Sat 8am–6.30pm; Sun 10.30am–5pm.
Café.
The grande dame of Edinburgh delis, established way back in 1934, V&C is a foodie's delight. Walking in is like stepping into a little Italy, where bottles of exquisite wines and spirits line the walls and stacks of indulgent pasta, biscuits and chocolates tempt both the tastebuds and the wallet. An array of salamis, hams and sausages hangs from the ceiling at the front, and the cheese display with its oozing dolcelattes and enormous parmesans is enough to put you off any health kick. The café at the back of the shop also serves lunches and snacks for those who prefer to sample the produce in situ.

GLENFINLAS

Good at food.

Whether it's the great taste of Green Mountain Coffee, the delicious dishes we cook in our cafes, or the highest quality food and drink you'll find in our farm shop, you'll experience the strength of our passion. **We're Glenfinlas – good at food.**

■ Valvona & Crolla Foodhall at Jenners

Princes Street, Edinburgh
0131 260 2242, www.valvonacrolla.co.uk
Mon 9am–6pm; Tue 9.30am–6pm; Wed 9am–6pm; Thu 9am–8pm; Fri/Sat 9am–6pm; Sun 11am–5pm.
Café.
2008 marked a major development for Valvona & Crolla when a tie-up with House of Fraser saw them take over the foodhall not just in Princes Street's most famous shop, Jenners, but also in the Jenners outpost at Loch Lomond. The foodhall at Jenners has a stronger emphasis on Scottish products than the Italian dominated Elm Row store, and while the shortbread is a strong seller, there's also smoked fish, cheese, preserves, chocolates and V&C's ever-solid range of wines and spirits. A caffè offers hot drinks and snacks, as well as perches beside a long window overlooking the Scott Monument and Princes Street Gardens.

■ Victor Hugo

27–27 Melville Drive, Edinburgh
0131 667 1827, www.victorhugodeli.com
Mon–Fri 8am–8pm; Sat 9am–6pm; Sun 10am–5pm.
Café.
With a history spanning over 60 years, Victor Hugo is a landmark deli overlooking the Meadows. Within the cherry red exterior is a small but well-stocked local shop with a good balance of everyday and more specialist items. Edinburgh's farmers' market is one principal source for a number of its lines, with other Scottish suppliers such as Ramsay of Carluke well represented. A table and chairs are squeezed inside – there are a few more outdoors – and a decent array of salads, bakes, daily specials and baked treats can be bought to eat on site or take away.

GREATER GLASGOW & CLYDESIDE

■ Ardardan Estate

Ardardan Estate, Farm Shop, Cardross
01389 849188, www.ardardan.co.uk
Tue–Sun 10am–5pm. Closed Mon.
Café.
Run by the Montgomery family, Ardardan Estate is set in a walled garden surrounded by its own farm. The estate consists of plant nursery, tearoom and farm shop which, recently refurbished, has extended its range to include an impressive cheese counter and olive bar. Priding itself on knowing the full traceability of its produce, it strives to stock as many Scottish and local products as possible. The farm's free-range eggs are a key ingredient in the delicious cakes hand-made on the premises. The tearoom's scones are the best for miles around. Visitors can pick strawberries in the summer months.

■ Berits & Brown

6 Wilson Street, Merchant City, Glasgow
0141 552 6980
www.beritsandbrown.com
Mon 8am–7pm; Tue/Wed 8am–8pm; Thu 8am–10pm; Fri 8am–11pm; Sat 9am–11pm; Sun 9am–7pm.
Café.
Glasgow's Merchant City has an increasing number of little boutiques, bars and cafés, and Berits & Brown is a jewel among them. The deli side stocks a good range of high quality, fresh and honest produce, sourced locally and from all over the UK and further afield, and sits alongside an impressive selection of wines from around the world. The café serves up delicious fare made on the premises using fresh ingredients. For breakfast, try the French toast served with shards of crisp smoked bacon and doused in maple syrup and have a delicious start to the day.

■ Deli 1901

11 Skirving Street, Shawlands, Glasgow
0141 632 1630, www.deli1901.co.uk
Mon–Sat 9am–7pm; Sun 10am–6pm.
Café.
Owned by award-winning chef team Colin and Aileen Campbell, Deli 1901 is a fine food emporium selling artisan products from around the globe, cheese from local supplier IJ Mellis, freshly ground coffees and own label jams and chutneys. There are also take-away meals hand-made in the kitchens using fresh local produce. Take home mouth-watering dishes such as salmon and pesto en croute and Morrocan spinach and feta flat breads. They source the wine selection of over 120 bins for quality and make a point of stocking the wines they love.

■ Delizique and Cafezique

66 and 70 Hyndland Street, Partick, Glasgow
0141 339 2000 / 0141 339 7180
www.delizique.co.uk
Mon–Fri 9am–9pm; Sat/Sun 9am–8pm.
Café.
Established in 2001, Delizique aims to be a one-stop shop providing the best of ingredients for when you have the time to cook and dishes to take away when you don't. The in-store bakery emits a distinctive, delicious smell, and produces bread and pastries daily as well as pizza for delivery. A range of fresh pies – such as free range-chicken and leek – typically sells out. Its beetroot cake with fresh berries is famed locally. A couple of doors down, Cafezique serves breakfast, lunch, coffees, high tea and dinner.

■ Dobbies Farm Foodhall

Boclair Road, Milngavie, Glasgow
01360 620721, www.dobbies.com
Mon–Sat 9am–6pm; Thu 9am–8pm; Sun 10am–6pm.
Café.
For two of Glasgow's most famously affluent suburbs, there aren't many outlets for local and specialist food in Bearsden and Milngavie. Dobbies is generally considered the best option in the area for a number of deli items. As with the four other Farm Foodhalls around the country, there's a decent commitment to Scottish produce, with chilled local meat available as well as a broad range of cheese, dried goods and fresh vegetables.

■ Grassroots

20 Woodlands Road, Glasgow
0141 353 3278
www.grassrootsorganic.com
Mon–Wed 8am–6pm; Thu/Fri 8am–7pm; Sat 9am–6pm; Sun 11am–5pm.
Café, Web/mail order.
Grassroots is a friendly, local wholefood haven, stocked with 2000 or so lines of all the grains, nuts, seeds, oils, herbs and spices your heart could desire. The main fridge is bursting with savoury treats – smoked tofu, gourmet vegetarian sausages, organic dairy goods – while the deli counter displays each day's freshly prepared meals and snacks such as frittata and hummus. As well as vegetarian and vegan, it caters for other special diets and makes many products without wheat, dairy or sugar. There's a good selection of organic fruit and vegetables, and it boasts the city's widest range of organic wine and beer.

■ Heart Buchanan

380 Byres Road, Glasgow
0141 334 7626
www.heartbuchanan.co.uk
Mon–Fri 8.30am–9.30pm; Sat 9am–9.30pm; Sun noon–7pm.
Café.
See photo on page 20.

■ Kember & Jones Fine Food Emporium

134 Byres Road, Glasgow
07717 828930
www.kemberandjones.co.uk
Mon–Sat 8am–8pm; Sun 9am–5pm.
Café.
Established in 2004, Kember & Jones is something of a gourmet superstore. Everything about it speaks of quality:

pale wood cabinets laden with fine continental delicacies, huge terracotta bowls of olives beside organic artisan bread (it stocks the delicious Poilane) and a table of hip cookbooks that invite browsing as you wait. Choose from authentic pastas and sauces, chutneys and jams, Rococo and Prestat chocolates, luxury mueslis and cheeses, charcuterie, home-made pâtés and salads from the deli counter. A small team of pastry chefs work tirelessly to produce an amazing array of cakes and tarts, and along with muffins, scones and giant meringues, these are available to take away. The food served in the café is influenced by the products sold in the shop. Always busy, so expect to queue.

▉ Peckham's

• 61–65 Glassford Street, Glasgow
0141 553 0666, www.peckhams.co.uk
Mon–Sat 8am–midnight; Sun
10.30am–11pm.
• 114 Kirkintilloch Road, Lenzie
0141 776 6050
Mon–Sat 8.30am–10pm; Sun
9.30am–10pm.
• 275 Mearns Road, Glasgow
0141 639 3782
Mon–Sun 8am–10pm.
• 124–126 Byres Road, Glasgow
0141 357 1454
Mon–Sat 8.30am–midnight; Sun
9am–midnight.

• 43 Clarence Drive, Glasgow
0141 357 2909
Mon–Sat 8.30am–midnight; Sun
9am–midnight.
A proper institution in the West End of Glasgow and beyond these days, Peckham's manages to be both a reliable all-hours food stop and a place to pick up treats, gifts and hard-to-find food items. There have been recent changes at the city centre branch on Glassford Street, with a rearrangement of the various facilities on site, which include a deli, wine store, café, restaurant and cook school. Other developments are also expected in 2009 with the opening of further stores in Glasgow, Livingston, Dundee and Aberdeen – the latter two locations a result of owner Tony Johnston buying up sites vacated by the failed McLeish Bros venture.

▉ Roots and Fruits

• 351 Byres Road, Glasgow
• 455–457 Great Western Road, Glasgow
See Fruit & veg specialists

▉ Valvona & Crolla Foodhall at Jenners

Lomond Shores, Balloch, Dunbartonshire
01389 722200, www.valvonacrolla.co.uk
See main entry for Valvona & Crolla Foodhall at Jenners in Edinburgh & Lothians, page 20.

SOUTHERN SCOTLAND

▉ Chisholms of Ayr

17 Carrick Street, Ayr
01292 269555
www.chisholmsofayrdeli.com
Now a well-established good food stop in central Ayr, Chisholms has always set out its store by the quality of produce available on its doorstep. Thus a broad range of cheese is headed up by examples from Dunlop and Arran, smoked fish comes from Fencebay at Fairlie, pies from down the road at Dalduff and bacon and puddings from Ramsays over in Carluke. Chisholms came under new ownership in late 2008.

▉ Deli Beans

7 High Street, Peebles
01721 723461
Mon–Sat 9am–5.30pm. Closed Sun.
Café.
Unlike many county towns around Scotland, Peebles has managed to hold onto its independent retailers and has a high street that's refreshingly light on national branded stores. In the mix are a handful of good food retailers, including Deli Beans. Supplying the locals with fresh local deli goods, it has become quite a popular favourite for its range of cheeses, meats and deli antipasti treats. There's also lovely fresh baked bread that you can sometimes grab when it's still warm.

Delizique

BERITS & BROWN Kippen isn't, perhaps, the most obvious place from which to embark upon world domination, but it might yet happen. Berits & Brown opened here in 2004, quickly establishing itself as a classy but friendly good food shop, coffee stop and wine emporium. The concept was then expanded into a franchise business, with shops now beginning to spring up in both England and Scotland.

■ Deli on the Corner
1/5 Main Street, Stewarton, Ayrshire
01560 482883
www.delionthecorner.co.uk
Mon/Tue, Thu & Sat 9am–4pm; Wed 9am–2.30pm; Fri 9am–5pm. Closed Sun.
Café.
Once Borlands Deli, in 2008 the business expanded and developed, renaming itself Deli on the Corner. An important part of the business is in sandwiches and catering, but for all aspects, including the retail deli, Ayrshire and other regional suppliers play an important part: there's food and drink from Arran as well as Graeme's local honey, Lime Tree Larder tablet, Galloway preserves and Little Doone's sweet balsamic dressing from Dalry. Dalduff Farm's ready meal range is also available.

■ Dobbies Farm Foodhall
Old Toll, Holmston, Ayr
01292 294750, www.dobbies.com
Mon–Sat 9am–6pm; Sun 10am–6pm.
Café.
The Farm Foodhall situated within Dobbies Garden World on the western edge of Ayr has an extensive food range including fresh vegetables, a wide delicatessen section, biscuits, jams and chutneys. Adding significantly to the local flavour, Dalduff butchers of

Maybole now has a concession within the site, selling its range of fresh farm meat, sausages, burgers and pies.

■ Fencebay Fisheries
Fencefoot Farm, Fairlie, Ayrshire
See Fish & Shellfish

■ Loch Arthur Creamery
Camphill Village Trust Ltd, Beeswing, Dumfries, Dumfriesshire
See Cheese & Dairy

■ Woodland Farm
Woodland Farm, Girvan, Ayrshire
01465 710700
www.woodlandfarm.co.uk
Apr–Oct: Mon–Sun 9am–5pm. Nov–Mar: Mon–Sun 10am–5pm.
Café.
Located on the coast just south of Girvan, Woodland Farm has become quite a landmark. The large stone complex encompasses a farm shop, 50-seater restaurant and coffee house, garden centre and trout pond – and there are even developments underway to add courtyard accommodation. At the right time of year the shop is well stocked with a fine selection of home-grown fruit and vegetables, fresh home baking and other deli items from oatcakes to Cream o'Galloway's ice-cream.

CENTRAL SCOTLAND & FIFE

■ Berits & Brown
Main Street, Kippen, Stirlingshire
01786 870077
www.beritsandbrown.com
Mon–Sat 9am–5pm; Sun 10am–5pm.
Café.
See photo on this page.

■ Blairmains Farm Shop
Manor Loan, Blairlogie, Stirlingshire
01259 762266
www.blairmainsfarmshop.co.uk
Mon–Sat 10am–5pm; Sun noon–4pm.
Café.
Located at the foot of the Ochil Hills not far out of Stirling, Blairmains is a busy place these days, with its 'coffee bothy' a well-established place for hearty home baking and filling lunches. The adjoining farm shop offers various local items such as eggs and bread alongside decent Scottish produce, imported and also flash-frozen fruit and vegetables, plus sweets, knick-knacks and even hardwood furniture.

■ Dalchonzie Fruit Farm Shop
Dalchonze, Comrie, Perthshire
See Fruit & Veg Specialists

■ Deli Ecosse
10 Ancaster Square, Callander
01877 331220
Mon/Tue & Thu–Sun 8.30am–5pm.
Closed Wed.
Café.
Tucked away in a converted church hall just off Callander's often busy high street, Deli Ecosse is a sanctuary for good deli basics, sweet treats, interesting beers and wines and a decent cup of coffee. A good place to stock up if you're in the Trossachs for a picnic or a longer holiday, it's also a pit stop worth knowing about if you're travelling through. There are a number of tables available for sit-in food, as well as take-away sandwiches and hot drinks.

■ JL Gill
26 West High Street, Crieff, Perthshire
01764 653011
www.scottishproduce.co.uk
Mon–Sun 8am–5pm.
A charming food shop that looks as if it belongs to times past. On the outside it seems to be a traditional greengrocer's and inside it lives up to its appearance. It stocks all the larder basics, such as oatcakes, preserves and cooking sauces. But you can also stock up the drinks cabinet with its extensive range of Scotch malt whiskies, Scottish wines and premium Scottish ales.

Gloagburn Farm Shop

Gloagburn, Tibbermore, Perth
01738 840864
www.gloagburnfarmshop.co.uk
Mon–Sun 9am–6pm.
Café.
Gloagburn is a friendly farm shop in Tibbermore, near Perth. It stocks a variety of home-made produce; such as oatcakes, jams and soup. It also impresses with its extensive range of locally produced meats, with Puddledub sausages, Hilton wild boar burgers and organic lamb and beef from the neighbouring farm. Demand for its quality local produce continues to increase and it's no wonder why.

House of Menzies

Castle Menzies Farm, Aberfeldy, Perthshire
See Whisky, Beer & Other Drinks

Jamesfield Farm

Jamesfield Farm Outlet Ltd, Jamesfield Farm, Abernethy, Perthshire
01738 850498
Mon–Sun 10am–5pm.
Café.
The large, purpose-built shop and restaurant built by Ian Miller on his mixed organic farm on the boundary between Perthshire and Fife at Abernethy has been around for five years. Once again under the management of the Miller family themselves, the centre still aims to be a showcase for produce that's mostly organic and definitely oriented to the local, not least the beef, lamb and vegetables from the surrounding 300-acre farm.

Loch Leven's Larder

Channel Farm, Channel, Kinross, Perthshire
01592 841000
www.lochlevenslarder.com
Mon–Sun 9.30am–5pm (6pm during summer months).
Café.
Heart and soul has obviously gone into creating the lovely shopping space at this family-run business. The contemporary open-plan shop houses fine foods from Scotland, as well as many delicacies from across Europe. There is also a gift shop, 'farm larder' and coffee shop section – as well as a range of bespoke hand-made kitchens by a local craftsman. It's a bit of a quirky mix, but that's what makes it such a treasure trove.

Mains of Taymouth Delicatessen

Mains of Taymouth Courtyard, Kenmore
01887 830 756
www.taymouthcourtyard.com
Mon–Sun 9am–5pm (later on summer evenings).
Café.
Mains of Taymouth is a U-shaped complex and has been built around an open view of Loch Tay. It sources products from around the world and closer to home. Its meat comes locally from Rannoch and its bread is delivered daily from Aberfeldy. With on-site parking and a courtyard cafe, you'll probably spend the best part of a day pottering around the complex and buying up tasty deli goods.

McNee's of Crieff

23 High Street, Crieff
01764 654582, www.mcneesofcrieff.co.uk
Mon–Sat 9am–5pm; Sun 11am–4pm.
McNee's has put time and care into sourcing the more unusual and interesting varieties of deli produce. It avoids brands stocked by supermarket retailers and instead sources new – and often local – suppliers. As a result, you will find products such as Woodalls dry cured bacon and De Cecco pasta. The business started as a chololatier and there's still plenty of cocoa-based confectionery to tempt you from your saintly ways.

Menzies of Dunkeld

1 Atholl Street, Dunkeld, Perthshire
01350 728028, www.scottish-deli.co.uk
See main entry for sister venue the Scottish Deli in Pitlochry, this page.

Pestle & Mortar

41–43 Glasgow Road, Blanefield, Stirlingshire
01360 771110, www.pestlemortar.com
Mon–Fri 9am–7pm; Sat 9am–6pm; Sun 10am–5pm.
Café, web/mail order.
Pestle & Mortar really is an act of indulgence. Based in the beautiful little village of Blanefield, this lovely shop is filled to the brim with fine foods. Its speciality is hampers and gift selections that come in wicker baskets wrapped with coloured ribbons. Many of the items in stock have won Great Taste awards – so you're just going to have to find an excuse to treat yourself.

Pillars of Hercules Organic Farm Shop & Cafe

Pillars of Hercules, Falkland, Fife
See Fruit & Veg Specialists.

Clive Ramsay

26–28 Henderson Street, Bridge of Allan, Fife
01786 833903, www.cliveramsay.com
Mon–Sat 7am–7pm; Sun 8am–6pm.
Clive Ramsay's award-winning delicatessen has been open since 1984 and continues to cater to those with the finest of taste buds. It sources its produce globally, aiming to bring customers the best that various regions around the world have to offer. Ramsay himself uses deli ingredients to cook up soups, pizzas and sweets. His gooey chocolate mousse is, understandably, a big hit.

The Scottish Deli

8 West Moulin Road, Pitlochry, Perthshire
01796 473322, www.scottish-deli.co.uk
Mon–Sat 8.30am–5.30pm. Closed Sun.
This was the first to open in what is now a trio of delis owned by husband and wife team Alec and Sarah Cruikshank. They have worked to build up a quality and varied range of produce – from Alec's personal selection of 70 cheeses to the finest local organic venison. They also provide organic veggie boxes and luxury hampers, and can rustle you up a picnic basket. Their outlet at the Highland Adventures Safari Lodge at Dull by Aberfeldy contains a fully fledged café, while the most recent expansion has been to take over long-standing deli-grocers Menzies of Dunkeld.

NORTH EAST SCOTLAND

Baxters Highland Village

Focabers, Moray
01343 820666, www.baxters.co.uk
Mon–Sun 9am–5.30pm.
Café.
For decades Baxters has been synonymous with traditional tinned soups and jars of beetroot. These days it drapes less tartan around the packaging and places more emphasis on convenience and the use of fresh, contemporary ingredients alongside the traditional staples. The Highland Village is a surprisingly large development, with four shops and two restaurants, and is up-front about welcoming tourists and trippers. Other stores can be found in Ocean Terminal in Edinburgh, Dunsdale Haugh in Selkirk, beside the A9 at Blackford and by the M90 at Kelty.

Bridgefoot Organics

Bridgefoot, Newmachar, Aberdeenshire
See Fruit & Veg Specialists.

Cairn Gourmet

52 High Street, Banchory
01330 825132
Mon–Sun 9am–5.30pm.
Cairn Gourmet is a nice delicatessen in the pretty town of Banchory. It has the

FINZEAN FARM SHOP & CAFE Finzean Farm Shop is now an integral part of Finzean Estate, which has been owned by the Farquharson family for 16 decades. So far, so regal. The shop itself is an attractively converted old stone building; on the ground floor, the well-stocked shop sells fresh fruit and vegetables, as well as other local supplies such as jams, bread and oatcakes. Meat comes from Aberdeenshire farms but also from the estate, with a good deal of small game often available. A hard-working kitchen produces takeaway items as well as food for the café, which has tables beside picture windows on the ground floor and also up one level.

usual deli fare, but it is the great selection of Scottish cheeses for which it is best known – with a few local restaurants using its fine cheeses on their menu. Cairn Gourmet also offers an outside catering service for parties and special occasions.

■ Deli-Cacies
32 Evan Street, Stonehaven
01569 765 941
Mon–Fri 9.30am–5pm; Sat 9am–5pm.
Closed Sun.
Web/mail order.
Housed in the original Cairn tearooms, this deli has a nice quirkiness about it. It is spacious, with light wooden floors

and a calm atmosphere. It stocks a comprehensive range of fine Scottish produce – from Mull cheddar to Achiltibuie smoked salmon, all the way through to the more obscure speciality of Scottish Beef Jerky. It also has a good range of continental produce on offer.

■ Finzean Estate Farm Shop & Tea Room
Balnaboth, Finzean, Banchory, Aberdeenshire
01330 850710, www.finzean.com
Mon–Sat 9am–5pm; Sun noon–5pm.
Café.
See photo entry above.

■ Gordon & MacPhail
George House, Boroughbriggs Road, Elgin
See Whisky, Beer & Other Drinks

■ Hammerton Store
336 Great Western Road, Aberdeen
01224 324449
www.hammertonstore.co.uk
Mon–Thu 8am–7pm; Fri 8am–7.30pm; Sat 8am–6pm; Sun 9am–6pm.
This is Aberdeen's version of the kind of all-round general food store that is as much influenced by farm shops and old fashioned provision merchants as it is by specialist continental delis. Owner Susan Watson has ensured that the bedrock of the shop is in local and organic fruit and veg, alongside meats and bakery. Then there are the extras which both extend the range and emphasise the values of the place: real ales, cook books, ceramics and art.

■ Lenshaw Organics
Upper Lenshaw Farm, by Rothienorman, Inverurie, Aberdeenshire
See Fruit & Veg Specialists.

THE SPEY LARDER Part of a dual operation that spans the Cairngorms (the Dee Larder is tucked down a side street in Banchory in Aberdeenshire), the Spey Larder gives the small town of Aberlour an extra foodie dimension beyond the giant Walkers biscuit factory and the many surrounding whisky distilleries. It is the range of produce that impresses here and, as the name would suggest, it is the perfect place to stock up on all the deli larder basics such as cheese, cooked meats and bread. It has a good selection of local real ale and local wines, as well as wines from more far-flung destinations.

■ Milton Haugh Farm Shop

Milton Haugh Farm Shop, Carmylie, By Arbroath, Angus
01241 860579, www.miltonhaugh.com
Mon–Sat 9am–5pm; Sun 10am–5pm.
Milton Haugh is a lovely farm shop near Arbroath, selling seasonal vegetables and home-made jams and jellies. It sells its own reared Shorthorn Cross Beef as well as free-range chickens and eggs. There are also plenty of store cupboard essentials, ready made meals and a selection of frozen game (also available fresh when in season), wild boar sausage and venison steaks.

■ Phoenix Community Stores

The Park, by Findhorn, Moray
01309 690110, www.phoenixshop.co.uk
Mon–Fri 10am–6pm; Sat 10am–5pm; Sun noon–5pm.
Café.
Located at the entrance to the famous Findhorn eco-village, the Phoenix Community Store started life as a specialist new-age shop. It has now turned into a thriving community store, specialising in organic, Fairtrade and artisan foodstuffs. But it has retained

some of its alternative tendencies and also houses an apothecary. What's more, the Phoenix is part of a community partnership and hundreds of local people own a share of the business.

■ Rock Salt & Snails

40 St Swithin Street, Aberdeen
01224 200012
Mon–Fri 8am–6pm; Sat 9am–5pm.
Closed Sun.
Café.
This brilliantly named delicatessen stocks lots of interesting products, with the emphasis on superior tasting foods. There's a good range of fine meats and cheeses, and it sells Piper's crisps, the wonder crisps that won no fewer than four Taste Awards in 2008. It also does a nice range of gourmet filled rolls and warm paninis for the lunchtime crowd.

■ The Spey Larder

96–98 High Street, Aberlour on Spey, Moray
01340 871243, www.speylarder.com
Mon–Sat 9am–5.30pm. Closed Sun.
See photo entry above.

■ Taste Fresh

11 Union Street, Dundee, Angus
01382 224300, www.tastefresh.co.uk
Mon–Fri 8:30am–5pm; Sat 9:30am–5pm.
Closed Sun.
Located in the heart of Dundee, Taste Fresh is a classy deli with a real passion for the products it stocks. The owner often personally sources and selects the products, deciding to stock them only once he is sure they are of the finest quality. Most recently, it has started selling fresh pasta from Luigino's in Fife. Made by an Italian, using local ingredients, it is the best of both worlds.

HIGHLANDS, ISLANDS & ARGYLL

■ Brin Herb Nursery

Flichity, Farr, Inverness
01808 521288
www.brinherbnursery.co.uk
Plant sales daily during daylight hours.
Apr–Sep only: Fri–Mon 11am–5pm.
Café.
Brin is a vibrant and prolific nursery, stocking over 300 herbs and wild flower plants, including 15 varieties of basil, 23 types of mint, lovage and many more. It is for producing Spoff muesli, however, that it is better known. Since 2003, it has added hot cereals, oats, oatmeal and snack packs to the signature stock, which includes wheat and gluten-free ranges, and is supplied to quality retailers throughout the country and as far away as the USA. A café/shop, the Schoolroom, stocks a good selection of local and Scottish cheeses, meat and fish, as well as locally brewed beers, fruit and flowers, wines and, of course, the largest selection of Spoff products available anywhere.

■ Corner on the Square

1 High Street, Beauly
0146 378 3000
www.corneronthesquare.co.uk
Mon–Sat 9am–5.30pm. Closed Sun.
(Open until 7pm in summer and at Christmas.)
Café.
Corner on the Square is a friendly delicatessen and eatery in the Highland village of Beauly, stocking an impressive range of local produce from Highland herb hams, artisan cheeses and haggis to heather honey and Highland wheat beer. A particular emphasis on wine means whether you're looking for an Old or New World wine, knowledgeable staff are able to advise you on your purchase. They can also recommend a cheese to go with it and offer a cheese board service all year round.

■ Kitchen Garden Delicatessen

14 George Street, Oban, Argyll
01631 566332
www.kitchengardenoban.co.uk
Mon–Sat 9am–5pm; Sun 11am–5pm.
Café.

Set right in the heart of Oban looking onto the harbour, the Kitchen Garden is a busy, well-run operation that combines serious commitment to stocking excellent Scottish produce with the day-to-day demands of a popular café. Inevitably there is a lot of crossover between the two parts of the business, with items such as Inverawe's smoked fish, Ramsay's Ayrshire cure bacon or Isle of Mull cheddar prominent both downstairs in the deli and upstairs in the coffee shop. The deli also stocks plenty of continental produce, around 100 cheeses in all, and twice that number of whiskies.

■ Lochaber Farm Shop

Unit 5, Lochaber Rural Complex, Torlundy, Fort William
01397 708686
www.lochaberfarmshop.com
Tue–Sun 10am–5pm. Closed Mon.
Café.

Lochaber Farm Shop was set up in 2004 to sell lamb, mutton, beef and free-range pork reared on the farm. It also stocks free-to-roam chickens, outdoor reared bacon, gammon steaks and wild venison. While meat remains its speciality, its range has expanded to include vegetables sourced as locally as possible, as well as home baking, jams and chutneys, smoked salmon, free-range eggs and special dietary goods such as gluten-free and dairy-free produce. With an aim to support small farmers in other parts of the world, it also stocks a range of Fairtrade teas, coffees, biscuits and chocolates.

■ The Original Orkney Hamper Company

78 Victoria Street, Stromness, Orkney
01856 850 551
www.orkneyhampers.co.uk
Mon–Sat 10am–5pm; Sun 11am–4pm (summer months only).

Nine years ago the Original Orkney Hamper Company was established to make the island's excellent produce available further afield, producing hampers of fine food for delivery straight to your door. Mixed hampers offer a selection of produce such as lobster, crab, salmon, mussels, oysters and scallops, the world-famous Orkney Island Gold beef, home-made traditional cheeses, preserves, sweet biscuits and oatcakes. There are also specific speciality cheese or seafood hampers as well as gift boxes. The company's smokery is located outside Stromness, where it smokes cheese, fish, garlic and even tomatoes, which are made into a delicious chutney. All food and hampers are available online, or from the Stromness shop on Victoria Street.

■ Rothiemurchus Farm Shop & Deli

Rothiemurchus Centre, Inverdruie, by Aviemore, Inverness–shire
01479 812345, www.rothiemurchus.net
Mon–Sun 9.30am–5.30pm.
Café, Web/mail order.

Established in 1985, Rothiemurchus Farm Shop started life selling fresh and smoked rainbow trout caught in the clear sparkling water flowing from the Cairngorms straight into its fishery. There soon followed the sale of the farm's tender venison – such was its popularity among the family's friends – and before long it was stocking a fully fledged farm shop, selling a range of local produce. Choose from a tempting selection of decidedly classic to boldly adventurous cheese, freshly baked bread, wines from around the globe and locally hand-made truffles and chocolates.

BEEF, LAMB & OTHER MEAT

In praise of grass

Cows eat grass, as every school child knows. Except that it's not always the case these days. In many parts of Scotland (thanks to all our rain) grass is what grows best and gives the animals that graze it a natural advantage. Catharina Day explains why the grass is greener.

PHOTOS: (PREVIOUS PAGE) SCOTTISH VIEWPOINT; (THIS PAGE) QMS

Remaining outdoors the entire year is not a particularly attractive prospect in the Scottish climate, but one of the characteristics of our native breeds of cattle is that they're hardy enough to endure it. When grazed on grasses and moorland flora, breeds such as Belted Galloway, Highland and Aberdeen Angus have fine marbled flesh that's low in saturated fats and contains a much higher percentage of omega three fatty acids than store-fed cattle.

In fact, if kept in natural conditions their meat shows a number of the health benefits more commonly championed in wild venison, as grass-fed ruminants are also higher in protein, vitamin E, beta carotene anti-oxidants and conjugated linoleic acid. Arguably most importantly of all they also offer wonderful flavour. Geese, chickens and turkeys have these health benefits too if they are allowed to feed on grasses and other plants.

Where our awareness of seasonality has been re-awoken for fruit, vegetables and, to a lesser extent, fish, consumers are not particularly attuned to the seasonal aspect of meat. Beyond an awareness of autumn and winter being a time for game, and widespread confusion over 'fresh Spring' lamb (in Scotland lambs are mostly born in spring, so anything you're eating around Easter either isn't Scottish or is no longer lamb), we don't tend to associate meat with a seasonal calendar.

In places where the seasons are less marked, or animals are fed predominantly on grain and silage, they are slaughtered all year around. In addition, a good deal of meat in the food chain is habitually frozen which also affects our appreciation of the seasonal dimension.

If an animal is taken to slaughter after a summer feeding on natural grasses and other flora, the flavour of their flesh is more complex as well as being sweeter and juicier, it is also darker and the fat has a yellowish tone because of the beta carotene in the animal's diet. The fact that a large majority of Scottish cattle and sheep graze grass when it's growing in the spring, summer and autumn is one reason why Scotch meat carries a premium. Compared to the rest of the world, Scottish livestock production is still notably extensive and pastoral.

Game still adheres to some rules of seasonality because it is, on the whole, grazing and foraging naturally the whole year round. Indeed, the shooting seasons for wild game are built around the breeding season, beginning only at the point in the year when birds have matured and fed well on the summer growth. While the grouse season starts with the 'glorious twelfth' of August (the traditional start of Queen Victoria's long summer holidays at Balmoral), a gamekeeper always favours reason over tradition and will maintain a strict control over the numbers shot in order to preserve a balance between the core breeding numbers and the old males. If it has been a bad breeding season and the grouse are not ready, shooting days will be cancelled. A day off to admire – and appreciate – the green scenery.

Below is a selection of outlets for Scottish grass-fed meat. Many sell direct to the public via mail/web order:

Angus Organics, by Forfar
www.angusorganics.com

Atholl Glens Organic Meat Co-operative, Blair Atholl
www.athollglens.co.uk

Buccleuch Scotch Beef, Castle Douglas
www.buccleuchfoods.com

Dalduff Farm, Maybole
www.dalduff.co.uk

Donald Russell Direct, Inverurie
www.donaldrussell.com

Fast Castle, Eyemouth
www.fast-castle.co.uk

Fletchers of Auchtermuchty, Fife
www.seriouslygoodvenison.co.uk

Highland Game, Dundee
www.highlandgame.com

Hardiesmill, near Kelso
www.hardiesmill.co.uk

Hugh Grieson Organic, Tibbermore, Perthshire
www.the-organic-farm.co.uk

Mey Selections, Wick
www.mey-selections.com

Peelham Farm Produce, Berwickshire
www.peelham.co.uk

Speyside Organics, Knockando
www.speysideorganics.com

The Store, Foveran, Aberdeenshire
www.thestorecompany.co.uk

Weatherall Foods, Dumfriesshire
www.blackface.co.uk

Well Hung & Tender, Berwickshire
www.wellhungandtender.com

CHEF'S CHOICE
CRAIG WOOD ON HENDERSON'S THE BUTCHER

I first discovered Henderson's while working in Edinburgh at the Hallion Club at a point when I was becoming increasingly frustrated by various butchers I had previously worked with. Alan Mattheson (now at Nick Nairn's Cook School) mentioned this small family butcher in Fife and gave me the contact details. I sampled some of the steaks and other meat and was hugely impressed.

Since opening the Wee Restaurant I have built a good relationship with both David and Andrew and speak with them both regularly. We change the menu at the restaurant every week and advice from David often helps me make these choices. I firmly believe that chefs should listen to their suppliers. Advice on certain cuts of meat, curing times, game seasons and pricing are all part of our regular conversations. The meat is often sourced from selected farms from the north of Scotland with whom they have built up a relationship. Sourcing great quality from the outset is obviously of the utmost importance – however without an understanding of the handling of the meat the final product can often be disappointing. At Henderson's the meat is hung for a lengthy period to ensure a mature flavour is achieved and that the meat is as tender as possible. I request that the ribeye we use are hung for a minimum of 28 days and I have to say the results are far better than any I have eaten before, including the famous Kobe beef.

■ *Craig Wood is the owner and chef at the Wee Restaurant, 17 Main Street, North Queensferry, 01383 616263, www.theweerestaurant.co.uk*

John Henderson Ltd Butchers is based at Unit 8, Fife Food Park, Faraday Road, Glenrothes, 01592 770 555

Cuts of meat

Scotch Beef has a great reputation, but there's little point in swooning over the prime cuts and ignoring the rest. Here butcher Jonathan Honeyman teams up with chef John Webber for a guided tour of a side of beef.

Feather Blade

The cut: It sits on the side of the shoulder blade and when sliced looks like a feather with the nerve like the quill. Cut like this it is good for casseroles. However, if the nerve is removed it gives two flat muscles that are very lean with a good flavour and firm texture. These are also good for daubes and casseroles but also for flash frying. Excellent value for money.
Alternatives: Topside.
Cooking: Brilliant slow cooked in curries. Char grill very rare for a Thai salad.

Fore rib

The cut: This is the bovine equivalent of rack of lamb, located between the shoulder and middle back. It's a good sized joint with a good proportion of inter-muscular fat which, when well conditioned, results in fantastic flavour and textures of beef. Undoubtedly a premium cut but worth every penny. When full trimmed back to the main muscle eye it gives one of the best steaks available: rib eye.
Alternatives: Wing rib.
Cooking: As a roast there is none better though it's more difficult to cook than sirloin. Don't undercook too much – if you like your beef rare go for wing rib. For the steaks simply grill or fry.

Leg of mutton cut

The cut: Sometimes known as thick rib or runner. Taken from the shoulder, it's typically sliced for braising steak or cubed for casseroles and the like. Occasionally used as an economy flash-fry steak or to make beef olives. Can also be used as an economical roast when properly de-nerved, but because this is a lean cut it will require barding with fat.
Alternatives: Something from the hind quarter – topside or thick flank.
Cooking: Braise in red wine with shallots and parsnips.

NECK

CHUCK & BLADE

FORE RIB

THICK RIB

THIN RIB

BRISKET

SHIN

Brisket

The cut: From the breast area, the brisket is typically boned and rolled allowing it to be trimmed of any excess fat. It's not best suited for quick cooking methods but responds well to slow cooking and is a very economical cut. Brisket is also a popular choice for making salt or pickled beef.
Alternatives: Silverside will react in a similar way to a long, slow braise, can be bought in the same manner and has a similar physical shape.
Cooking: A cheap source of good eating – five hours in a slow cooker and it is butter tender.

Fillet

The cut: There are two fillets per animal (one on each side), located in the lumbar region beneath the back bone, on the opposite side of the bone to the sirloin. The fillet does very little work so is very tender and also very low in fat hence it has a delicate, light flavour and will benefit from good hanging. Almost no external fat is present so marbling through the meat is essential to avoid dryness.

Alternatives: There isn't one, really, but you could try heart of rump.

Cooking: Best suited to quick cooking but a successful roast can be obtained using the head or thick centre section. This is by far the tenderest cut on the carcass but it is also the most subtle in flavour. This tenderness makes it ideal for serving underdone or even raw in a carpaccio or steak tartare. For steaks, pan fry them in olive oil with a little butter added half way through cooking. Don't cook them any more than medium and avoid too strong a sauce.

Sirloin

The cut: This describes the lower middle of the animal's back. It can be used on or off the bone as a roast but more often nowadays it's seen as a premium steak. The sirloin is basically a single muscle with good marbling and a nice cover of fat on the outside. It benefits from good maturation which results in tenderness and developed flavour.

Alternatives: Rib eye or pope's eye depending on budget.

Cooking: Sirloin is the best bet for an easy home roast beef and it's great served cold. Char grill the steaks and lightly rub with a bruised garlic clove. For something a bit different try a smoke roast on a kettle barbecue.

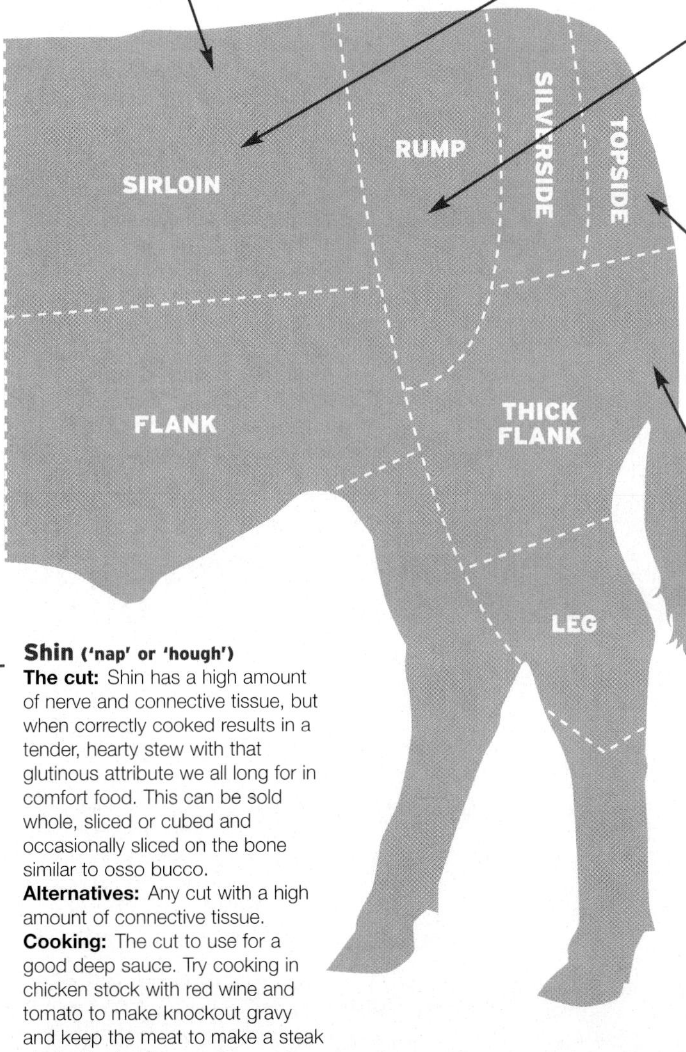

Rump (or 'pope's eye')

The cut: Located at the base of the spine where the back joins onto the leg. This cut is made up of a few muscles and is usually cut into thick steaks, though it can also be seam cut into individual muscles and then portioned. This is a full-flavored steak when properly matured and has more texture than the fillet. Cheapest of the 'premium' steaks.

Alternatives: Sirloin could be substituted in any recipe for pope's eye.

Cooking: A great steak for the barbecue as you get good flavour from the meat and it will take a marinade well.

Topside

The cut: From the hind quarter, an economical roast of more than acceptable quality when prepared correctly from good meat. This is a lean cut with reasonable texture and flavour. Also good for braising, minute steaks, and for curing as in salt beef or bresola.

Alternatives: Any hind quarter cut such as point of rump.

Cooking: Topside is a lean meat that can dry out easily, so if it's being roasted any over cooking or reheating can leave it appearing to be tough. It's better as a pot roast with plenty of vegetables to make a full flavoured sauce.

Shin ('nap' or 'hough')

The cut: Shin has a high amount of nerve and connective tissue, but when correctly cooked results in a tender, hearty stew with that glutinous attribute we all long for in comfort food. This can be sold whole, sliced or cubed and occasionally sliced on the bone similar to osso bucco.

Alternatives: Any cut with a high amount of connective tissue.

Cooking: The cut to use for a good deep sauce. Try cooking in chicken stock with red wine and tomato to make knockout gravy and keep the meat to make a steak pie for the family.

Oxtail

The cut: Have your butcher trim well and joint ready to go. Oxtail will respond wonderfully to long slow cooking resulting in a gelatinous meat full of flavour that falls effortlessly off the bone. This is real comfort food and considering there's only one per animal it's good value too.

Alternatives: Is there an alternative? The next best bet is slow cooked shin.

Cooking: Try serving the meat off the bone for your less adventurous guest or get the butcher to bone and stuff the tail. Then braise whole and serve as a joint.

Diagram labels: SILVERSIDE, RUMP, TOPSIDE, SIRLOIN, FLANK, THICK FLANK, LEG

• Master butcher Jonathan Honeyman runs the Aberfoyle Butcher and John Webber, who has twice won a Michelin star, is best known as a chef at Nick Nairn Cook School. They have recently joined to form Umami Culinaire, a small specialist artisan food company which sells a range of goods prepared by Honeyman and Webber, including hand-made charcuterie, meat and deli products. These are available through the Aberfoyle Butcher (see listings, p44).
• Quality Meat Scotland (www.qmscotland.co.uk) offers various guides to beef cuts and cooking for both professionals and public, including a series of video tutorials available on its website.

PHOTO: SCOTTISH VIEWPOINT

The crofting century

Lewis-based food writer Barry Shelby argues that, far from clinging to a dying way of life, crofting's time is right now.

Crofting can be a conundrum. It was a modern improvement to subsistence farming on the mostly marginal lands of the Highlands and islands, but it neither fitted into the mainstream nor ever quite managed to shake off a bias against it as inefficient. Though crofts are indeed a type of small farm or smallholding, very few crofters have ever been full-time agriculturalists: in the past they also fished or collected kelp and today might be joiners and weavers. Yet official solutions to the perceived problems have nearly always offered only agricultural prescriptions – and then they have tended to favour large farming systems over small.

Yet I would argue that crofting's time has come. Consider various current issues: whether concerns over food security or demand for locally produced food, environmental issues or the reassessment of the values of self-sufficiency and sustainability. Crofting essentially offers a tick in all these boxes, though very real issues of reasonable profitability for crofters linger. Crofting systems need to be accepted as a fair and perhaps even equal partner by agri-business – and in the eyes of government policy makers who acknowledge that crofting keeps rural areas populated where, elsewhere, vast areas are controlled by only the wealthy.

'Crofters can't feed the entire country, but they can contribute in a healthy way,' says Lewis-based shepherd, weaver and retired engineer Neil Macleod, who is chairman of the Scottish Crofting Foundation (formerly the crofters' union). Macleod is bullish if realistic. But he thinks crofters need to do more to promote the elements that people increasingly hold dear, for example food produced in pristine environments, offering traceability and, generally speaking, additive free.

Crofting counties represent a third of the Scottish landmass, a quarter of which is in the hands of crofters. One traditional contribution that crofting has made to agriculture across the UK has been the breeding of 'store lambs' – that is livestock sold for finishing down south in lowland Scotland or England. While that must continue – 'crofters are good at breeding hardy, healthy stock,' says Skye crofter Donald Murdie – it also puts crofters at the bottom of the food production chain, subject to low prices as everyone above them trims margins. Murdie has looked at food policy from various angles. He and wife Susanna Robson have been part of the Highlands and Islands Food Network and run fruit and veg box schemes (delivered sometimes by a local GP).

One answer is more finished products: whether local staples for the local market or speciality goods for a wider audience. Murdie, who has worked as the Crofting Foundation's land use project manager, says that means less centralisation of the processing, particularly abattoirs – a topic that 'consumers don't really want to hear about,' he adds. But neither do they want to hear that live animals have been shifted huge distances, suffering stress as a result.

Another solution may be the Crofting Produce Mark (see side panel), certifying the provenance of crofting goods. Still, the reality of most crofting lives is that their plots are not large enough to provide a full income. So Murdie says they need to be 'flexible' as they traditionally have been. That means local economies have to provide the part-time jobs, too.

Up on Shetland, Ronnie Eunson – who has some 675 hectares at Uradale Farm for organic sheep and rare breed cattle – has met first-hand local resistance to his attempts to set up a

local abattoir ('A million and one hoops to leap through,' he says). He believes that the crofting brand, to really succeed, will need a bit of the PR juice that someone like HRH Prince Charles can give to his Mey Selections products. Alas, says Eunson, a relatively recent appointment to the Crofting Commission, 'crofters are not always good at organising themselves.'

In the end, crofting has its limitations, for sure. Yet, it has proven that it can

keep people (and not just the wealthy) on rural land; it can provide produce to local consumers as well as niche or speciality goods for the wider market; breed livestock for mainstream farms; and help to ensure bio-diversity in the countryside – sometimes spectacular landscapes – for people to visit and enjoy. Today it is less of an anachronism than it has been for over a century.

■ For more information:
www.croftingfoundation.co.uk
www.croftinginquiry.org
www.crofters commission.org.uk

Crofting keeps rural areas populated and satisfies a demand for locally produced food. Photos on this page show Woodside Croft, Strathpeffer (www.woodsidecroft.com)

> CROFTING PRODUCE MARK

Crofters are building consumer confidence with a label that promises wholesome, environmentally friendly produce, while celebrating the crofting lifestyle.

One recent innovation to help promote crofting goods is the Crofting Produce Mark. While essentially a branding exercise, European regulation means that it cannot technically be called a brand. But with this label, crofters are hoping that consumers will develop the confidence that whatever they buy – whether soft fruit, honey or Shetland lamb – comes from a system of farming that is wholesome, environmentally friendly, and trustworthy. It's also an opportunity for crofters to sell their oft-admired lifestyle. The mark can be applied to textiles made in the crofting regions, too.

While it is unlikely to assist the wholesale livestock market – once 500 live lambs have been shipped to central UK for finishing, the provenance is largely lost – the Scottish Crofters Mark should aid in many ways.

When he attaches the mark to his meat, crofter Neil Macleod says he 'gets such a thrill.' It is a 'tremendous opportunity' for crofters, he says. It doesn't cost them much (£20 per annum) and it shows that they have achieved a discernable standard of quality, animal health and welfare, hygiene and total traceability.

But as Laurent Vernet, senior manager of marketing for Quality Meat Scotland, warned the annual gathering of the Scottish Crofting Foundation on Barra in 2008: 'A brand is a promise, a moral contract between the producer and the consumer. With a collective brand, you are only as strong as your weakest product. If someone has a bad experience with one single product . . . this consumer will often be resistant to trying others.'

Scottish Crofting Produce

Highlands and Islands Croft Origin

Sheepish about mutton

Sheep farming faces many challenges as the economics of meat and wool production prove unreliable, but Barry Shelby reports on the renewed interest in an aged lamb product.

PHOTO: WETHERALL FOODS

Foods fall in and out of fashion, but over the past 100 years arguably nothing lost its appeal quite as badly as mutton. Its ignominy is confirmed by the well-known backhanded compliment that compares it unfavourably to its now dominant rival, lamb. But mutton – that is the meat from sheep no less than two years old – is making a comeback. At least among gourmands, who appreciate its depth of flavour (and who know how to prepare it).

From his farm in Dumfries and Galloway, Ben Weatherall reports that he's seen a ten-fold increase in internet sales in the past few years. In addition to the general public, particularly keen buyers include some top London-based chefs whose business he has cultivated: well-kent names such as Jeremy Lee and Fergus Henderson.

On Shetland, sheep and rare-breed cattle farmer Ronnie Eunson is less sanguine. 'Plenty of food writers want to talk about it,' he says wryly from Uradale Farm, 'but that hasn't necessarily translated into customers.' Before mutton can make a true comeback, butchers and consumers need to have more confidence in the meat's preparation. Too many remain unfamiliar with the product, even if mutton dishes prove a big hit when served in restaurants or at Slow Food gatherings.

One key to turning raw mutton into virtual spun gold is a long, slow cook. In the Weatherall household, the trick is to salt and pepper a leg, place it in a low oven for about a dozen hours (eg over night), finish for 40 minutes in a hot oven and then let it rest for another three quarters of an hour.

It's too soon to be certain, but one day we might be talking about how someone is 'lamb dressed as mutton'.
■ *For more information on Wetherall Foods visit www.blackface.co.uk; Uradale Farm contact www.uradale.com*

Other sources of Scottish mutton

Ardalanish Farm:
www.ardalanish.com

Fast Castle:
www.fast-castle.co.uk

Mey Selections:
www.mey-selections.com

Scottish Organic Lamb:
www.scottishorganiclamb.com

Shetland Food Directory
www.foodshetland.com

Pie of the Land

Claire Ritchie looks at the life and times of a national icon.

'**S**cotch Pie' - the very words conjure up unsavory images of football grounds across the country, where mediocre, gristly pies are served to warm the heaving ranks on cold winters' days, entirely unpalatable without the requisite cup of Bovril alongside. Right? Well, not necessarily, no.

The Scotch pie – or mutton pie as it was once commonly called – actually seems to have originated in England some 500 years ago, although records are predictably vague. Today the pie is almost synonymous with Scotland, and can be found served hot from the oven in any bakery in any town. Costing little, and eaten without the need for cutlery or plates, this is the food of the everyman.

The method is simple: each pie is an individual serving, made from an outer casing of crisp hot-water pastry (four parts flour to one part fat) that is moulded into shape and left to harden overnight before the filling is added. The lid of the pie is placed about a centimetre lower than the sides to allow for toppings such as baked beans, peas or even mashed potatoes to be added.

Although historically mutton was the meat of choice for the pie filling, creating a use for the tougher, older meat, these days beef is the more common ingredient, despite the re-emergence of mutton in food fashions. The meat is usually highly spiced, and although every baker claims to guard his own secret recipe, a blend of pepper, mace and all-spice would be the standard components.

So revered is the humble pie that the Scotch Pie Club was formed in its honour in 1996, and holds the annual World Scotch Pie Championship to judge the best pie in the country. The 2009 winner of this coveted trophy was Paul Boyle of Boghall Butchers in Bathgate, whose family business has been baking pies since 1982.

› FIELD TO FORK: THE HARDIESMILL EXPERIENCE

Donald Reid reports on a Border farm offering an insight into the food chain.
Hardiesmill is Robin and Allison Tuke's 482-acre farm at Gordon, near Kelso in the Scottish Borders. As a way of introducing the public to their herd of pure-bred Aberdeen Angus cattle, they spend certain Friday afternoons taking small groups on the Hardiesmill 'Ten Steak Experience'. Following a trip out to see the cattle, on-farm butcher Lee demonstrates how a side of beef is divided up into different cuts, and there's then an opportunity to taste your way through ten different steaks from feather steak to onglet.
For Robin Tuke, the idea is to give more people 'a hands-on understanding of what to look and ask for when buying beef in order to get the best eating experience for your money. Is the fillet the best, or only the most expensive? Every steak has a different flavour and level of tenderness.' The tour also provides an insight into the effects of breeding, feeding and handling on the final product, along with hanging and maturing.

■ *Tickets are £35 per person, with a maximum eight people to a group. For more, call 01573 410797, www.hardiesmill.co.uk*

CHEF'S CHOICE
HECTOR MACRAE ON REESTIT MUTTON

It's important to me to source quality Scottish produce. As a youngster I worked in a local fish factory in Skye and it was heartbreaking to see about 99 per cent of the langoustines and scallops being shipped abroad. Times are changing and chefs are getting more supportive and demanding, which can only be a good thing. We started sourcing reestit mutton when a chef from Shetland, who was working in the restaurant, suggested we try it.

'Reestit' is an old-style Scottish dish; it is basically a heavily salted meat that is cured over peat fires in Shetland. Before freezers were invented, this was a way of treating the meat to last through the winter. We get ours from Globe Butchers in Lerwick.

It's great in a hearty broth, as it has a really intense mutton-y flavour. I'd slow cook the meat and use it to make a stock. However, it's so salty that – depending on the batch – I sometimes have to dilute it a little. You can also cut it up thinly, lightly fry it and use it in a salad. It's not as refined a meat as parma ham, but it has a much more appealing bite to it. I'll sometimes have it in a roll before service to keep me going.

■ *Hector MacRae is head chef at First Coast, 97–101 Dalry Road, Edinburgh, 0131 313 4404, www.first-coast.co.uk Globe Butchers is at 49–53 Commercial Road, Lerwick, Shetland, 01595 692819 www.globebutchers.co.uk*

Wild and free (or, at least, inexpensive)

Small game - wild pheasant, duck, pigeon, partridge and rabbit - was once a staple food in Scottish working-class households. Gordon Davidson hunts around to see where it has all gone.

Cheap, plentiful and nutritious, no self-respecting butcher's shopfront was without its garland of wild birds, freshly shot and bound into braces, then hung on purpose-built chrome rails in the windows above the red meat. Rabbits, meanwhile, were traditionally strung around butchers' doors, and were so popular – and plentiful – that there was an export market, with great wicker hampers full of fresh Scots bunny slung onto the London train each evening, to be sold the next day at Smithfield meat market.

Game-eating was, quite simply, a centuries-old Scottish habit and its presence on the family dinner table was as common and unremarkable as that of chicken today.

It was, of course, chicken that displaced game, in the years after the Second World War, when battery farming, created to supply the hungry nation with plentiful eggs, began churning out its side-product of young hens, burnt out as egg-layers but fat on intensive feeding and minimal exercise.

An avalanche of white meat tumbled out of these new factory farms, plucked and oven-ready, perfectly placed to ride the post-war consumer trends of convenience and modernity, and Scottish shoppers were soon no more inclined to buy a bird with its feathers and head still attached than they were to bake their own bread. In time, we simply forgot how tasty wild meat was.

However, our 50-year flirtation with factory-farmed chicken, though not entirely over, is certainly looking pretty jaded these days and a fresh public appetite for meats outwith the abilities of the factory farmers has been seized on by a new generation of firms dedicated to reconnecting Scots with their game heritage.

'In the last five years, the small game industry has really leapt forward – I think it is looking absolutely fantastic,' enthuses Craig Stevenson, managing director of Braehead Foods, the Kilmarnock company currently supplying ready-to-cook small game meat to a stellar list of top Scots restaurants.

When Stevenson, a veteran of both

the bakery and beef sectors, took over Braehead's speciality foods business in 1999, he found that demand for Scottish small game was all from overseas, in continental markets that had never lost the taste for it, while the home market was sadly indifferent.

'So we started encouraging Scottish chefs to put game on their menus – even if it meant giving it to them for free,' he says. He confesses to randomly adding pheasant breasts to orders for other goods, then when chefs phoned up to query the delivery, he'd tell them they were a free sample, why not cook them up for your staff?

'I just had to get chefs to try gamebirds and start thinking of them as food again – and once they'd had a taste of it, pheasant and partridge and pigeon soon started appearing on their menus.'

Television's celebrity chefs have since embraced game as an opportunity to widen their repertoire – and fill airtime – and in so doing have persuaded a new generation of home cooks to experiment with the meat.

Newcomers to cooking gamebirds should be aware that they can most definitely not be treated as a substitute for domesticated chicken. With their natural diet and lots of exercise, wild birds and rabbits are not inclined to be fatty, and that must be taken into account during preparation.

Chef Jacqueline O'Donnell, of Glasgow's The Sisters restaurant, which runs regular cookery demos, finds that the look of a feathered or skinned pheasant often creates a stir of fear in her audiences, but that is easy to get over with just a little practice at the 'fiddly bits'.

'I sometimes cook breasts on the crown as that can help prevent them

> SEASONALITY

It is legal to shoot a variety of birds, wildfowl and mammals in Scotland, but for many of these species, there is also a closed season during which time they must be left undisturbed to breed and disperse. As such, small game is generally unavailable during the spring and summer months.

Pheasant > 1 October to 1 February
Partridge > 1 September to
1 February
Grouse > 12 August to 10 December
Duck and goose > 1 September to
31 January
Woodcock > 1 September to 31
January
Pigeon and rabbit are seen as pests, so can be shot all year, but it is better to wait until autumn to take advantage of a well-fed crop of birds and bunnies. As retired Stirlingshire gamekeeper Alastair Davidson puts it: 'The best way to think of small game is that it's wild fruit, like brambles or mushrooms – a seasonal treat to be sorely missed when you can't get it, then savoured with relish when it returns.'

Game is the green alternative to factory farming

becoming dry, and it's essential to always use the bones to make a stock – too many discard the bit with all the taste,' says O'Donnell. 'Instead of trimming all the tiny bits from the carcass, we braise everything then the excess meat falls off, which gives you much more for your money and all the longer cooking times make a tastier piece of meat, although mostly people use loin or breast for quickness.

'I personally love complementing all the different types of game with other Scotch things which are also in season. Often Mother Nature just guides us to put them together and suprisingly it works! In the correct season we have such an abundance of these products – we should have them appearing on menus up and down the country to showcase the excellence of the Scottish produce.'

But shoppers looking to buy the raw product won't have much luck in the major supermarkets, which are geared up to sell centrally distributed and homogenous product, not wild animals.

Though there are moves afoot to get more oven-ready small game into the major retailers, the best bet at the moment is to seek out vacuum-packed portions available through delicatessens, farmers' markets and, increasingly, internet mail order.

It is small beer compared with the volume of chicken sold every day, but as Ross Montague of the Scottish Countryside Alliance notes, small is beautiful: 'The fact that game is not an ideal supermarket product shouldn't be a worry. The essence of game is as a local, low-food-miles product.'

Speaking for Borders game suppliers, Burnside Farm Foods, Johnny Rutherford agrees that, aside from the superior taste of game meat, shoppers are getting a better environmental deal. All the game that goes through Burnside's plant is sourced within a 30-mile radius. 'We pick up gamebirds at local estates, process them right here, then put them back out to local hotels and the farmers' markets at Kelso and Hawick. That's the kind of food miles we had a century ago – as a product, small game is about as green as it gets.'
■ *Braehead Foods: www.braehead foods.co.uk; Burnside Farm Foods: www.maxton.bordernet.co.uk/ burnside; Weatherall Foods: www. blackface.co.uk*

WHERE TO BUY

Outlets for buying beef, lamb and other meat, listed regionally then organised alphabetically.

EDINBURGH & LOTHIANS

■ Andersons Quality Butcher

36 High Street, North Berwick
01620 892964
Mon–Fri 7am–5pm; Sat 7.30am–4.30pm.
Closed Sun.
A real family affair, this award-winning North Berwick butcher shop is run by John Anderson with his wife Elizabeth and three sons. They sell high quality meat, sourced locally – sometimes within two miles – and more often than not they place a note in the window to let customers know where from. There is often a queue of people lining up to buy the various cuts of meat on offer, as well as the popular haggis, bridies and Scotch pies. Chatty and friendly staff are always around to give a helping hand and advise on your purchases.

■ Ballencrieff Rare Pedigree Pigs

Ballencrieff Gardens, by Longniddry, East Lothian
01875 870551
www.ballencrieffrppigs.co.uk
Tue–Fri 10am–4pm; Sat/Sun 1–4pm and at Haddington and Edinburgh farmers' markets.
Award-winning Ballencrieff offers an alternative to intensive farming. It farms old fashioned pigs, in an old fashioned way, to produce a flavour second to none. Berkshire, Saddleback and Gloucester Old Spot sows run outside all year round, and piglets are born and reared completely free-range. It mixes its own feed, adding no growth promoters or drugs, and allows the pigs to grow at the speed that nature intended – very slowly. The resulting bacon is all home dry-cured with nothing added. It makes 20 varieties of sausages from shoulder pork with no gristle, very little fat and of course never any additives, artificial colours or flavourings.

■ Belhaven Smokehouse

Beltonford, Dunbar, East Lothian
See Fish & Shellfish

■ Boghall Butchers

65 Margaret Avenue, Boghall, Bathgate
01506 630178
www.boghallbutchers.co.uk
Mon–Fri 7am–5pm, Sat 6am–4.30pm.
Closed Sun.
There is a focus on quality pies and pastry goods at this butcher's shop on the outskirts of Bathgate, with the proud motto 'Say Aye Tae a Pie'. Award-winning Scotch pies, speciality steak pies and ready meals have all garnered awards for the family-run shop, which was refitted in 2007 to cope with the growing demand from hungry customers. For pudding, it provides a range of cakes and pastries. Deliveries are available in West Lothian.

■ George Bower

75 Raeburn Place, Stockbridge, Edinburgh
0131 332 3469
www.georgebowerbutchers.co.uk
Mon–Sat 8am–5pm. Closed Sun.
In the heart of the foodie mini-village of Stockbridge, Bowers has earned itself a reputation as one of the best quality butchers in Edinburgh. Specialising in traditional meat products including sausages, haggis and black pudding, it also offers harder to find goods such as tripe or wild boar, and a range of cooked meats, pies and meatloaf. Its game and poultry range comes highly recommended, with a seal of approval from Heston Blumenthal and Nick Nairn among others.

■ Crombies of Edinburgh

97–101 Broughton Street, Edinburgh
0131 557 0111
www.crombiesofedinburgh.co.uk
Mon–Fri 8am–6pm; Sat 8am–5pm.
Closed Sun.
Founded by Jonathan Crombie's grandfather in 1956, award-winning Crombies of Edinburgh is a rare combination of tradition and innovation. Its haggis is made on the premises (halal version available), and there are all the expected and well-sourced meats, game, and poultry. The real stars, however, are the award-winning sausages. Expect a remarkable selection of flavour combinations: wild boar, apricot and brandy; venison, pork and calvados; whisky, hog and wild thyme; cumberland; Scottish beef; chorizo; toulouse and merguez. There is something here to suit every palate. Available for delivery anywhere in the UK so no one need miss out on these delectable bangers.

■ Findlay's of Portobello

116 Portobello High Street, Portobello, Edinburgh
0131 669 2783
www.findlayofportobello.co.uk
Tue–Sat 8am–5pm. Closed Sun & Mon.
A family-run butcher providing free-range meat and poultry from selected farms around the Scottish borders, Findlay's has been trading since 1974. It uses only free-range cattle, selected by Mr Findlay himself and then hung for a period of no less than two weeks to mature and enhance the flavour of the meat. It sources free-range pork from a farm in Hawick and lamb from farms in Peeblesshire. Renowned for its award-winning products, which are all hand-made on the premises, it holds titles for its haggis, black pudding, beef sausage and bacon.

■ Gosford Bothy Farm Shop

Gosford Estate, Aberlady, East Lothian
01875 871234
www.gosfordfarmshop.co.uk
Mon–Sun 9.30am–5pm.
Café.
Down Gosford way there's a caring, sharing attitude, selling as it does a range of products from local specialist suppliers as well as its own Northwood wild boar. The bothy incorporates a butchery and the farm shop has a fresh meat counter with boar, beef, lamb and organic rare-breed pork. Locally sourced seasonal vegetables and deli items sit alongside. The café adjoining serves lunches, snacks, and has an attractive outdoor decking area.

■ John Saunderson

40 Leven Street, Edinburgh
0131 229 8348
www.johnsaunderson.co.uk
Mon–Fri 7.30am–5.30pm; Sat 7.30am–1pm. Closed Sun.
John Saunderson is the fourth generation of butcher to run this award-winning shop and, with 80 years of experience between him and his staff, they are well placed to give advice. Stocking an impressive range of products from reputable and award-winning suppliers – Copas' turkeys, free-range chickens and duck eggs from Linda Dick; game from George Bower; venison from Lochaber Game Services; and pork and bacon from Ramsay of Carluke – it guarantees quality produce with absolute traceability. Call into the shop on Leven Street where you are assured of a warm welcome.

■ The Store

13 Comely Bank Road, Stockbridge, Edinburgh
See Delis & General Food

GREATER GLASGOW & CLYDESIDE

■ James Allan

85 Lauderdale Gardens, Glasgow
0141 334 8973, www.craftbutchers.com
Mon–Sat 8am–5.30pm. Closed Sun.
This family-run business deals with only the best suppliers of organic meat from

SCOTCH BEEF.
GREAT QUALITY OF LIFE.

GREAT QUALITY OF TASTE.

Exceptional farming methods and a favourable climate are the reason that Scotch Beef tastes so naturally delicious. Couple these with stringent assurance schemes and you have, in our opinion, the tastiest beef in the world. Simply look for the PGI and Scotch Beef symbols. This guarantees that your beef is of a higher quality.

the Orkney Islands. It carries a wide range of game and poultry, and makes its own highly acclaimed sausages, haggis and meat pies on the premises. Every animal can be traced back to its farm of origin on Orkney where they led idyllic, grass-fed lives, and where there has never been a single case of BSE.

■ Carmichael Estate Farm Meats

Carmichael Visitor Centre, Warrenhill Farm, A73 between Biggar and Lanark, Lanarkshire
01899 308336, www.carmichael.co.uk
Mon–Sun 10am–5pm (Nov–Feb hours restricted: phone ahead to confirm).
Café.
In the wake of various animal disease scares, this single estate farm in southern Scotland strives to provide meat with 'total traceability', ensuring that every animal is born, reared, fattened, slaughtered, butchered, packaged and processed on the farm. Beef, lamb and venison (including lean venison and mushroom sausages, and cuts of smoked venison) are specialities. A home delivery service is available, as well as the option to order by phone or online and then pick up in person.

■ Ramsay of Carluke

22 Mount Stewart Street, Carluke, Lanarkshire
01555 772277
www.ramsayofcarluke.co.uk
Mon 8am–4pm; Tue–Fri 8am–4.30pm; Sat 8am–12.30pm. Closed Sun.
Web/mail order
Ramsay of Carluke has been a local family butcher for over 150 years. Using only farm-assured outdoor free-range pigs specifically selected from carefully chosen farmers, it produces traditional Ayrshire bacon, home-cured in large vats of old fashioned pickle. After curing, the sides are left to mature before being divided into traditional Ayrshire cuts, after which much of the bacon is slowly smoked in its own smokehouse. In addition it produces a range of award-winning sausages, puddings, haggis and cooked hams using closely guarded old family recipes. It also supplies Scottish grass-fed beef and makes all products available by mail order throughout mainland UK.

SOUTHERN SCOTLAND

■ Dalduff Farm Shop

Crosshill, Maybole, Ayrshire
01655 740271, www.dalduff.co.uk
Mon–Sat 8am–4.30pm. Closed Sun.
(Dobbies counter open Mon–Sun 9am–6pm.)
GM produce is strictly off the menu at this farm kitchen and shop in South Ayrshire. Instead, it offers a range of locally reared beef, lamb and pork, covering steaks and chops, via mince rounds and pies, through to quality home-made frozen meals, including luxury lasagne or beef olives in onion gravy. It will deliver to the west coast of Scotland and customers can pop in to the Maybole farm shop or buy from the Dalduff counter at Dobbies Garden World on the outskirts of Ayr.

■ WTS Forsyth & Sons

21 Eastgate, Peebles, Peeblesshire
01721 720833, www.scottish-food.co.uk
Mon/Tue & Thu/Fri 7am–5.15pm; Wed 7am–1pm; Sat 7am–4.45pm. Closed Sun.
WTS Forsyth & Sons is a family-run butcher set in the Scottish Borders selling traditional Scottish fare. It sources its beef exclusively from quality herds and its lambs from farms in the surrounding area of Peebles. Specialities include home-cured bacon, haggis, white and black puddings and pies. In addition, an in-house bakery produces shortbread, gingerbread, Selkirk bannocks and a selection of breads. Gluten-free pork sausages are available, as are other products on request. Expect to queue on a Saturday – an encouraging sign.

■ Lindsay Grieve Traditional Butchers

29 High Street, Hawick
01450 372109, www.angus.co.uk/haggis
Mon–Fri 7am–5pm, Sat 7am–3.30pm. Closed Sun.
Web/mail order.
St Andrew's Day, Hogmanay and Burns' Night are the busiest times of the year for Lindsay Grieve, whose award-winning haggis is prepared by hand, following a family recipe. The Borders butcher offers a mail order service for haggis, dispatching the mutton and oatmeal speciality from Hawick's High Street to the rest of the UK and Europe. It also offers a range of tips on the customs for celebrating Burns' Night in traditional style.

■ Hardiesmill

Hardiesmill Place, Gordon, Berwickshire
01573 410797, www.hardiesmill.co.uk
Web/mail order.
A privately owned family-run farm set in the Scottish Borders, Hardiesmill is a 482-acre farm focusing on its herd of free range pedigree Aberdeen Angus cattle. Committed to a concept of 'farm-to fork', owners Robin and Alison Tuke believe in the balance of taste, flavours, texture, look and aroma achieved by rearing their cattle the natural way. In addition to the farm, Hardiesmill has acquired the renowned Tombuie Smokehouse and, as a result, it sells a range of smoked Aberdeen Angus beef products, as well as smoked Scottish cheeses, venison, duck breast, lamb, chicken and hams.

■ Whitmuir Organics

Whitmuir Farm, Lamancha, West Linton, Peeblesshire
01968 661908
www.whitmuirorganics.co.uk
Mon–Fri 10am–6pm; Sat 10am–4pm; Sun noon–4pm.
Whitmuir Organics is a small, award-winning organic farm set in the Borders. Beef, lamb, mutton and pork is reared, and butchered on the farm. Committed to the highest standards of animal welfare, it keeps pigs in family groups on open ground, woodland and in traditional pig arcs, while it gives free-range hens space to roam and spend their days happily scratching around. In addition to providing individually requested cuts of meat, it will also supply larger quantities in the form of 'stash packs', allowing you to purchase a whole lamb, half a pig or 5kg–15kg quantities of beef. As well as organic meat, Whitmuir grows organic vegetables and soft fruit to sell, and also eggs.

CENTRAL SCOTLAND & FIFE

■ The Aberfoyle Butcher

Mayfield, 206 Main Street, Aberfoyle
01877 382473
www.aberfoylebutcher.co.uk
Mon–Sat 8am–5pm. Closed Sun.
See photo entry on page 46.

■ Ballathie Good Food Company

Ballathie Estate, Kinclaven, Stanley, Perthshire
01250 876219
www.ballathiegoodfood.com
Tue–Sun 9.30am–5.30pm. Closed Mon.
Café, Web/mail order
The specialities in this farm shop with an adjoining café-restaurant, the Ballathie Country Kitchen, are the pies, gourmet sausages, burgers and speciality cooked meats produced from the Ballathie estate. It also sells meat from the herds of Aberdeen Angus beef, Tamworth and Saddleback pigs and seasonal game, with packages shipped for next day delivery.

■ Brig Farm Shop

Gateside Home Farm, Bridge Of Earn, Perth, Perthshire
See Fruit & Veg Specialists

HIGHLAND *Organics*

SUPREME

HIGHLAND *Organics* FREE RANGE CHICKEN

THE ABERFOYLE BUTCHER Running a traditional family business in the heart of the Trossachs, Jonathan Honeyman has established himself as one of Scotland's foremost butchers. At ease passing on his skills and knowledge to trainee butchers, chefs and the general public, Honeyman has always placed quality, heritage and the seasons at the heart of his operation. This is obvious in a recent innovation, Legend, a range of meat and game individually assessed and chosen by Honeyman from specialist producers which reflects the true characteristics of the breed, cut, and area in which it was raised, giving full provenance from breeder to plate. Very few products qualify to be included in the Legend selection, but each one carries the unique qualities imbued by tradition, individual selection, maturation and careful preparation. See page 44.

■ Gloagburn Farm Shop
Gloagburn, Tibbermore, Perth
See Delis & General Food

■ Jamesfield Farm
Jamesfield Farm Outlet Ltd, Jamesfield Farm, Abernethy, Perthshire
See Delis & General Food

■ D&A Kennedy
36 High Street, Blairgowrie, Perthshire
01250 870358, www.kennedybeef.com
Mon–Sat 8am–5pm. Closed Sun.
Web/mail order.
Opened in 1982, D&A Kennedy has established itself as one of Scotland's leading butchers. Alan Kennedy visits Forfar market every Wednesday to purchase livestock from tried and trusted local farms and suppliers, keen to assure traceability from farm to plate. His beef is then hung for at least three weeks to ensure tenderness and flavour. The Kennedys have been based at their Blairgowrie premises for the last ten years, and offer a nationwide mail order service.

■ Rannoch Smokery
Kinloch Rannoch, Perthshire
01796 472194
www.rannochsmokery.co.uk
Web/mail order.
Rannoch Smokery was founded in the late 1980s following a bad winter which prevented Ben Barclay's deer cull getting to market. Not to be defeated, he brined and smoked all of his meat, stopping it from going to waste and, in so doing, created the first ever Rannoch Smokery smoked venison. The family business now produces smoked pheasant, chicken, goose and turkey as well as the venison, and distributes through a wide network of supermarkets and delis, as well as by mail order through its own website.

■ Tombuie Smokehouse
Hardiesmill Place, Gordon, Berwickshire
01887 820127, www.tombuie.com
Web/mail order.
See entry for Hardiesmill

NORTH EAST SCOTLAND

■ Finzean Estate Farm Shop & Tea Room
Balnaboth, Finzean, Banchory, Aberdeenshire
See Delis & General Food

■ HM Sheridan
11 Bridge Street, Ballater
01339 755218, www.hmsheridan.co.uk
Mon–Sat 7am–5.15pm. Closed Sun.
Web/mail order.
The village of Ballater in Aberdeenshire has been home to butcher HM Sheridan for nearly 40 years. It sources beef from local farms and hangs it for 21 days. It also goes to local sources for lamb and pork, both of which boast a distinctive flavour having been reared outdoors. It purchases venison from Deeside estates and also sells local game including pigeon, pheasant and partridge. In addition, it makes a large range of products in the shop, including traditional puddings, haggis and over 20 varieties of sausage.

■ The Store
Foveran, Newburgh, Ellon, Aberdeenshire
01358 788083
www.thestorecompany.co.uk
Mon & Wed–Fri 11am–5pm; Sat/Sun 10am–4pm. Closed Tue.
The Booth family farm in Foveran is the source of much of the fresh produce for sale in its shops both on site and in

Edinburgh's Stockbridge. It feeds its lamb on grass and rears its Aberdeen Angus naturally in small numbers. The farm shop's meat counter has a range of products from steaks and sausages to freshly made shepherd's pie, curry and lasagne, and various cuts and joints for the Sunday roast. In addition, there's poultry, fish, deli products, vegetables and cheeses, as well as fresh breads and home baking, wines and chocolates. It sets aside three small paddocks for educational tours to learn about farming.

■ Wark Farm
Wark Farm, Cushnie, Alford
01975 581149, www.warkfarm.co.uk
10am–4.30pm on monthly open days (last Thu, Fri and Sat each month).
Details on website.
Web/mail order.
Wark Farm is a family-owned business run by Dugie and Jenny Foreman in the low hills of Aberdeenshire. Specialising in the production of traditional breed meats and charcuterie, they are on a quest to produce fantastic meats and products that are worthy of being eaten and do justice to the animals and their environment. A variety of organic produce is always available to purchase from the farm, including Belted

Galloway beef, Oxford, Sandy and Black pork, Hebridean lamb and Aylsebury duck. Their impressive range includes bacon, hams, sausages and pork pies, as well as home-made confits, rilettes and even corned beef.

HIGHLANDS, ISLANDS & ARGYLL

■ The Dounby Butchers
Dounby, Orkney
01856 771777
Considered by some to be the best beef in Scotland, Orkney beef comes from Aberdeen Angus cattle, reared in the area's clean, natural environment and fed on a grass diet. The Dounby Butcher is proud of its commitment to providing the best quality cuts, with high standards of animal welfare and with meat matured for a minimum of 21 days.

■ Globe Butchers
49–53 Commercial Road, Lerwick, Shetland Isles
01595 692819, www.globebutchers.co.uk
Web/mail order.
Established over 100 years ago, this Lerwick-based butcher knows a thing or two about quality cuts. Tender Shetland-reared lamb is a particular

speciality (available August to March) but it also stocks beef and pork sourced from the north-east of Scotland. It caters for summer barbeques with sausages and burgers, as well as quality ready meals. Recipe ideas and helpful cooking instructions are also dished out regularly by staff.

■ Charles MacLeod
Ropework Park, Stornoway, Isle of Lewis
01851 702445
www.charlesmacleod.co.uk
Mon–Sat 8am–5.30pm. Closed Sun.
Mail order.
Charles MacLeod on the Isle of Lewis has done more than any other family butcher to help establish the humble black pudding as one of Scotland's distinctive regional foods. The shop in the heart of Stornoway sells a full range of meat and other grocery items, including fruit and veg, while it sells puddings (black, white and fruit) and an own-brand haggis by mail order through its website. Recently, Charles and Iain MacLeod, sons of the founder of the business, have been among a group of local butchers involved in pursuing European geographical protection for Stornoway black puddings, or *marag dubh* as the Gaelic-speaking locals have it.

BREAD, CAKES & CHOCOLATE

TONY SINGH ON UGLY BREAD

Nothing beats freshly baked bread. The smell, the taste, the diversity – it is always hard to resist newly baked bread but it's not always easy to find genuinely fresh, flavoursome products. In Scotland, we boast a small number of artisan bakers but one that really stands out for me is Edinburgh's Ugly Bread – a new Scottish bakery tucked away on North Castle Street. Their wide range of products always promise quality tastes and textures.

The bakery serves surrounding hotels and restaurants but has also just started selling its products to consumers and diners. They make quality Scottish favourites, baked using traditional hand-craft techniques and recipes with a focus on taste. All ingredients used are natural and sourced locally and they offer a fantastic range of breads, scones, cakes and pastries – including truly Scottish fly cemetery – all prepared fresh on site throughout the day.

Master baker Graeme Ayton is always looking to try out new recipes and ideas. Soon they will be introducing butties, bran scones and some unique, fresh wild mushroom sausage rolls. It's simple baking at its very best.
■ *Tony Singh is chef proprietor of Tony's Table and Oloroso restaurants in Edinburgh, www.oloroso.co.uk*
Ugly Bread is at 58a North Castle Street, Edinburgh, 0131 226 6743

MAIN PHOTO: COURTESY DAFTMILL DISTILLERY

Grains of truth

Oats and barley have been Scotland's main cereal crops since the Middle Ages, simply because, unlike wheat and maize, both are willing to grow in our damp, sun-deprived climate. Gordon Davidson traces their fortunes.

Things were going great for oats in Scotland until they legalised whisky. Before 1823, oats had enjoyed two centuries as a staple food grain, having relegated barley to animal feed. But once Scotch whisky was legitimised, barley's fortunes shot up. Oats were usurped as farmers switched to growing spring barley for malting.

The money on offer prompted the breeding of new, higher yielding barley strains and the crop moved away from its hardy origins, becoming something of a racehorse – a great earner, but vulnerable to disease and adverse conditions.

Having slogged along in barley's shadow for a century or more, oats are enjoying an upswing in fortune as a cheap and cheerful superfood – something granny knew all along.

The organic boom has also favoured oats as, closer to their wild genetic roots, they grow with less artificial help and are particularly resistant to the diseases that plague the more refined barleys and wheats. In the seven-year rotations used by organic farmers, oats are effectively biological bouncers, able to clear a field of disease and fungal problems.

Organic oats are now taking a novel route to the market via the mobile Stoats Porridge Bars, often to be found standing alongside the burger vans at Scotland's music festivals.

In contrast to this renaissance, barley growers have been hit by the global market. The multinational maltsters, with ready access to imported barley, have pushed down the farmgate price. Officially, the big players insist that around 90 per cent of the barley used to produce Scotch whisky is still grown domestically. But they refuse to guarantee that domestic origin, arguing that without imports to fall back on, the whisky industry is only one bad harvest away from disaster.

Scotland's recent horribly wet summers have only fuelled the fierce disagreements over the price on offer to those farmers willing to take a risk and plant for the malting market – and much saber-rattling over the long-term veracity of the term 'Scotch' if local growers carry through their threats to abandon the crop.

But, among the independent distilleries some operations have made a virtue of their small size by leaping back several centuries and sourcing barley from their farming neighbours. Islay's Bruichladdich distillery, for example, now offers individual caskings traceable to barley grown on the island itself.
■ *For more on oats and Scottish suppliers see www.allaboutoats.co.uk*

Scotland's cakes

Robert Burns described Scotland as a 'Land o' Cakes'.
Nicki Holmyard discovers whether there's still a heritage of
regional speciality cakes beyond the high-street bakery chains.

Pancakes

Scotch pancakes, made from a simple sweet batter poured, or dropped, onto a girdle, are one of Scotland's distinctive and fondly-regarded foods, an icon of the nation's affinity with baking. They're best, of course, warm from the girdle (Scots term for flat iron baking plate or griddle), their taste always compromised the moment time or packaging are involved. As far back as 1599, Culross in Fife was granted a Royal Charter for making girdles.

Bannocks

Girdles were used to make everything from oatcakes to bannocks and have survived the passage of time in Scots cookery. Original bannocks were loaves made from barley flour or oatmeal, but over time the recipe changed to use wheat flour and yeast, enriched with butter and dried fruit, and cooked in an oven. Selkirk Bannock, first made by a

baker in the town, was initially made for festive occasions but tends to be a year-round fixture these days.

Tarts

Edinburgh Tart also has a link to Mary, Queen of Scots, and was supposedly developed in honour of her visit to the city. It is a traditional Scottish butter tart, similar in basic recipe to Ecclefechan and Border tarts, and uses butter, sugar, eggs, candied peel and dried fruit. Butter tart recipes were taken by Scots migrants all over the world and are popular in Canada and the US. The American Pecan Pie takes its influence from the same route.

Orkney & Shetland

Orcadians used oatmeal in their broonie, which is a type of gingerbread. The term comes from *brüni* – Norse for a thick bannock. In Shetland, a Bride's Bonn or Bun was traditionally broken over the head of a bride as she entered her new marital home. The bonn was historically knows as infar-cake and the tradition has links back to Roman times, when the eating of a consecrated cake in the rite of *confarratio*, solemnised a marriage.

Dundee Cake

While legend tells that the first Dundee cake recipe was developed for Mary, Queen of Scots, who wanted a fruit cake without cherries, it was first made

commercially at the beginning of the nineteenth century by marmalade makers, the Keillers, using left-over peel. Similar fruit cake recipes were widely in use, but the Keillers decorated theirs with blanched almonds and branded them with the name of their home town.

Black Bun

A dark spicy fruit cake full of fruit encased in shortcrust pastry case, Black Bun is a pretty solid piece of baking, and was referred to by Robert Louis Stevenson in his *Notes on Edinburgh Life* (1879) as a 'dense, black substance, inimical to life'. It is one of three gifts carried by New Year first footers, along with whisky and a lump of coal, the three representing food, drink and warmth for the year ahead.

Butteries

Aberdeenshire butteries, also known as rowies, are a savoury, flattened, flakey roll, high in fat and salt. Dating to the 1880s, they were created for the growing population of fishermen to take to sea, as they kept longer than traditional bread. They were immortalised in a street cry, 'bawbee baps and buttery rowies,' and remain the strongest of regional baking traditions today.

Oat cuisine

Oatcakes are the definitive Scottish biscuit, but there's a vast range. The Larder got together with Mary Contini in the Valvona & Crolla Food Hall in Jenners to sample a selection.

Nairns Organic Oatcakes

In their green tartan box with convenient, individually portioned packets, these are one of the more 'polished' oatcake varieties available. They contain no added sugar and are made using rough oatmeal and without the addition of wheat flour – which cannot be said of all oatcakes, so those with intolerances beware. A relatively neutral taste, they would perhaps make a good vehicle for a strong cheese or game pâté.

Macleans Cocktail Oatcakes

From the small Outer Hebridean island of Benbecula come these lovely little bite-sized oatcakes, produced by Macleans' small but successful family business. They have a home-baked feel to them and smell fresh and sweet, although they contain no sugar. Darker in colour and flavour from a longer bake, with their unusual grainy texture they are both rich and moist. Also made in a larger, triangular size, these are one of our favourites.

Isle of Skye Baking Co Original

These attractively packaged oatcakes are one example of a wide range of goods from a small independent bakery in Portree, Skye. Made in the traditional way – using lard and a combination of fine oats and pinhead oatmeal – these oatcakes have a rough, dry texture and a rustic, home-baked style. Notable more for their texture than any distinctive flavour, they're designed as a good carrier for cheese or perhaps marmalade.

Paterson's Olive Oil Oatcakes

Paterson's markets these oatcakes as being orang-utan friendly, as they avoid the use of contentious palm oil, the cultivation of which endangers vast numbers of rainforest wildlife in south-east Asia.

This particular variety has a crisp, high-baked texture, though there's no doubting the olive oil gives them a distinctive taste. Made using the bare minimum ingredients – oats, oil and salt – these are good for vegetarians and those with wheat intolerances.

Stockan & Gardens Cocktail Oatcakes

Another island entry, this time from Stromness in Orkney. These elegant little oatcakes benefit from the addition of a little sugar as well as the usual salt, giving them an appealing sweet and salty tang. The texture is grainy and mealy – almost buttery – thanks to the combination of oats and wheat. Also sold in quarter round (triangular) packs of varying thickness – which itself alters the way the oatcake tastes.

Wooleys Arran Oatcakes

In general oatcakes suffer from flimsy and unattractive packaging, so these stand out from the crowd with their easily resealed or folded bag. Their crisp texture, high-baked flavour and fresh, home-baked smell are appealing, but as a thick oatcake they offer more than a hint of digestive biscuit – possibly thanks to the addition of brown sugar to the mix.

Adamson's of Pittenweem
These well-known hand-made oatcakes have a distinctive triangular shape and are rough-and-ready in appearance. Unfortunately they don't travel well and tend to break easily, not helped by rather flimsy packaging. While they are nutty, rustic oatcakes with an old-fashioned and traditional charm, their thickness and large size make eating just one quite an undertaking.

Mitchells
These oatcakes have been made using the same Inverurie family recipe since 1928, and are a good example of the fact that many small local bakeries still produce their own oatcake. Unusually for an oatcake recipe, they contain a splash of milk, which gives them a crumbly, soft texture. Very thin and with a high fat content, these oatcakes taste unlike any of the other brands on the market.

Handmade Oatcake Company
This small independent Perthshire bakery makes four different styles of oatcake, all in a distinctive rectangular or square shape. The green-packaged 'Traditional' variety are pale in appearance and have a fairly soft, floury texture. The yellow-labelled 'Thin and crispy' variety are sweeter, with a crisp, crunchy texture that finds an affinity with cheese. A popular artisan product, the range also includes a thicker sweet oatcake and a black pepper version.

Walkers Fine Oatcake
These factory-produced oatcakes are very different from their hand-made cousins, both in appearance and texture. Vegetarian and with a high oat content, this variety is fine and slightly floury – although curiously contains no wheat flour. They are savoury, with no sugar added, but are on the bland side. The packaging features text in a variety of languages, reflecting these oatcakes' scope in the export market.

Isle of Skye Baking Company – Dill & Black Pepper
Another strong contender from the little Skye bakery. Plenty of pinhead oatmeal in the recipe creates a nutty texture, with a taste that is spicy and savoury, with just a hint of the herby dill at the end. Peppery without being too intense, they would go well with a mild creamy goat's cheese or crowdie, perhaps with the addition of some smoked salmon for a bit of luxury.

Stoats Cracked Black Pepper Oatcake
These are very 'short' oatcakes, made without the addition of flour. Crispy but not crunchy, they are light in both taste and texture. The black pepper is definitely present, but not so intense as to mask the good-quality basic oatcake underneath. An underlying sweetness comes through the spice, which makes these oatcakes a great match for a smoked fish pâté.

The earliest oatcakes were made in the seventeeth century using a mixture of barley and oats, creating a filling breakfast biscuit that could keep a worker going until evening. With little wheat flour available to bake bread, oatcakes were also valued for their keeping qualities, offering a traveller sustenance for many days into his journey.

Brown sugar

A sticky guide to toffees, tablets and other uses
for boiled sugar, by Jo Ewart Mackenzie.

A ccording to the *Penguin Companion to Food* (2002), we Scots have a sweet tooth. Ever since the 15th century, when sugar started to be imported in significant volume, Scottish people have developed not just a love of confectionery but 'an international reputation for the quality of their products'. In particular, toffee has a strong heritage in Scottish towns and cities: think tangy Moffat Toffee, creamy Helensburgh Toffee and golden syrup enriched Glasgow Toffee, not forgetting the iconic soft toffee bars by McCowan's Highland Toffee, established in the 1920s.

What's not fully appreciated by non-cooks is that sweet treats such as chewy toffee, unctuous caramel, yieldingly soft fudge and delectably toothsome tablet are all simply different versions of boiled sugar.

What gives each confection its own distinct characteristics are the temperature and stage it is boiled to as well as slight variations in recipe. Fudge and tablet, for instance, is the fondant result of sugar, butter and condensed or evaporated milk boiled to between 112° and 116°C, or the 'soft ball' stage. Soft caramel, meanwhile, is the molten consequence of sugar enriched with butter, milk or cream and boiled to between 118° and 121°, or

the 'firm ball' stage. And last but not least, toffee is the glossy product of sugar and butter boiled to between 121° and 130°C, or the 'hard ball' stage.

The different stages are tested by dropping a little syrup into ice-cold water where it will form either a soft, firm or hard ball under the surface, which on contact with the air immediately disintegrates (soft ball), quickly loses its shape (firm ball), or maintains its shape and is quite

malleable (hard ball).

That's the science part!

The truth is that the secret to good caramel, toffee, tablet and fudge is experience. Sugar thermometers have been around since the late-19th century and are certainly an essential tool for the novice confectioner, but Carole Inglis of the Isle of Skye Fudge Company says there's a skill in knowing when it's ready.

'I did use thermometers to begin with,' Inglis explains, 'but now I do it by timing and by eye.'

A classic cottage industry, the Isle of Skye Fudge Company started in Inglis' kitchen in 2002. Using the same recipe handed down to her by her great grandmother who, at one time, owned a confectioner's in Glasgow, now Inglis sells her traditional Scottish tablet in local shops and at tourist attractions as well as through her website. She also produces the hand-made confection for the Baxter's Specially Selected Foods label.

So what exactly is the difference between fudge and tablet? 'It's to do with the texture,' Inglis explains. 'Tablet is smooth but slightly grainy and has a bite to it; with fudge you leave teeth marks when you bite into it – I'd say it has a more cloying texture than tablet.'

So why does Inglis call her company Skye Fudge rather than Skye Tablet? 'People south of the border don't know what tablet is!'

■ *You can find more about Scottish producers of tablet, fudge and other sweets at www.thelarder.net, including www.skyefudge.co.uk, www.crymblesconfectionery.co.uk, www.gallowayfudge.com, www.hebrideantoffeecompany.com*

Chocolate climbers

Balnakeil village, just outside Durness, is a community of artists and artisans housed in a Cold-War era RAF early warning base. In 2006, Paul Maden (40) and James Findlay (35) made it the base for their gourmet chocolate making operation, Cocoa Mountain. Barry Shelby spoke to Findlay about the business.

Could you give us a bit more about your backgrounds?

I was raised in Rutherglen, attended Stirling University, lived for two years in Austria, one year in Sweden and then moved back to Glasgow, where I worked in IT at IBM and as an academic researcher. Paul is from Blackburn, Lancashire, and studied marketing at Strathclyde Uni and had a varied career before Cocoa Mountain. He was working as a lecturer in entrepreneurship and studying for a PhD. We both lived in Glasgow before moving to Sutherland.

Chocolate making was a hobby turned into an enjoyable business. We both have a passion for good quality real chocolate and experimentation with different flavour combinations.

You use local produce when possible: raspberries, cream, and what else?

We source local raspberries, strawberries, cream and crème-fraiche. We also purchase a lot of our ingredients from [Inverness-based] Highland Wholefoods. We use chocolate from all over the world: Cuban, Venezuelan . . . different ones for different products: for example, organic chocolate for our range of chocolate bars that you can see on our website.

A white chocolate, coconut and chilli is one of your innovative chocolates: what are some others?

We have an orange and geranium truffle, a blood orange and mandarin and a fresh strawberry and black pepper. We are inventing new flavours all the time. Our most popular truffle is the chilli and lemongrass, the fresh raspberry and the classic French, which is made with a 70 per cent Cuban chocolate. We use fresh cream in our truffles – and no preservatives, which means they are always consumed fresh and thus taste the best.

Aside from the mail order business, what else is part of your operation?

We sell our range online and via mail order. We sell direct to the public at food fairs and farmers' markets. We also supply wholesale to select shops in the Highlands. We also do favours for weddings.

The Chocolate Bar is our refreshment bar at Balnakeil village where customers can enjoy the best hot chocolate, organic tea and coffee and a range of organic soft drinks, pastries and of course our truffles. Customers can visit and watch from the chocolate bar through to the production area as we make the chocolates.

Balnakeil is a bit of a surprising place. What makes it work for your business?

Balnakeil has a lot of visitors throughout the year. The craft village is close to Balnakeil beach and is a busy place especially during the summer months.

You got some start-up support from Highlands and Islands Enterprise, which has sung your praises. What's next?

We are in talks with partners to open a Cocoa Mountain in Bridge of Allan in 2009. We also plan to increase the wholesale business.

■ *For more information go to www.cocoamountain.co.uk*

PHOTO: JOHN BLAIKIE/MEY SELECTIONS

WHERE TO BUY

Outlets for buying bread, cakes and chocolate listed regionally then organised alphabetically.

EDINBURGH & LOTHIANS

■ The Chocolate Tree

Struie, 3 Bankrugg Cottages, Gifford, East Lothian
01620 811 102
www.the-chocolate-tree.co.uk
Aiming to create excellent quality chocolate at affordable prices, the Chocolate Tree is the brainchild of Friederike Matthis and Alastair Gower. With the original idea of touring their chocolate around the British music festivals, they can still be found travelling the length and breadth of the country every summer. Always choosing local and organic ingredients where possible, they hand-craft all of their products in small batches in their country kitchen. The product range stretches from chocolate bars and truffles to dairy-free hazelnut spread, chocolate-dipped strawberries and cakes, and can be ordered online or found in quality retailers around Scotland.

■ Coco Chocolate

174 Bruntsfield Place, Bruntsfield, Edinburgh
0131 228 4526
www.cocochocolate.co.uk
Mon–Sat 10am–6pm; Sun noon–4pm. Café.
A haven for the sweet-toothed in classy Bruntsfield, this is so much more than just a chocolate shop. All of the sweet treats are produced by hand in Coco's Edinburgh kitchen, using only the best chocolate with a high cocoa content and full of indulgent cocoa butter. Owner Rebecca Knights-Kerswell also runs a twice-monthly chocolate school and a Friday night Connoisseurs evening in her beautiful shop. Here you can purchase pretty bags of the finest dark, white and milk chocolate and linger over the papers with a mug of real, decadent, 64 per cent cocoa hot chocolate made right there in the shop. Better still, a bar of good quality chocolate is rich in antioxidants, and has one tenth of the calories of mass produced chocolate, so you can feel good about each mouthful.

■ Falko Konditormeister

• 1 Stanley Road, Gullane, East Lothian
01620 843168, www.falko.co.uk
Wed–Fri 8am–5.30pm; Sat 9am–5.30pm; Sun 11am–5.30pm. Closed Mon/Tue.
• 185 Bruntsfield Place, Edinburgh
0131 656 0763, www.falko.co.uk
Wed–Fri 8.45am–6.30pm; Sat 9am–6pm; Sun 10.30am–6pm. Closed Mon/Tue. Café.
German-born Falko Burkert caused something of a storm in Edinburgh when he started selling his baked goods at Edinburgh farmers' markets in 2005. Such was the demand for his wares that he opened a shop in Bruntsfield soon after, followed a couple of years later by one in Gullane. Meanwhile, he remains a fixture at the farmers' market. The intoxicating aroma that seduces you as you near the stall or enter one of the shops tells you this is no ordinary baker. Indeed, this is a *konditormeister*, a master baker who has trained hard for his craft. Gaze upon the vast array of artisan breads made with an endless list of seeds and flours, pretzels, cakes and cinnamon-scented German pastries. The only problem you'll encounter here is choosing what to have.

Peter's Yard

Hot Chocolates

40/8 Littlejohn Road, Edinburgh
0131 477 9902, www.hotchocolates.biz
Web/mail order.

Sharon Grimshaw's passion for chocolate was sparked by a trip to Spain, a particularly good cup of thick hot chocolate and doughy churros. Based in Edinburgh, she creates luxury hand-made chocolates to secret recipes that have won awards. Though based entirely online, Hot Chocolates' friendly staff are available at the end of the phone to offer advice and guide you through the process of buying, whether it's a treat for yourself, wedding favours or a corporate gift. With a mind-boggling selection of chocolates ranging from hand-made bars studded with whole fruit and nuts to exotic dark chocolate infused with warming chilli, you'll be spoilt for choice.

The Manna House

22–24 Easter Road, Edinburgh
0131 652 2349
www.manna-house-edinburgh.co.uk
Tue–Thu 8am–7pm; Fri/Sat 8am–6pm. Closed Sun/Mon.
Café.

The Manna House is a treasure trove of sweet delights, hidden well off the beaten track near the top of Easter Road. It is worth seeking out for the bread alone, all made without flour improvers, preservatives or other nasties, and all made using Scottish produce where possible. Call in for a loaf or two of freshly baked artisan bread and you're bound to be tempted by one of the beautiful fruit tarts as well. Or choose from sandwiches, soup, quiches and pies, all of which are available to eat in or take away.

Peter's Yard

Quartermile, 27 Simpson Loan, Edinburgh
0131 228 5876, www.petersyard.com
Mon–Fri 7am–6pm; Sat/Sun 9am–6pm.

An extraordinary emporium dedicated to fresh, natural and quality produce, Peter's Yard is a haven for foodies. It has a passion for bread, believing it to be fundamental to a modern, healthy lifestyle, and is determined to establish a food culture in which bread plays the starring role. This should not be a problem as its range of artisan breads, produced using a stone wood-fired oven, is phenomenal and includes authentic Swedish rye and *kavring*. It sells sandwiches, muffins (sweet and savoury), innovative breakfasts and cakes to take away or enjoy in situ, as well as a staggering range, from biscuits and baking to conserves and chocolate. Quite simply a must.

Trusty Crust Organic Bakery

5–7 The Glebe, East Saltoun, East Lothian
01875 340939, www.trustycrust.co.uk

This small but growing artisan bakery produces a range of organic hand-crafted breads, pastries and cakes on a daily basis, using traditional baking skills and practices. It uses lengthy fermentation processes to give the products full rough development and keeps ingredients to an absolute minimum with no additives or anything artificial – the Pain au Levain contains only flour, water and salt. Other breads include basil and onion, caraway, rye and sourdough. It sells continental goods such as croissants and Danish pastries as well as home-made cakes made from domestic recipes. Pick the bread up at farmers' markets as well as organic outlets across the central belt.

W T S Forsyth & Sons

21 Eastgate, Peebles, Peeblesshire
See Beef, Lamb & Other Meat.

GREATER GLASGOW & CLYDESIDE

Tapa Bakehouse & Coffeehouse

• 21 Whitehill Street, Dennistoun, Glasgow
0141 554 9981
www.tapabakehouse.com
Mon–Sat 8am–6pm; Sun 10am–5pm.
• 721 Pollokshaws Road, Glasgow
0141 423 9494
www.tapabakehouse.com
Mon–Thu 8am–6pm; Fri/Sat 8am–9pm; Sun 9am–5pm.

The Tapa Bakehouse boasts not only a bakery, but a café and coffee roastery where it roasts its 100 per cent Arabica beans in small batches every week to ensure freshness. It bakes its breads the old fashioned way, using basic, good quality organic ingredients and lots of time to release all the flavours and nutrients in the dough. The range of breads produced is staggering, from rye and caraway to sourdough, brioche and pane italiano (and even one based on an old Scottish recipe – see the panel on p59). In both the original Dennistoun and newer Strathbungo cafés, organic seasonal ingredients are to the fore; sandwiches are of course made with its own bread and its cakes alone are worth a visit.

SOUTHERN SCOTLAND

In House Chocolates

128 King Street, Castle Douglas
01556 503037

www.inhousechocolates.co.uk
Mon–Fri 7.15am–5pm, Sat 9am–5pm.
Web/mail order.

Based in Castle Douglas, Gillian Houston and Bobby McLeary set up In House Chocolates in July 2003. Since then it has flourished to become a prolific award-winning business (it has won gold at the Great Taste Awards for five years running), creating chocolates entirely by hand in its workshop using traditional methods – from tempering to moulding, filling, sealing and finally cooling. Its cream and chocolate ganaches are blended with fruits and the finest liqueurs to create delectable melt-in-your-mouth treats. Pay a visit and watch the chocolates being made, before choosing from boxed selections, chocolate hampers and hand-dipped fruit (also available to order from its website).

Simple Simon's Perfect Pie Factory

Units 1 & 2, Coulter Park Farm, Coulter, Lanarkshire
01899 220118
www.simplesimonspies.co.uk
Mail/web order.

Nestled in the pastures of the Scottish Southern Uplands is the nineteenth-century farm building which houses Simple Simon's Perfect Pie Factory. It is from this location that chef Bernard Alessi prepares and bakes his now famous pies. Using fresh, natural ingredients and no artificial additives, the pies contain Aberdeen Angus beef from Blackmount Organics, Organic black faced hill lamb from Easton Farm and Jimmy Bogle's haggis, as well as other meats, cheeses, vegetables and herbs from other local suppliers. Danny Wild's Magnificant Cheese and Onion and Mince and Tattie pie are just some examples of over 20 types available

CENTRAL SCOTLAND & FIFE

Fisher & Donaldson

21 Crossgate, Cupar, Fife
01334 656433
www.fisheranddonaldson.com
Mon–Sat 6am–5pm; Thu 6am–4.45pm. Closed Sun.

Fisher & Donaldson is a local institution. Multiple generations of Fife families have bought their wedding, christening and birthday cakes here and the bakers continue to give a much-valued personal service. But this is much more than a local bakery, with a continental edge you won't find anywhere else. It can't be said that it hasn't moved with the times, for alongside tea fancies, morning rolls, bridies and oatcakes you'll find croissants, baguettes and crisp French rolls. In addition to the shop in central St Andrews, the company's branches in Dundee and Cupar have in-store cafés where customers can enjoy a leisurely tea or coffee with (of course) some freshly baked goodies.

■ Gordon & Durward

14 West High Street, Crieff, Perthshire
01764 653800
www.scottishsweets.co.uk
Mon–Sat 9am–5pm. Sun 11am–5pm.
Web/mail order.

A quaint, old-style sweetie shop famed for its sugar mice, Gordon & Durward in Crieff manufactures its own range of confectionary as well as selling traditional sweets made by other Scottish producers such as McCowan's Highland Toffee and Ross's of Edinburgh. The treats on offer are quintessentially Scottish, traditionally made using copper boilers, and sweet enough to melt your teeth. Make like a kid in a sweetie shop and gaze upon the vast array of brightly coloured wrappers, while trying to make the difficult choice between butter tablet, macaroon, fudge and coconut slices.

■ Mhor Bread

8 Main Street, Callander
01877 339518, www.mhor.net
Mon–Sun 8.30am–5pm.
Café.

Another arm to the Lewis family's burgeoning foodie empire in and around Callander, Mhor Bread is a re-branding for the Scotch Oven bakery which has been in the area in one form or another for over 100 years. Mhor is, however, commited to producing artisan bread made traditionally by hand, entirely

without preservatives and using flour milled in Scotland. Varieties include olive and rosemary, fennel and caraway seed and multigrain, alongside a plain pan loaf, sliced and packaged to compete with processed breads. With an aim to keep alive that which is best in Scottish quality baking, it also sells a range of black buns and bannocks.

■ Tunstall's Organic Bakery

Unit 6, Birnam Industrial Estate, Station Road, Birnam, Perthshire
01350 724310

Baker Justin Tunstall spends around four hours lovingly crafting one of his artisan breads before even thinking about putting it in an oven. Relying not on additives, flour improvers or pre-mixes, but rather on his skill, he produces an organic bread that is snapped up for its extraordinary texture and flavour. A resolutely organic and traditional craftsman, he insists on using only windmill-powered renewable energy to power his bakery and refuses to invest in weighing or shaping machines. He sells a variety of specialist breads, including pain au levain, Italian pagnotta, and honey, sunflower and pumpkin seed, at farmers' markets and specialist food shops.

NORTH EAST SCOTLAND

■ The Chocolate Shop

74 High Street, Banchory
01330 820209
www.thechocolateshopbanchory.co.uk
Mon–Sat 10am–5pm. Closed Sun.
Café.

Banchory's little wood-lined speciality chocolate shop stocks a large and diverse range of top-notch cocoa products. Alongside its own hand-made

chocolates are examples of some of the most famous international producers such as Amedei and Valrhona. The in-house range includes one called Black Gold which, with its dark chocolate, whisky, heather honey, cream and gold leaf, pays tribute to the key local industries of oil, whisky distilling and farming. Sit-in options include hot chocolate, teas and milkshakes with double chocolate chip cookies among the baked treats available.

■ Phoenix Community Stores

The Park, by Findhorn, Moray
See Delis & General Food

HIGHLANDS, ISLANDS & ARGYLL

■ Argo's Bakery

50 Victoria Street, Stromness, Orkney
01856 850245, www.argosbakery.co.uk
Café.

Owned and run by the Argo family, Argo's Bakery in the heart of Stromness has been in business since the early 1940s, making it one of the oldest family-run businesses in the area. Artisan bakers make some of the finest bread, cakes and biscuits in the islands every day in their bakery, using only the finest ingredients. Ten years ago it created a bread made from beremeal (a type of barley that grows in the Orkney Islands and can be traced back to Neolithic times), and soon afterwards also launched a savoury biscuit made from bere, which goes equally well with cheese, pâté or just good old plain butter.

■ Cocoa Mountain

19A Balnakeil Craft Village, Durness, Lairg, Sutherland
01971 511233
www.cocoamountain.co.uk
Summer 9am–6pm; winter 11am–4pm.

They call themselves the most geographically remote chocolatiers in Europe but, not to be deterred by geographical constraints, the guys behind Cocoa Mountain have been producing delicious hand-made chocolates since 2006, using organic, Fairtrade cocoa where possible and combining unusual flavours such as chilli and lemongrass with the more standard nuts, fruits and pralines. The well-organised nationwide delivery system means you don't have to make the trek all the way up to the north-west Highlands but, if you do, you'll be rewarded with stunning views over Cape Wrath while visiting the delightful café for a hot drink and, of course, a chance to sample some of the chocolates up close.

Cocoa Mountain

■ Hebridean Toffee

Castlebay, Isle of Barra, Western Isles
01871 810898
www.hebrideantoffeecompany.com
Mon–Sat 9.30am–5pm. Closed Sun.
Café.

Softer than the traditional chewy stuff which pulls teeth, Hebridean Toffee is a luxury tablet made entirely by hand on the Isle of Barra. No automation is used in either the cooking or packaging process and the tablet contains no additives, preservatives or colourings. Situated in Castlebay and overlooking Kisimul Castle, the gift shop offers a devilishly good sticky toffee pudding to take home as well as a range of local arts and crafts. Hebridean Toffee can be made to order and when purchased online, can be shipped within 24 hours of production ensuring freshness and guaranteeing a six-month shelf life.

■ The Isle of Skye Baking Company

14 Rathad an Fheoir, Portree
01478 611114, www.iosbakingco.co.uk
Operating from their home kitchen in the community of Portree, Barry and Liza Hawthorne run the Isle of Skye Baking Company, a tiny independent bakery set up originally to make oatcakes and shortbread for Skye. A pastry chef by profession, Barry trained under a German master baker nearly 20 years ago and now uses his skills to produce an increasing range of shortbread, oatcakes, gingerbread, biscotti and fruitcake. The company's artisan breads in particular have attracted a huge amount of attention and are available, by request only, to be collected by arrangement from the kitchen or a farmers' market.

■ Oban Chocolate Company

9 Craigard Rd, Oban, Argyll
01631 566099
www.oban-chocolate.co.uk
Tue–Sat 10am–5pm. Closed Sun/Mon.
Café, web/mail order.

A visit to the Margaret River Chocolate Factory in Australia was the inspiration for the Oban Chocolate Company. Established in 2003, this originally small business has grown to become an award-winning enterprise, making sweet treats entirely by hand on its premises in Oban. The shop and café are open plan, and viewing windows allow you to watch the chocolatiers at work in the factory, with interpretive panels to explain the process. It produces two types of chocolate: truffles and moulded chocolates, and all recipes are developed in-house with no artificial additives. Choose from a range of over 30, including strawberry and champagne hearts, walnut cappuccino and even Marmite chocolate.

■ The Shetland Fudge Company

135–137 Commercial Street, Lerwick, Shetland
01595 694324, www.shetlandfudge.co.uk

A small family business hand-making fudge and truffles on the remote Shetland Islands, the Shetland Fudge Company uses the finest ingredients, no additives and local produce where possible. With products ranging from Scottish tablet and truffle fudge to Belgian chocolates and the obscurely named 'puffin poo', there is something to suit every taste. Order fudge online and it will be hand-made that day for delivery, guaranteeing that your products will arrive as fresh as possible.

■ Tobermory Chocolate

56/57 Main Street, Tobermory, Argyll
01688 302 526, www.tobchoc.co.uk
Mon–Sat 9.30am–5pm; Sun 11am–4pm.
(Oct–Apr: closed Sun).
Café, web/mail order.

Established in 1991 in a derelict stone workshop, Tobermory Chocolate has been producing hand-made chocolates for nearly 20 years. Now operating from larger premises, it has room for a gift shop and café where you can choose from an array of cakes, pastries and luxury hot chocolate. For those further afield than Mull, an online shop allows access to its selection of chocolates, from bars, mixed boxes and truffles to a range of wedding favours.

■ Ullapool Bakery

Ullapool Bakery, 6B1 Morefield Trading Estate, Ullapool, Ross-shire
01854 613034, www.ullapoolbakery.co.uk
Mon–Fri 8am–1pm. Closed Sat/Sun.

Allan and Alex Doherty took over the Ullapool Bakery in 2002 when they embarked on producing traditional bakery products. With a real passion for creating speciality breads, oatcakes and shortbreads, they soon realised that local farmers' markets and country shows provided an ideal market place to sell their wares. Visit the bakery and try to choose from an incredible 30 speciality breads including chickpea, coriander and cumin, Irish soda bread and pain de campagne, or be swayed by the variety of savoury and sweet biscuits. Committed to sourcing and supporting local suppliers, they use only Scottish milled flour, Scottish grown garlic, Isle of Mull cheese and local beef, venison, lamb and pork in their products.

> NEW BREAD FROM OLD TRADITIONS

Tapa Bakehouse was established six years ago by Robert Winters and Virginia Webb in the unlikely setting of a side street in Glasgow's East End. Native New Zealanders, they had a love of good coffee and good bread but struggled to find anywhere doing that in the city.

Winters began attending baking classes at what's now Glasgow Metropolitan College. He would have struggled to learn about the old-fashioned techniques of baking had it not been for the older members of staff who had learned their trade before the domination of industrial plant baking.

Proper artisan bread-makers who believe the best way to make good bread it to use simple ingredients and give their doughs time to allow flavours and nutrients develop, Tapa include in their range a loaf they call Struan, which follows a style of bread traditionally baked throughout the Western Isles on the eve of Michaelmas to celebrate the harvest. Wheat didn't grow in the Western Isles so the original bread would have been a dense cake made of barley with grain, seeds, berries or fruit added, according to each family's recipe. Winters and Webb found out about the loaf in North America, where they found descendants of Scottish emigrants making it. The Tapa version – which does include wheat – is mixed in with millet, oats and seeds, is flavoured with milk and honey. With a moist, sweetish, oaty denseness, Struan has impressive keeping qualities – up to two weeks in a bag or terracotta bread bin, and makes lovely toast. Worth celebrating.

■ *Tapa Bakehouse, 21 Whitehill Street, Dennistoun, www.tapabakehouse.com*

CHEESE & DAIRY

Big Scottish cheeses

Scotland has a small but talented band of cheesemakers, and it also has a significant champion in cheesemonger Iain Mellis. Here Iain and his colleagues Benjamin Newell and Alistair Marr select their top ten cheeses.

Isle of Mull Cheddar

Isle of Mull Cheddar is considered by many as the daddy of Scottish cheddars. Strong, fruity and brooding, Isle of Mull cheddar is made from unpasteurised cow's milk on Sgriob-ruadh (pronounced 'Ski-brooah') farm on the tranquil Isle of Mull in the Inner Hebrides by Chris and Jeff Reade and their sons. What stands out about Isle of Mull in relation to other cheddars in the British Isles is its colour. Whereas most cheddars are insipid or rich in yellows, Mull is more ivory in colour. Herein lies its instant attraction. This ivory veneer gives off a sense of what the palette may expect.

There is no doubting that Mull is a complex cheese that evokes a plethora of tastes. It's deep and strong, ballsy in its outlook and at times can be quite severe on the palette, but it is rewarding when fully devoured. The prominent overtones of grass and fruit are due to Sgriob-ruadh's cows having their feed supplemented by leftover fermented grain supplied by the nearby Tobermory malt whisky distillery. (See also Chef's Choice on page 70.)

Grimbister

Grimbister Farm Cheese is a family-run business producing traditional Orkney farmhouse cheese made to an age-old recipe handed down through the generations.

Made from unpasteurised cows' milk, Grimbister is a gentle soul of a cheese with a mild and fruity taste. In Orkney it is eaten at a very young age in its maturity (around six weeks) and offers a smooth and silky taste while retaining a subtle zestiness. Here at Iain Mellis Cheesemongers we tend to mature Grimbister to around 10–12 weeks, therefore offering a different blend of taste and texture. In this case Grimbister becomes more crumbly in texture and offers a deeper lemony taste. It blends wonderfully with grapes (or any fruit for that matter) and it's certainly one to drink with a nice Pinot Grigio or for that matter a can of frosty beer.

Blarliath

If Isle of Mull cheddar is the elder statesmen of Scottish cheddars, then Blarliath is the Young Pretender to the throne. Conceived by Ruaraidh Stone at Highland Fine Cheeses near Tain, this cheddar is a 'tongue sucker' of an experience, evoking the farm yard environment it comes from.

Blarliath is without doubt mild cheddar, but it has many layers of taste and texture. It has a rubbery and murky yellow exterior. Once placed within your mouth you feel as if it may melt instantly but then offers up a lottery of tastes. Perhaps that's the defining character of Blarliath: its unexpectedness. Gentle on the palette but with an exquisite aftertaste you yearn for more and it seems to demand repeated tasting. A dark horse, but a worthy one.

Lanark Blue

First produced by Humphrey Errington in 1985 at Walston Braehead in Lanarkshire, Lanark Blue was the first British blue sheep's cheese for centuries, and most likely the first ewe's milk cheese made commercially in Scotland in the 20th century.

With its mild ewe's milk tang and graceful blue veining, Lanark Blue is certainly one for eating on its own, but would also work wonderfully wedged in between two hefty slices of soft brown bread accompanied with a full bodied red wine.

Very much in the style and flavour of Roquefort, Lanark Blue changes from season to season due to twice yearly lambing. Early season cheese has an enduring, persistent sweet flavour with a prickly undercurrent; late season cheese is rigorous and more savoury. (For more on Humphrey Errington see page 64.)

Criffel

Made at the Dumfries-based Loch Arthur Creamery, Criffel is a strong semi-soft cheese that attacks the palette with the subtleness of a hammer and leaves you craving more of its dense and grassy-rich flavours. Undoubtedly pungent, it flares the nostrils and its stays with you long after the initial tasting. The farm, dairy and creamery at Loch Arthur are run to strict biodynamic principles, helping to produce a cheese completely in tune with its environment, the flavour of the land in every mouthful.

Strathdon Blue

If Ruaraidh Stone's Strathdon Blue were a film it would be classed as avant-garde. This is an inventive, original, devastatingly tasty and vibrant cheese capable of bringing out all the emotions in great cheese lovers. Though essentially mild, it has a wide range of flavours, tastes and textures. It leaves you tingly and numbs the mind with its delightful salty aftertaste. Also, it not only tastes fabulous, but also one of the most visually enticing of cheeses being made in Scotland today. The perfect accompaniment to freshly baked bread.

Dunsyre blue

Humphrey Errington's Dunsyre Blue is a deep and soily cheese that will challenge all cheese lovers with its dark and flat undertones. Gorgeously creamy with a soft, long, blue mellowness, each flavour is distinct but perfectly poised, before a stunningly long aftertaste. Not one to be taken lightly, Dunsyre can be a versatile and rewarding cheese if eaten in the correct context. In some circles it is known that Dunsyre blends well with pears and ice cream.

Anster

Anster (pronounced 'Ain-Ster') hails from the small fishing village of Anstruther in Fife, and is produced from unpasteurised cow's milk within the converted cow shed at the St Andrews Cheese Company. The crumbly, light texture of the cheese opens up the depth of its fresh citrus flavors.

The farm itself is located just north of Anstruther and not only can visitors buy the cheese direct from the farm, they can also see it being made and talk with the makers as they go about producing Scotland's newest cheese.

Clava

Made by Connage Dairy, based on an organic farm at Ardersier by the shores of the Moray Firth. Their herd of Holstein Friesian with Jersey crosses and Norwegian Reds graze on clover-rich grasses producing full, rich milk that in turn produces wonderful cheese. Clava brie is a mild and engaging cheese. With hidden depths of bitterness and coolness it can be best eaten either straight from a chilled fridge or left to ripen to bring out its funky, buttery taste and unique grassy flavor.

Connage Crowdie

One of Scotland's oldest cheeses, and the natural accompaniment to a pre-ceildh whisky, crowdie is a half-fat curd cheese made by Connage Dairies. The traditional recipe produces a soft, creamy cheese with a mousse-like texture, a fresh zesty aroma and a slightly sour aftertaste. (For more on crowdie, see panel on page 65.)

IJ Mellis Cheesemongers has six shops across Scotland: further details can be found in the listings starting on page 70. For further details on the makers of the cheeses listed above as well as details of other farmhouse and artisan cheesemakers in Scotland, see the panel on page 72.

The man who saved Scottish cheese

Nearly 15 years ago Humphrey Errington's tiny but highly regarded cheesemaking operation was threatened by closure under a harshly enforced health regulation. Nicki Holmyard recalls his landmark battle.

Lanark Blue is a firm favourite on Scottish cheeseboards and without it, there might not be such a thing as a Scottish cheeseboard at all. Certainly not one where terms such as 'farmhouse,' 'hand-made' and 'unpasteurised' could attach themselves to the best of the selection upon it.

The man who created Lanark Blue, Humphrey Errington, farms 400 sheep near Carnwath in the Lanarkshire countryside and began making cheese in the mid-1980s as a diversification exercise to add value to his flock. In doing so he created the first new Scottish blue cheese for centuries. 'Cheese making in the past was always a part of farming and I wanted to revive the tradition,' he says.

By the mid-1990s, having perfected his unpasteurised cheese and found plenty of regular buyers, Errington fell foul of the local environmental health authorities, who wanted him to produce a 'safe' pasteurised cheese.

Problems escalated when Clydesdale Council claimed to have found *Listeria monocytogenes* in a sample and demanded all produce be recalled. Devastated by the news, Errington had his own tests done, the majority of which failed to find any listeria, while a few found minute amounts of a non-dangerous strain. He decided to appeal against the council's decision and the case went to court. Legal arguments dragged on for over a year, making Errington and his flock a regular news item.

'We fought the case on a couple of grounds,' he says. 'Firstly that the government's test methodology was incorrect and secondly that the listeria strain in question was not a harmful one. Professor Hugh Pennington championed our cause and eventually sense prevailed and we won the case.

'We were tremendously lucky in that so many customers stuck by us and continued to take our cheese and also that people all over the country helped to raise funds to pay our escalating legal bills. But it was a fight that needed to be fought for small producers everywhere and it touched a lot of people.'

The cheese is hand-made by introducing *Penicillium roquefortii* mould at the start of the process to encourage blue-green veining, along with vegetarian rennet to set the curds. These are ladled into forms and allowed to settle into shape. During the maturing process, the cheeses are twice dipped in brine then put into clean forms. They are removed after a month, wrapped in foil to prevent growth of surface mould and left in a cool room for a further two months. Turning three times a week ensures they ripen evenly. Before sale, they are hand-scraped and wrapped in the distinctive foil pack designed by Humphrey's brother Tom Errington.

Errington explains that cheese made at different times of the year can vary, as the ewes' milk is affected by seasonal changes in their diet. The sheep are only milked between January and September, but Lanark Blue is available all year. 'Following the

success of this cheese we developed Dunsyre Blue a cow's cheese which is also mould ripened and hand-made,' he says. The unpasteurised milk for this cheese comes from a neighbouring farm at Dunsyre – hence the name.

Two white cheeses followed, one made with ewes' milk named Lanark White and another, Maisie's Kebbuck, from cows' milk. This cheese was made for Humphrey's mother-in-law Maisie, who does not like blue cheese, and very proud she is of it.

In 2005 he developed Fallachan, a

fermented alcoholic drink made from the whey left over when curds are separated from the milk. It uses an ancient recipe and needs to mature for a year in oak casks before bottling.

Errington's skill as a cheesemaker took him to Romania recently to investigate how local sheep farmers could make their products acceptable for general sale under European Union regulations. 'What we saw there was amazing – people milking up to 800 sheep by hand and making cheese without refrigeration or water. The taste was superb, but they have a lot of work to do before they can market it outside their country.'

Errington's cheese is sold all over Scotland and the UK and can be found as far afield as Hong Kong and the USA. With his daughter Selina working full-time in the business, he takes time to make regular personal deliveries to many of his Scottish customers and values the feedback he receives.

Errington may have earned a special place in Scottish cheesemaking and the hearts of many small-scale food producers, but his energy and enthusiasm seem undiminished. 'I am currently developing a small, hard-pressed cheese with both sheep and cows' milk,' he reveals. 'But it is not perfected yet.'

■ *www.lanarkblue.com*

> A WAY WITH CURDS

Jo Ewart Mackenzie tells the story of crowdie – an essentially simple but historic Highland cheese.

Possibly Scotland's most ancient cheese, crowdie is thought to date back to Viking and Pictish times, and might have disappeared completely had it not been for an enterprising farmer's wife in the 1960s.

Made at one time by every crofter in the Highlands, crowdie involved souring fresh milk by a warm fire or sunny windowsill, then cooking gently until it curdled. Once separated, the whey was drained then salt and cream added to the curds, making a crumbly white cheese. The Pictish version would have been firmer and saltier, pressed into crocks and covered with melted butter, to make a longer lasting cheese.

Crowdie production declined following World War II and the demise of crofting, but years later in the Ross-shire village of Tain, Susannah Stone continued to make it at home. One day in 1962, she made too much and offered the surplus to a local grocer. Heralding the return of crowdie to the Highlands, Susannah's crowdie became the first artisan cheese produced by family business Highland Fine Cheeses, now run by her son Ruaraidh.

Further artisan cheese makers now produce their own crowdie, the version made by Connage Highland Dairy being crowned Best Scottish Cheese 2008 at the Great British Cheese Awards. 'Crowdie was traditionally eaten before ceilidhs to line the stomach to help alleviate the ill effects of whisky,' says Jill Clark, partner in Connage. Characterised by its whipped mousse-like texture, Connage crowdie goes particularly well on scones with jam, for a 'Highland twist on the traditional cream tea'.

■ *Producers of crowdie in Scotland are Connage Highland Dairy www.connage.co.uk, Highland Fine Cheeses 01862 892034, West Highland Dairy www.westhighlanddairy.co.uk, and Devenick Dairy www.devenickdairy.co.uk*

PHOTOS: GRAHAM'S FAMILY DAIRY

The return of the small family dairy

The milk industry is a pertinent example of how the link between the consumer and the countryside has changed in two decades of consolidation, industrialisation and homogenisation. David Pollock goes to check if milk still comes from cows.

'A lot of people's attitude to milk now,' says Hamish Miller of North Street Dairy in Forfar, 'is that as long as it's white and colours their tea, they couldn't care less.' North Street is a small processor so it doesn't actually deal with the business of raising and milking the cows themselves, but it's still part of that fading tradition of dairy produce being sourced and sold locally – the good old days of cream-capped milk which originated no more than five miles away being delivered to the customer's doorstep in a foil-top glass bottle.

'We don't homogenise,' says Miller simply. 'Homogenisation, standardisation – all that's doing is skimming off all the cream and then pasteurising at a higher temperature. It gives the milk enough of a shelf-life to be sold in supermarkets, but it kills the flavour of it.'

By diversifying into the local sale of home-made dairy products, the owners of many family dairy farms have found a handy new stream of revenue. The Devenick Dairy has been based near Banchory for over half a century, but it was only two years ago that they installed a processing plant to allow a move into the production of cheeses and yoghurts. 'Quite simply the farm wasn't big enough to support everyone,' says Kenny Groat, who manages Devenick with his parents and brother, 'and we weren't going to make much more money by selling our milk. Now we supply hotels, restaurants, farm shops and delis, and we have a small farm shop of our own.'

As well as dairy produce, they also sell meat – itself a by-product of the dairy process.

Before this diversification, Devenick supplied one of the large dairy brands which was the only one in the area. The lack of competing buyers meant it felt they were being 'held to ransom' on the price of milk. Yet the wild fluctuations in the price of milk don't exactly lend themselves to stability anyway. The price they were getting went as low as 16p a litre, before rising again to around 30p at the end of 2008. With the current financial crisis, though, he doesn't expect that upward trend to continue, and speaks with a clear sense of relief when he describes the popularity of Devenick's farm shop with local customers.

Where Devenick uses around 20 per cent of its milk for dairy produce and continues to sell the rest on, other farmer/processors seek to cut out the middleman and bottle their own milk. Donald Laird of Bonaly Dairy Farm in Loanhead is one example: 'It cuts right down on the food miles if you produce your own milk for the local market, and there's full traceability in there – you can make sure the cows are kept outside and fed on grass as much as possible, and that nothing is then added to the milk.' Or, as Hamish Miller puts it, 'you just hope the customers appreciate the personal touch.'

■ *Bonaly Dairy Farm, Unit 8 Enterprise Centre, 1 Dryden Road, Loanhead, 0131 440 0110, www.bonalyfarmdairy.co.uk*

The Devenick Dairy, Banchory, Aberdeen, 01224 782476, www.devenickdairy.co.uk

Graham's Family Dairy, Airthrey Kerse Farm, Bridge of Allan, www.grahamsfamilydairy.com

North Street Dairy, 22 North Street, Forfar, 01307 643796

> SOURCING LOCAL BUTTER

In search of a product that really melts in your mouth

It's not too hard to track down Scotland's many fine local cheeses, but uncovering farm-made butter can be a challenge. Why? According to Brenda Leddy at Stichill near Kelso, who has been making butter, cheese and clotted cream from her small herd of Jersey cows for over 30 years, she is virtually unique in the practice. 'It is a lot easier for people to sell their milk to a big dairy, rather than making the effort to churn it into butter and hand shape it,' she says.

Brenda's daughter Susan milks the cows and helps with production, making butter three times a week. They produce 200 or so 250g packs every week and sell them at farmers' markets, delicatessens, garden centres and local hotels.

The Loch Arthur Creamery, a social project for people with learning disabilities, also produces a small quantity of butter, which is sold in its farm shop at Beeswing near Dumfries. Manager Barry Graham explains that 'someone is assigned every day to churn the butter using cream from our small herd, but it is very much on a craft scale'. Up in Aberdeenshire, visitors to the farm shop at Devenick Dairy might also come across pats of butter hand-made from the farm's Jersey cows.

Operating with a much higher profile is Graham's Family Dairy at Bridge of Allan, a family business which began producing butter four years ago using traditional churn methods to make 1000 litres at a time. It has since developed a range encompassing both salted and unsalted versions, as well as organic and Jersey-cow milk 'Gold' butters. 'We saw a gap in the marketplace and are delighted to see demand growing steadily,' says managing director Robert B Graham.
■ *Stichill Jerseys, 01573 470263 www.locharthur.org, www.devenickdairy.co.uk, www.grahamsfamilydairy.com*

INSET PHOTO: KRISTA FOGLE

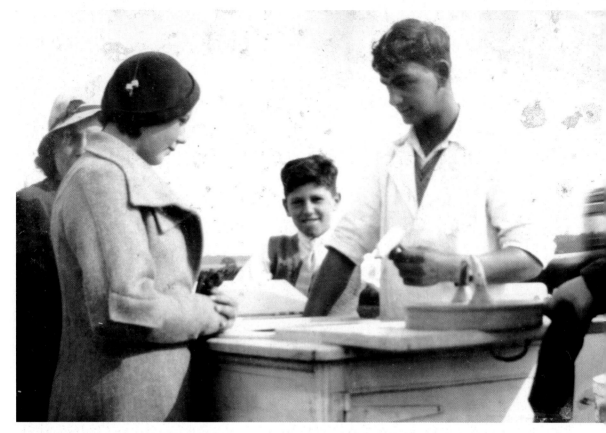

Ice cream days

What brought the first Italian ice cream makers to Scotland?
Mary Contini describes growing up in a Scottish-Italian ice cream parlour.

PHOTOS: COURTESY OF VALVONA & CROLLA

t took two men, my father and Tommy Dougal, to lift up each milk churn and tip it into the stainless-steel vat. It could be four or five churns at a time – even more in July and August when the factory was working at full capacity. Once the 20-gallon vat was full of creamy full-fat milk, the alchemy began. Bags of sugar; scoops of white powder; packets of yellow butter, peeled from their shiny greaseproof wrapping; pint bottles of cream and dark, voluptuous drips of glossy vanilla were added in a mesmerising ritual.

Often work went on into the night as the men decanted the mix from the vat along stainless-steel pipes and down corrugated coolers into waiting pails. There they lay, full of steaming, creamy, vanilla-flavoured custard, lined up oh-so-temptingly,waiting to cool. If left alone, I would guiltily stick my

fingers in, sucking up the sweet concoction with delight.

And still the magical transformation into ice cream was not yet complete. The next morning I would be woken by the jolt of the compressor starting up and the long, low rumbling of the mixer, churning steadily, back and forth, while the custard was whisked

into ice-cold deliciousness.

To me it was second nature to eat fresh ice cream from morning till dusk. I don't recall ever drinking milk. There was no need: I licked cones instead.

The Italian ice cream trade in Scotland dates back over 150 years, started by impoverished immigrant families from the south of Italy. Few came directly to Scotland, many having started in London before returning to Italy and bringing back youths and family to Britain to start the next shop, in the next town.

Although records exist of ice cream being made in Clerkenwell, London, as early as 1850, it was no more than a boiled concoction of milk and sugar chilled in a hand-cranked freezer in the street and offered to passers by on a 'licking glass'. This unhygienic practice resulted in a law that forbade the selling of ice cream in the streets, forcing the itinerant immigrants to go home, or settle.

Those who arrived first seized the opportunity and quickly built up businesses – not in ice cream but in chain migration. They built up trade in one area then returned to the impoverished south of Italy to cajole, tempt and con an inexperienced and naïve set of new migrants to rent from them and work in their trade.

A process of renting properties developed right across Britain so that by 1905 men and families could set up shop in Glasgow by committing £150 for rent and stock. Records from that year show 89 such shops in Glasgow. Within ten years there were 336, and thousands more across the rest of Scotland.

With the shop's rent came an ice cream recipe, most likely repeated by word of mouth as few immigrants were literate. But these men were all shepherds, with an instinctive knowledge of milk, seasons, food preservation and survival. They were also Italian and so understood the value of a 'brand'.

It was survival of the fittest: only the strongest took the risk and left their homes in Italy, and only the strongest of those made that scrap of a chance, a rented shop and a recipe into a brand. The brands that have survived are testament to their family's sacrifice, hard work and integrity: Nardini in Ayr; Gizzi in Hamilton; Conetta in Glasgow; Yanetta in Fife; Lucca in Musselburgh; Crolla in Edinburgh and, sadly no longer, my father, Di Ciacca in Cockenzie.

■ *Mary Contini is a director of Valvona & Crolla, which runs three establishments in Edinburgh: the original shop and caffe bar on Elm Row, VinCaffè on Multrees Walk and the Foodhall at Jenners on Princes Street. www.valvonacrolla.co.uk*

The softest ice cream required the hardest work from generations of Italian immigrants to Scotland

> BIG LICKS

David Pollock gets the scoop on the modern Scottish farmhouse ice-cream scene.

'Ice cream is a very competitive market,' says Wilma Finlay, managing director of Castle Douglas' farm-based ice cream producers Cream o' Galloway, 'and the big boys can always do it cheaper than you can. The difference is that the smaller manufacturer can try lots of different flavours, whereas those at the top end of the scale have to concentrate on maybe six lines that sell and produce a huge amount of each.'

With the price of milk having taken a battering recently, many smaller but more entrepreneurial farms have taken to making ice cream as a means of maximising their return. Cream o' Galloway's line of flavours, distributed nationally to supermarkets and delis, complemented by small specialist runs for restaurants. Previous orders have included Roquefort, spruce oil and lavender flavours.

Improved technology plays a part in small producers' ability to diversify. Thorntonhall Farmhouse Ice Cream began production three years ago, after seeing an advert in *Scottish Farmer* for a machine that would allow them to create ice cream at home. Says Thorntonhall's Micki Henderson: 'The machine actually pasteurises the milk first and then freezes the ice cream, which most small farms like ours wouldn't otherwise be able to do.'

Yet beyond their obvious enthusiasm for the product, just why might farm ice creams be better than the big brands? 'Some farms might tell you that theirs is best because it comes from a certain type of dairy cow,' says Finlay, 'but the real reason it's good is because there's a lot of cream in it. There are three things which make a good farm ice cream: lots of cream, good quality fruit or chocolate, and not putting in too much air, so that the finished product is nice and solid rather than ready to disintegrate.'

Cream O' Galloway Dairy Co, Rainton, Gatehouse of Fleet, Castle Douglas, 01557 814040, www.creamogalloway.co.uk
Thorntonhall Farmhouse Ice Cream, Meikle Dripps Farm, Waterfoot Road, Thorntonhall, 0141 644 2226, www.thorntonhallicecream.co.uk
■ *For more of Scotland's ice cream producers see the listings on pages 70–73 and the searchable online directory at www.thelarder.net*

CHEF'S CHOICE
FI BUCHANAN ON ISLE OF MULL CHEESE

The very first day we opened, brimming with pride, expectation, and a couple of glasses of Prosecco, we had virtually nothing in the shop. We had metal shelves sparsely filled with olive oils and spices, a handful of wines we knew were fantastic, and a cold counter with home-made pesto, spider crab spring rolls, olives and a great big block of Isle of Mull cheddar.

Everything at Heart Buchanan has changed, but nothing has changed. We've done a thousand things, some of them folly, some of them brilliant, but we still fall in love with ingredients and Isle of Mull Cheddar is one of them. The wonderful Reade family, based just outside of Tobermory, make a cheese that changes with the seasons – the lush, moist, pastures change from spring to summer to winter when the cows eat sweet hay, and these qualities translate though the milk into the cheese. What doesn't change is the quality of the cheese. It's a gentle, pastoral reminder of a season past. It's a perfect light lunch with apple and walnut chutney, a great way to open or close a dinner, or the simplest, most comforting supper in an omelette or on toast.

Isle of Mull is an ambassador for Scotland throughout the world (I saw it recently on a cheese menu in New York) and most importantly to the Scottish people. Affordable, artisanal and delicious, it's enjoyed by everyone who gets it at Heart Buchanan, from Billy the *Big Issue* seller to A-list film stars.

■ *Fi Buchanan runs Heart Buchanan Fine Food and Wine, 380 Byres Road, Glasgow, 0141 334 7626, www.heartbuchanan.co.uk Isle of Mull Cheese, Sgriob-Ruadh farm, Tobermory, Isle of Mull, 01688 302235, www.isleofmullcheese.co.uk*

WHERE TO BUY

Outlets for cheese, ice cream and other dairy produce listed regionally then organised alphabetically.

EDINBURGH & LOTHIANS

■ Clarks Speciality Foods
202 Bruntsfield Place, Edinburgh
0131 656 0500, www.clarksfoods.co.uk
Mon–Fri 10am–6pm, Sat 9am–5pm, Sun noon–4pm.
Clarks Speciality Foods is run by Chris Clark, while his parents, Alastair and Jill, take care of the wholesale side of the business and supply to some of the best hotels and restaurants in Scotland. A gourmet emporium focusing on farmhouse and artisan cheese from around the UK and Europe, it finds that Scottish cheese remains among the most popular, with over 30 varieties on offer. In addition there are pastas, olive oils, olives, vinegars, charcuterie and Sardinian wine on sale and every week a selection of fruit and vegetables arrive directly from the renowned Parisian market, Marché d'Intérêt National de Rungis.

■ Harvey Nichols Foodmarket
30–34 St Andrew Square, Edinburgh
0131 524 8322, www.harveynichols.com
Mon–Wed 10am–6pm; Thu 10am–8pm; Fri/Sat 10am–7pm; Sun noon–6pm.
Café, Web/mail order.
See Delis & General Food.

■ S Luca of Musselburgh
• 16 Morningside Road, Edinburgh
0131 446 0233
www.lucasicecream.co.uk
Mon–Sat 9am–10pm; Sun 10am–10pm.
• 32–38 High Street, Musselburgh
0131 665 2237, www.lucasicecream.co.uk
Mon–Sat 9am–10pm; Sun 10.30am–10pm.
Café
From its beginnings in 1908, S Luca of Musselburgh has been a family-run business producing authentic Italian ice cream. From its traditional parlour outlets in Morningside and Musselburgh, it sells a selection of ice creams, cakes and confectionary. Tuck into a knickerbocker glory, an ice cream sundae or glorious confectionary, and take something away to be enjoyed at home. If there's a special occasion coming up, it can produce a tailor-made cake through its bespoke service. Still very much a family business, it is being steered into the 21st century by the third generation Lucas.

■ IJ Mellis Cheesemonger
• 6 Bakers Place, Edinburgh
0131 225 6566, www.mellischeese.co.uk
Mon–Fri 9am–6.30pm; Sat 9am–6pm; Sun noon–5pm.
• 330 Morningside Road, Edinburgh
0131 447 8889
Mon–Fri 9am–6.30pm; Sat 9am–6pm.
• 30a Victoria Street, Edinburgh
0131 226 6215
Mon–Sat 9.30am–6pm; Sun noon–5pm.
See photo entry opposite.

Cream o' Galloway

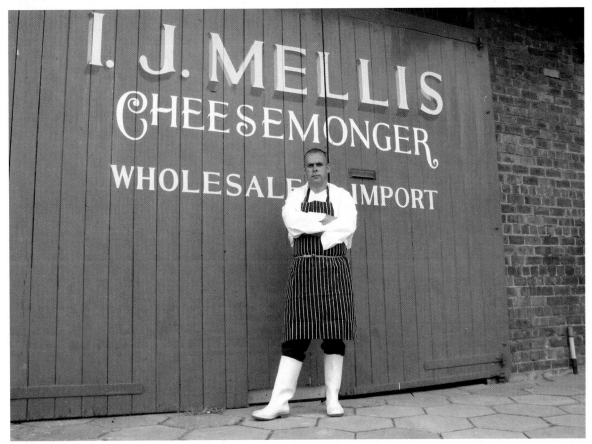

GREATER GLASGOW & CLYDESIDE

■ Delizique
66 Hyndland Street, Partick, Glasgow
See Delis & General Food.

■ Dobbies Farm Foodhall
Boclair Road, Milngavie, Glasgow
See Delis & General Food.

■ Heart Buchanan
380 Byres Road, Glasgow
See Delis & General Food.

■ IJ Mellis Cheesemonger
492 Great Western Road, Glasgow
0141 339 8998, www.mellischeese.co.uk
Mon–Fri 9.30am–7pm; Sat 9am–6.30pm;
Sun 11am–6pm.
See photo entry above.

SOUTHERN SCOTLAND

■ Chisholms of Ayr
17 Carrick Street, Ayr
See Delis & General Food.

■ Cream o' Galloway Dairy
Rainton, Gatehouse-of-Fleet
01557 814040
www.creamogalloway.co.uk
Apr–Jun Mon–Sun 10am–6pm.

IJ MELLIS CHEESEMONGER Since opening his first premises in 1993, Iain Mellis has established a mini empire of traditional cheesemonger's shops between Edinburgh, Glasgow, Aberdeen and St Andrews, with a reputation for supplying only the best British farmhouse cheeses. Well-trained, friendly staff are on hand to advise and guide you through the tricky decision-making process, and are happy to let customers try before they buy. An array of crackers, bread and chutneys are for sale to accompany your dairy purchases, and with the variety of cows', goats' and sheeps' cheeses on offer, and that enticing smell in the air, new customers will surely want to make it part of their weekly shopping routine.

Jul–Aug Mon–Sun 10am–8pm.
Sep–Oct Mon–Sun 10am–5pm.
Nov–Mar Sat/Sun 10am–4pm. Closed Mon–Fri.
Café.
Established in the early 1990s, Cream O' Galloway has been producing Fairtrade dairy ice cream and frozen smoothies for over a decade. Using only the finest organically grown ingredients to produce its ice creams, it is serious about its commitment to reduce its impact on the environment and trades ethically. Keep the kids entertained on a day out at the visitor centre where they can spot wildlife and let off steam in the natural adventure playground. Afterwards, enjoy a treat in the tearoom or ice cream parlour where there are nearly 30 flavours to choose from before buying more to take home from the shop.

■ Loch Arthur Creamery
Camphill Village Trust Ltd, Beeswing, Dumfriesshire
01387 760296, www.locharthur.org.uk
Mon–Fri 9am–5.30pm; Sat 10am–3pm.
Closed Sun.
Web/mail order.
Grown out of the productive efforts of a diverse and vibrant community, Loch Arthur Creamery is a social enterprise committed to creating meaningful work and making a positive contribution to the local community. From humble beginnings in 1985 using the milk from their two Jersey and two Ayrshire cows, their cheeses have since grown to become recognised and sought after, winning awards and accolades in some of the UK's top competitions. Their extensive range of cheeses and yoghurts are sold in their farm shop and other shops throughout the UK.

> SCOTLAND'S FARMHOUSE AND ARTISAN CHEESEMAKERS

Connage Highland Dairy,
Milton of Connage,
Ardersier, Inverness
www.connage.co.uk

Dunlop Dairy, West Clerkland Farm,
Stewarton, Ayrshire

Grimbister Farm Cheeses, Grimbister,
Orkney **www.oqfd.co.uk**

Highland Fine Cheeses,
Blarliath Farm, Tain

HJ Errington & Co, Walston Braehead
Farm, Carnwath, Lanarkshire
www.lanarkblue.com

Isle of Mull Cheese, Sgriob-ruadh
Farm, Tobermory, Mull
www.isleofmullcheese.co.uk

Inverloch Cheese Company,
22 Kirk Street, Campbeltown
www.inverlochcheese.com

Loch Arthur Creamery, Camphill
Village Trust, Beeswing, Dumfries
www.locharthur.org.uk

St Andrews Farmhouse Cheese Co,
Falside Farm, Anstruther, Fife
www.standrewscheese.co.uk

Standhill Cheesery, Standhill Farm,
Minto, by Hawick
www.standhillcheesery.co.uk

Wester Lawrenceton Farm, Forres

West Highland Dairy, Achmore, by
Kyle of Lochalsh
www.westhighlanddairy.co.uk

St Andrews Farmhouse Cheese Company

■ Standhill Cheesery

Standhill Farm, Minto, by Hawick,
Scottish Borders
01835 870225
www.standhillcheesery.co.uk

Jim Shanks' father bought Standhill
Farm in 1951, bringing dairy cows from
Lockerbie to Hawick. Through his love
of the breed, the farm prospered and
today Jim and his wife Annie continue
to care and nurture the continuing
generations of these cows. Looking for
a fresh challenge, they looked to turning
the cows' milk into cheese. After lots of
hard work converting the old milking
parlour into a modern food production
area, Borders Brie and Roxburgh
Roondie came into being very soon
afterwards. Available to buy at farmers'
markets in Kelso, Hawick and
Langholm.

CENTRAL SCOTLAND & FIFE

■ McDonalds Cheese Shop

Westfield, Balmoral Road, Rattray,
Blairgowrie
01250 872493
Tue–Sat 9am–5pm. Closed Sun/Mon.
With a history stretching back nearly 50
years, McDonalds is a mini emporium of
cheese owned by Caroline Robertson.
The stock runs to 80 varieties of British
and continental artisan styles and Swiss
in particular – this is the place to go if
you're looking to buy a whole wheel of
Gruyere. If there's something in
particular you're looking for, Caroline will
take orders and have the cheese
ripened and ready for collection. The
shop also stocks general delicatessen
fodder as well as chocolate from
Bendicks of Mayfair.

■ IJ Mellis Cheesemonger

149 South Street, St Andrews
01334 471410, www.mellischeese.co.uk
Mon–Sat 9am–5.30pm; Sun noon–5pm.
See photo on page 71.

■ St Andrews Farmhouse Cheese Company

Falside Farm, Anstruther, Fife
01333 312580
www.standrewscheese.co.uk
Café.
Falside Farm is home to Robert and
Jane Stewart, whose family have been
farming there for 50 years. Dairy has
always been central to their business
and their herd of home-bred Holstein
Friesian cows produces the
unpasteurised milk which is used to
produce Anster cheese. Fresh and dry,
the cheese has an almost crumbly
texture which dissolves in the mouth to
leave a full-flavoured finish. A visit to the

farm allows you to watch the cheese making process from the specially constructed viewing gallery, before calling into the Butterpat Coffee Shop for some home baking. Don't forget to buy some cheese to take home.

■ Stewart Tower Dairy

Stewart Tower Farm, Stanley, Perth, Perthshire
01738 710044, www.stewart-tower.co.uk
Mon–Sun 10am–4.30pm.
Café.
Using fresh whole milk from its herd of Pedigree Holstein Friesian cows, Stewart Tower produces hand-made ice creams in a staggering range of flavours, as well as fruit ices and frozen yoghurts to sell from its parlour in converted farm steadings. Visit the Round House coffee shop for home-made soup and a slice of cake or, in finer weather, relax on decking overlooking the Strathmore Valley. The Farm Shop stocks a variety of Scottish produce including fruit and vegetables sourced from local farmers and a range of preserves, cheeses and meats.

NORTH EAST SCOTLAND

■ The Cheesery

9 Exchange Street, Dundee
01382 202160, www.thecheesery.co.uk
Mon 10.30am–5.30pm; Tue–Fri 9.30am–5.30pm; Sat 9.30am–5pm.
Closed Sun.
Based in Dundee, this award-winning independent cheese specialist sells quality regional and continental artisan cheeses. With an aim to offer customers new cheeses on a weekly basis, its range stretches to around 50

THE CHEESE COUNTER While the number of cheesemongers and specialist cheese retailers in Scotland is relatively limited, local cheeses are always among the most popular items in good delis and farm shops, such as in the display here at Craigies Farm Shop near South Queensferry. A large number of the outlets listed elsewhere in *The Larder* carry good cheese selections; in addition, the majority of cheeses are suitable for sending through the post by cheesemakers and other companies offering web/mail order.

varieties, around half of which hail from the British Isles and Ireland. Choose from an impressive array of accompaniments including olives, chutneys and savoury preserves to oatcakes and biscuits and, for real cheese aficionados, there's a selection of kitchenware and utensils including hand-carved cheese and breadboards, platters and domes.

■ Devenick Dairy

The Devenick Dairy, Banchory, Aberdeenshire
01224 782476, www.devenickdairy.co.uk
Mon–Fri 10am–6pm, Sat/Sun 10am–5pm.
A local family-run dairy farm based on the outskirts of Aberdeen, Devenick Dairy produces quality, hand-crafted Scottish cheeses and yoghurts. Cows graze on luscious grass which in turn yields the creamy milk essential for giving the products their unique and fresh taste. Visit the farm shop to take home fresh cream, butter, free-range eggs and vegetables from the farm, as well as produce sourced from other local businesses including wild venison, preservatives, chutneys, puddings and oatcakes. Devenick also supplies to other retail outlets and its products can be found in quality shops and delicatessens throughout Scotland.

■ IJ Mellis Cheesemonger

201 Rosemount Place, Aberdeen
01224 566530, www.mellischeese.co.uk
Mon–Fri 10am–5.30pm; Sat 9am–5.30pm. Closed Sun.
See photo on page 71.

HIGHLANDS, ISLANDS & ARGYLL

■ Corner on the Square

1 High Street, Beauly
See Delis & General Food.

■ The Island Cheese Company Ltd

Home Farm, Brodick, Isle of Arran
01770 302 788
www.islandcheese.co.uk
Apr–Oct: Mon–Sun 9.30am–5.30pm.
Nov–Mar: Mon–Sun 9.30am–5pm.
Web/mail order.
A family-run business established 15 years ago on the home farm of Brodick Castle, the Island Cheese Company produces a range of wax-sealed flavoured and deluxe cheddars for sale in its shop, through farmers' markets and a number of other outlets including farm shops, delicatessens and restaurants throughout the UK. A further array of Arran preserves and oatcakes, Scottish drinks and hand-made chocolates are also available.

FISH & SHELLFISH

The sustaining seas

Malcolm MacGarvin surveys the past, present and future of Scottish fishing.

PHOTOS: (THIS PAGE) JOHN BLAIKIE/MEY SELECTIONS; (PREVIOUS PAGE) SCOTTISH VIEWPOINT

According to the 1849 *Report of the Fisheries Board*, 'The fisheries of Scotland present a remarkable contrast to the soil. They seem almost destined by nature to compensate for the natural infertility and insuperable difficulty for cultivation of large tracts of land.'

It's perhaps not surprising, then, that the first Scottish settlers followed the coast, leaving vast middens of shellfish. These contained mostly limpets, but also fish bones, notably of saithe (coalfish) but also cod, which suggests that even then they have fished some way from land.

Trade and industry

In the Middle Ages many fisheries had become locally important, with herring and salmon together making up one of three principal Scottish exports along with wool and hides. Whitefish (variously 'mullones', 'stockfish' and 'haberdynes') were also exported. These were probably large cod, suitable for salting, but ling, saithe, hake and haddock could also have been salted, and turbot, flounder, and plaice were certainly caught.

By the late-18th century increasing division between labour, risk and profit were becoming established. Lairds in Shetland provided the capital for the 'haaf' fisheries: in effect, bonded labour for four-oared 'fourern', and then 'sixern' boats long-longing (baited hooks on a line, even then up to seven miles per boat) for saithe but also catching ling and cod. A similar system emerged for the herring drift net fishery with the curers providing the 'golden handcuffs' of capital for boats, captured in Neil Gunn's *The Silver Darlings*, centred on the Moray Firth. On the west coast, Pennant, in his 1769 *Tour*, describes not only the Loch Fyne herring fishery, but also that for tunny, 'called here Mackerel-Sture' – the Scandinavian root suggesting a long association with the area.

Stocks away

The Age of Enlightenment brought better statistics, and those for the Moray Firth fisheries led to a prescient voice speaking out against the assumed inexhaustibility of fish stocks. James Bertram observed that, between 1818 and 1863, the area of herring drift nets per boat grew from 4500 to 16,800 square yards, yet the catch fell from 125 to 82 crans (barrels).

Statistics also help illuminate the salmon fishery, initially mainly by net at estuary mouths. In the late 1700s some 500,000lbs (225 tonnes) of salmon were caught annually on the Dee and Don, falling to 80,000lbs (35 tonnes) a century later. By then salmon were also being targeted offshore with stake and bag nets. These are remarkable numbers, but, even allowing for other rivers, they are dwarfed by Scotland's current aquaculture production of around 130,000 tonnes annually.

Steam power created another revolution. Steam trawlers, often funded by share-owners, were powerful, mobile and hugely controversial. They were strongly resisted by those inshore fishermen who had neither the resources nor inclination to join in. A Royal Commission Inquiry, held in the 1860s, was inconclusive about the impact of trawling on fish quality and environment impact. However a precautionary decision was taken and, as a result, between 1867 and 1897 trawling was banned throughout the Moray, Tay, Forth and Clyde firths. However, the ban couldn't be enforced on foreign boats, and eventually, Scots started to drag purse seine (encircling) nets along the sea bed, and by the 1920s the protected areas had effectively been abandoned.

The deep water fleet
New deep-sea trawlers able to exploit near-virgin stocks, icing, the railways, and the perfection of the deep-fat frier combined to make a 'pile-it-high, sell it cheap' approach profitable. The era of fish and chips had come. This may have sustained the working classes, but left a legacy and attitude regarding sustainability and quality which has perhaps still to be fully overcome. There were also other deep sea methods, notably long lining out of East coast ports for halibut between Scotland and Iceland, where the fish during the 1930s were still abundant, and so large to be considered a real problem to handle. But in many areas closer to home, by the early years of the 20th century, levels of fishing pressure and stock depletion were – surprisingly, perhaps – not so different from now. Fishing immediately after the First and Second World Wars, when fishing was constrained, saw a major bounce in landings of cod, plaice and rays, although not of salmon. In the first five years after the

Second World War, boats fishing out of Aberdeen could make a quarter of a million pounds, an enormous amount of money in those days, and crew joked about film-star salaries. All of which shows that stocks can recover rapidly with sharp cuts in fishing, and probably quite fast with more manageable transitions.

The Present: inshore fisheries
From Scottish Sea Fisheries Statistics 2007 we learn that there were some 1494 Scottish boats under 10m in length. These, along with a few larger boats, make up the bulk of the inshore day boats, to which a restauranteur would naturally turn for local fish caught that day and of the highest quality. What is immediately striking, compared with an area such as Cornwall, is the lack of variety. There were 1292 creel fishing boats (crabs, lobsters, langoustine), 95 langoustine trawlers, but just 29 liners and ten demersal gill netters throughout Scotland. There were also 35 diver boats, mainly scallopers. Put positively, there may be an opportunity here for boats switching to fish for top-end local restaurants who are after the very highest quality.

The Present: offshore fisheries
Mackerel and herring fisheries, the historic focus for thousands of Scottish boats, are now dominated by 23 large (50m and over) modern trawlers and seiners. The fisheries are highly controllable and, due to the shoaling nature of the fish, highly selective. For this reason in December 2008 these vessels received MSC certification, a remarkable turn-around from the first half of the decade.

In 2007, demersal trawling landed 62,534 tonnes of fish (typically haddock, whiting, saithe, plaice, anglers (monk) and cod), worth

£88million, while langoustine (Nephrops) trawling landed 30,484 tonnes, also worth £88million. Compared, for example, to Norway, it is again noticeable how narrow the fishing methods are, with very little long-lining, trapping or netting. The single most valuable category, langoustine trawling, is also associated with the worst concerns, of by-catch of immature whitefish, seabed damage and high fuel use.

The Future
Warmer water species, including anchovy, red mullet, bass and john dory are beginning to make an appearance and other species, such as the Moray Firth squid fishery and spoots (razorshells), are beginning to be exploited. As for the mainstream Scottish fisheries, how intensely, and by what method, they are exploited will make the difference between a lost opportunity and a renaissance. Current slight signs of recovery of stocks, and of the industry, should not be squandered, although history warns this is the usual outcome. It does seem that it is with the Cinderella of inshore small-scale fisheries that the most immediate opportunities now lie for diversification, higher quality, greater employment on and off boats, local restaurants and markets. Having gone through phases of subsistence, trade, capitalisation and industrialisation, such diversification – taking into account wider sustainability and other interests (such as anglers), quality of life and food miles – fits with the current spirit of the age.

■ *Malcolm MacGarvin is a marine ecologist, researcher and environmental consultant based in the Highlands of Scotland. He has recently worked on the Pisces Responsible Fish Restaurants scheme, which seeks to link restaurants directly with small-scale fishing boats using sustainable practices.*

Smoke filled rooms

The smoking of fish is one of the few Scottish traditional practices related to food to be flourishing today. Here we provide a spotters' guide to the differences in Scotland's best-known smoked fish, while Michelin-starred chef Martin Wishart offers his insights on some of his own favourites.

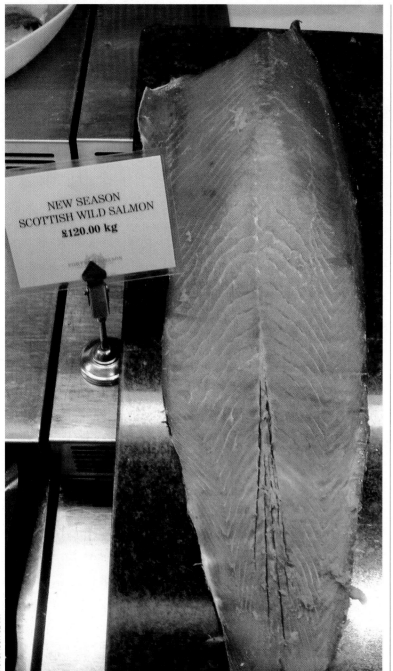

NEW SEASON SCOTTISH WILD SALMON £120.00 kg

PHOTO: IGOR CLARK

Cold smoked salmon

This is what most people recognise as smoked salmon, typically served in thin slices cut horizontal to the skin. Smoking was originally employed as a means of preserving fish, and while a longer shelf life remains a useful benefit, the principal role smoking has today is for the effects of flavour and texture it offers.

First the fresh salmon is salted, either in a brine solution or sometimes simply dry salt; additions to the cure play a role in the final flavour. Sugar is a common ingredient, but molasses, treacle, spices, rum, whisky and wine are also used. After curing, the salmon is smoked for a reasonable length of time (12–48 hours) at a lowish temperature (below 30° Celsius) – insufficient to cook the fish. It's then normally left to rest and mature for about 12 hours.

Martin Wishart: 'The best and most traditional way to make cold smoked salmon is to use wild salmon. You are looking for a salmon with a low fat content of around 14–16 per cent, as this allows a good quality of firmness and means that it won't weep any oils when you cut into it. You don't want a fish that has a lot of excess oil as it will affect the flavour. If you can't get wild salmon then the best alternative is organic farmed salmon. I get mine from Benbecula and Shetland.

'I remember being in Stornoway and buying some smoked salmon, but instead of being plastic wrapped it was carefully folded in greaseproof paper; it had a wonderfully authentic taste. Good things to serve with smoked salmon are those with a bit of bite: obviously citrus and lemon zests are the most common, but pickled cucumber, horseradish or long white radish with wasabi all work.

'I prepare it differently from most chefs in that I slice it vertically straight down the meat and serve it with the surface pellicle; that way you get the beautiful intense smokiness followed by a light creaminess of flavour.'

Hot smoked salmon

Also known as hot roast salmon, or sometimes flaky salmon, the basic processes are similar to cold smoking, except the fish is smoked in a hotter kiln or the heat is turned up at the end of the process.

Oak or oak chips are most commonly burned (or smouldered) for both kinds of smoked salmon, with many smokehouses using 'recycled' oak staves from old whisky barrels. Larch, ash and beech are also used, as is peat (for example by the Summer Isles Smokehouse). Kilns range from older fashioned brick kilns (such as those at Inverawe) to widely-used stainless steel smokers.

'This has become more popular and is widely available in supermarkets, but it's best to eat it straight after it's been warmed and smoked, when the flakes of meat will just break and crumble off. Because it is hot smoked, it works well in a warm dish like pasta. Just flake it in at the last minute, but be careful not to re-heat the fish. It is also nice served as it is, with a butter-based warm sauce such as a home-made hollandaise with herbs like tarragon and chervil.

'You can also smoke it at home. Buy your own wood chips, put them in a pan with a trellis over the top, lay in the fish and cover the pan tightly. It might take a couple of attempts to get it right, but the fish really lends itself to smaller, individual smoking.'

Arbroath Smokie

Smokies are one of the few Scottish foods granted Protected Geographical Indication (PGI) by the EU. This limits the name Arbroath Smokies to haddock which have been smoked in the traditional manner within an eight-kilometre radius of Arbroath. A whole haddock is headed and gutted, then dry salted for around two hours, washed, tied in pairs by the tail and hung over metal bars, air dried then placed over a fire pit for 30–45 minutes. Iain Spink prepares them in the original way in a half-barrel laid over with hessian sacking, a portable system that allows him to prepare fresh smokies at food festivals around the country.

'This is one of the best smoked fish. Last year I went over to Fife and had one of Iain Spink's smokies; he pulled it straight out from under the hessian and gave it to me from the barrel. It has a rich creaminess and moisture, and fresh like that is undoubtedly the best way to eat Smokies. It is also nice flaked up and served with potatoes.'

Finnan Haddie

Finnans are also whole haddock headed and gutted, but in this method they are split and opened up, dry salted overnight then cold smoked over peat for 8–9 hours. The method originates from Findon, a village south of Aberdeen. A Finnan needs to be cooked before eating.

'I get my haddie from Anstruther fishmonger David Lowrie, who gets it from Findon. We actually don't use it a lot in the restaurant, but my favourite way to serve it is in a potato mash. I'd use a nice floury potato, like a Golden Wonder, and then add reduced double cream, butter and salt. I'd then flake the haddie in raw. If you've cooked it right the flakes should retain a slight translucency and you should be able just to flake them off with your thumb.

'It's also great in soups like Cullen skink or served with a grainy mustard or braised leeks. It's an all-rounder.'

Smoked Haddock

This is simply a fillet of haddock cold smoked, so it's similar to a Finnan but off the bone and without the definition provided by a traditional method. Yellow dyed haddock fillets are still seen: they were originally used to mimic the colour of a properly smoked fish.

'I recently ate smoked haddock served raw with crème-fraiche and mixed herbs and the taste of the fish really came through. Often with fish it's about simple flavours, as you want to show off the fish itself. But just as much it is about the chef's skill in balancing the flavours.'

Kippers

Kippers are a different fish entirely – herring – which are gutted, split and brined for about half an hour, then cold smoked for anything between 4 and 24 hours. Though associated with Loch Fyne (see page 81), it's not a distinctively Scottish method and kippering traditions are strong elsewhere in the British Isles.

■ *Martin Wishart has held a Michelin star at Restaurant Martin Wishart in Leith since 2001. In 2007 he opened Cookschool by Martin Wishart, also in Leith, and a year later set up his second restaurant in Cameron House at Loch Lomond. He also produces his own brand of smoked Shetland salmon. www.martin-wishart.co.uk*

> SCOTLAND'S FISH SMOKEHOUSES

Belhaven Smokehouse, by Dunbar 01368 864025

Burns Country Smokehouse, by Maybole www.burnsmoke.com

Creelers of Arran Smoked Products, Brodick, Isle of Arran www.creelers.co.uk

Dunkeld Smoked Salmon, Dunkeld www.dunkeldsmokedsalmon.com

Fencebay Fisheries, Fairlie www.fencebay.co.uk

Hebridean Smokehouse, North Uist www.hebrideansmokehouse.com

Inverawe Smokehouses, by Taynuilt www.smokedsalmon.co.uk

Isle of Skye Smokehouse, Broadford www.skye-seafood.co.uk

Jolly's of Orkney, Kirkwall www.jollyfish.co.uk

Macdonald's Smoked Produce, Glenuig, Lochailort www.smokedproduce.com

Marrbury Smokehouse, Newton Stewart www.visitmarrbury.co.uk

St James Smokehouse, Annan www.stjamessmokehouse.com

Salar Smokehouse, South Uist www.salar.co.uk

Sleepy Hollow Smokehouse, Aultbea, Wester Ross, www.sleepyhollowsmokehouse.com

Summer Isles Seafood, Achiltibuie, Ullapool www.summerislesfoods.co.uk

Iain R Spink, Arbroath www.arbroathsmokies.com

M&M Spink, Arbroath www.arbroathsmokies.co.uk

Ugie Salmon Fishings, Peterhead www.ugie-salmon.co.uk

Uig Lodge Smoked Salmon, near Stornoway, Isle of Lewis www.uiglodge.co.uk

PHOTO: JAMIE GRANT

The scallop hunter

Nicki Holmyard speaks to scallop diver Hector Stewart about
what happens in the murky depths of Scotland's scallop beds.

'Fresh, locally dived scallops,' reads the menu at many a restaurant, portraying a romantic picture of sparkling blue seas and a lone diver working at one with nature. But is this the reality?

'Partly,' says Hector Stewart, a professional scallop diver from Skipness on the Kintyre Peninsula. He happens to think that his job is one of the best in the world, but it is hard work and requires dedication, for Hector dives seven days a week, 52 weeks a year, when the weather permits. He is also bound by a host of rules and regulations, designed to make diving safe, to ensure shellfish is safe to eat, and to stop unlicensed divers selling shellfish through the 'back door'.

'Unfortunately there are still divers out there who ignore the rules, and hotels and restaurants that aid and abet them. It is a difficult industry to police,' he says.

Stewart switched to professional diving just over six years ago, having been a creel fisherman for many years, catching langoustines, crab and lobster. 'We were having too many conflicts with trawlers in the loch and losing our gear to them, so I decided to dive for shellfish instead,' he says.

His ten-metre catamaran, *Pride and Joy*, steams out from Tarbert harbour at the crack of dawn each morning, taking the crew towards the rich diving grounds in the Firth of Clyde. Onboard are three divers plus an observer, who also sorts out the shellfish and returns undersized specimens to the sea.

Stewart explains that his policy is to take scallops at least 10mm above the minimum landing size of 100mm, leaving plenty to spawn and repopulate the stocks. 'We do our bit for conservation, and hand-picking from the seabed – unlike dredging – ensures that no damage is done. Our methods also mean the animals are not stressed.'

Scallops account for around one third of his daily take, with the remainder made up of razor clams (spoots) and sand gapers. Spoots are captured using a low pressure water pump which is held over the tell-tale holes they make in the seabed. It washes the sand away from the base of the shellfish, which is then carefully removed by a diver. Sand gapers are collected in the same way, but are deeper in the seabed.

Markets remain buoyant and Stewart says he could sell 'a thousand times' more than he can land. Most of his produce goes through ScotPrime in Ayr, which deals with all the paperwork and ensures the shellfish is properly packed for distribution, he says. From there it is sent throughout Scotland and the wider UK, and as far afield as Spain, Portugal, Hong Kong and Korea.

So what makes a dived scallop so good? 'They are succulent, sweet, free from grit, and unsoaked. Dredged scallops can have sand in the meat and some processors plump up the meats in water,' explains Stewart. 'And when landed legally, there are no health risks to consider. In short, their popularity is well deserved!'

Seaweed and urchins - a modern food industry?

From skincare to carbon sequestration, detox to fertiliser, seaweed is more versatile than we realise, finds Catharina Day.

Compared with the Japanese, we don't have a particularly broad or adventurous sea-borne culinary lexion. Seaweed – a novelty to most of us – appears often in Japanese cooking, not least in miso soup. Carrageen puddings and stews augmented by dulse used to be normal fare along the coasts of Scotland – a botanist in Victorian times

noted down 40 words for seaweed in the Western Isles – though it's in Ireland that the tradition lingers on today. It is still used as fertilising material by coastal gardeners and crofters, but various industrial uses for seaweed in Scotland over the centuries, such as the Leverhulme processing plant in Harris, failed due to overseas competition, changing markets and over-ambitious schemes. However, cottage industry BloominBute (www.justseaweed.com) sells fresh seaweed harvested in Bute waters for skincare, bathing and detox, as well five separate types suitable for eating. Those in the know, meanwhile, forage

for their own. The authors of a recent wild foraging guides for families, *Seaweed and Eat It*, are based in Edinburgh and inspired a local baker to bake a loaf flecked with seaweed. Possible uses as biofuel or in wave-based renewable energy schemes are being investigated, while sugar kelp and dulse are being grown alongside the sustainably farmed salmon at Loch Duart (www.lochduart.com), where they prove useful in carbon sequestration, helping to minimise the impact of pollutants. This company is also growing 20,000 native *Paracentrotus lividus*, an edible species of sea urchin. They graze on leftover feed and clean algae off the sides of the pens. Rich, creamy sea urchin roes are prized, especially in Japan; with no added antibiotics or growth promoters, these little urchins may yet become a Scottish delicacy.

■ *Seaweed and Eat It: a family foraging and cooking adventure by Fiona Houston and Xa Milne (Virgin Books, £10.99)*

> A FYNE TRADITION

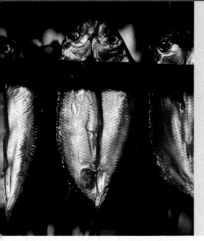

Loch Fyne was once synonymous with herring and kippers. However, the herring have all but disappeared and so have the kipper houses. Nicki Holmyard finds out about the last of a famous line.

In the Old Smokehouse in Campbeltown, one of the very last of Scotland's traditional kipper houses, Archie MacMillan keeps the Celtic traditions, skills and local knowledge alive with his Original Kintyre Kippers.

The kilns may be new and fully compliant with EU regulations, but the age old methods remain the same, according to MacMillan. 'We only source the very finest Scottish herring, bought at their

best during the season when the fat content is just right, and we use no dyes or additives,' he says.

The fish are hand-split, cured using an age-old recipe, then hung on kipper hooks prior to smoking over oak chippings made from local whisky barrels. The gentle smoking process takes around seven hours, before the kippers are ready for dispatch to customers including Loch Fyne Oysters, local hotels, restaurants and wholesalers. MacMillan also sells them at the twice-monthly farmers' market in the West End of Glasgow.

■ *MacMillan Foods are at the Old Smokehouse, Campbeltown, 01586 553580*

A guide to
cooking shellfish

Shellfish are often paraded as the very best of Scotland's larder, but many of us are intimidated by the prospect of dealing with them at home. Expert fish and shellfish chef, Jim Cowie of the Captain's Galley restaurant in Scrabster, gives us his personal guide to selecting and cooking his favourites.

Mussels

A fantastic species, healthy, versatile and widely available. You can make a basic moules marnière with stock, cream, shallots and garlic. But it's just as easy to do an Asian-style dish with coconut milk, Thai basil, lemongrass and lime. From start to eating, it shouldn't take more than two minutes. It's basically a really hot pan for a minute or so, then in with the ingredients for a few seconds and you're done. If you have any left, use them to make a stock.

Scallops and queenies

I get my queenies from Orkney; the quality of the water there makes a big difference to the flavour. First I remove the barnacled side and then sit the scallop in the cupped part of the shell. Then I grill it with some garlic butter, fresh coriander and parsley – and perhaps a sprinkle of lemon juice. The more you complicate it, the more you risk spoiling it. King scallops are good as a main dish: three diver king scallops from Orkney barely fit on our restaurant plates.

Cockles and clams

Although technically a different species, cockles and clams are very similar and, with my supplier, the two are interchangeable. I'll often make a huge pot of New England clam chowder with onions, garlic, bacon and potatoes. Taste-wise, clams are a superior shellfish and they can add a lovely flavour to pasta or risotto. I also find them to be visually superior; so it's sometimes nice just to steam them to open using stock or white wine, and then place them as a garnish around a larger piece of fish.

Whelks

Whelks are underutilised in Scotland, because we're not adventurous enough. They are lovely lightly boiled in salted water and sliced thinly to taste. The meat is fantastic minced up and used in a Caribbean conch chowder, as the whelk is a perfect alternative to conch. I would never fly conch round the world when you can always find a local alternative. This chowder is tomato, rather than cream, based – with bacon, green peppers, chillies, bay leaves, tobacco, lime juice and spices. Any time I've had it in the Caribbean I've been given a bottle of sherry with it. A few glugs in the dish sets it off.

Winkles

A winkle is like a smaller version of a whelk. They are small, black shellfish found around the coastline of Scotland. To me they are a snacking food. I boil them up in heavily salted water, as it's about trying to re-create the seawater environment they came from. I then add a dozen peppercorns and a couple of bay leaves, boil for a maximum of five minutes and then eat them as finger food. They are also good in a stir-fry: just take the pan off the heat and fold them through at the last minute. Due to their size they will cook in the steam.

Crabs

The first thing to look for is whether the crab is male or female. On the underside of the shell, between the small legs, the female has a wider 'purse' and the top side of her shell is more rounded. The female has more brown meat, because of her bigger body, and the male has bigger claws and so more white meat. Always pick a crab with a rich, brown coloured shell and lots of energy (ie fast moving legs). Feel for a weight of meat – depending on season, they can be light and watery. Often I use both white and brown meat in the same dish, like a nice crab salad with chunky guacamole, home-made crispy tortilla and lime granita. The brown meat gives an intense flavour and the white meat adds a nice texture.

Spoots (Razor clams)

A nice way of doing them is in a ribbed steak griddle pan. Get the pan fairly hot and then angle the clams into the spars of the griddle and it will help keep them closed for long enough. Cook them for a minute to 90 seconds in butter and wine, then take the clams out and put the pan back on the heat, reduce the juices and add butter and chopped herbs. Serve them as they are, with just the clams and a little of the juice. And get away from the idea that it has to be piping hot to serve, that's often when you ruin the fish.

Lobster

This is the king of fish to me, but be careful when choosing lobster – usually you can instinctively tell a good one, as it will be lively and heavy of body. They shed their shell each year, so you want one with a strong shell that hasn't just been cast. If it's not in season, I refuse to put it on the menu. The first thing I do when lobsters enter my kitchen is put them in a pan of salted boiling water for three to four minutes. This puts them out of their misery, as I believe that nothing gives us the right to be cruel to another creature. Then it's a case of deciding whether to grill the meat in olive oil and herbs or steam it and use it as it is; it can also be left to cool for a salad.

Langoustine

The ethics of fish use are changing and we're beyond the days of just using part of a fish and discarding the rest. Langoustine is a good fish for allowing you to use all parts – even with the shell you can make good bisque. Be careful only to heat the meat through once, however, because if you stir it through a pasta, for example, and then continue cooking it, you will ruin the meat. It's also particularly good in a stir fry with chilli, ginger, fried rice and some crunchy vegetables – but there's no need for a sauce. No fish needs a heavy sauce – it's about complementing it, not smothering it.

Shrimp

Shrimp is excellent for poaching and shelling in risottos, pastas and stir-fries – but potted shrimp is a favourite. Take the shrimps and add butter, herbs, mace, cayenne pepper and nutmeg and cook in a hot pan. Then put it in little clay ramekins and let it all mingle together, before leaving it to set in the fridge. The butter solidifies and then you can serve it with warm toast. I don't have shrimp on my menu, because I can't get it locally and I don't buy fish outwith a 50-mile perimeter. It just means I look forward to shrimp when I travel elsewhere.

CHEF'S CHOICE

KEVIN BROOME ON LOCH TORRIDON LANGOUSTINES

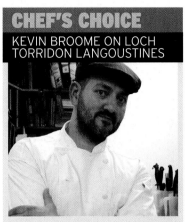

To some, the langoustine or Dublin bay prawn is the jewel in the crown of shellfish. Many top London restaurants pay high prices to allow this wonderful prawn a prime position on their menus. Nephrops norvegicus (the binomial name) are commercially fished around Scottish shores and some 40 per cent of the world's stocks caught and sold from Scotland, with Spain being one of the main buyers.

Based in Shieldaig, the award winning Loch Torridon fishermen are among a handful of collectives in the world to be accredited as a Marine Stewardship Council sustainable fishery and they're the only certified crustacean fishery in the UK today. Around the loch there's a three-mile ban on large commercial trawling which allows the langoustine to be caught only in traditional creels. This allows the prawns to grow to a proper size and protects healthy stocks for years to come.

Typically we'll serve Lorch Torridon langoustines grilled simply with basil, lemon and chilli butter. We place the fresh, live langoustines in the freezer which sends them to sleep, allowing a humane way of cooking without all the movement you get in the pot or oven. Spread the flavoured butter over the cooled prawn then put them under a hot grill for eight to ten minutes, finishing in a hot oven for a couple of minutes further, then serve on fresh summer leaves.

■ *Kevin-John Broome is head chef at the Torridon, www.thetorridon.com*

Flat out in Gigha

Jane Wright visits Scotland's only organic halibut farm.

I f anything symbolises the success of Gigha's thriving island economy since the islanders' historic buy-out in 2002, it is Alastair Barge's sustainable, organic halibut farm, the only one of its kind in Scotland. Perched above the shoreline on the east coast overlooking the Mull of Kintyre, the fishery uses sea water pumped through a system powered by the island's own windfarm. Organic, sustainable, producing high-quality fish, using renewable energy, creating local jobs: Gigha Halibut is a heartening success story for Scotland's rural economy, leading the way in organic practices that are both environmentally sound and profitable.

But the farm has been a long time in the making; 15 years of development drawn from formative experiences in trout and salmon farming and a long, slow painstaking process building up the country's only halibut hatchery – Alastair Barge is a man of infinite patience. And when you consider that only one per cent of hatchlings make it to tiddler stage, when they are transferred to tanks to begin a journey that sees the adult fish eventu-ally harvested at three years old, this is a long and labour-intensive process. But at Gigha Halibut there are no chemicals, no pollutants, no machinery – everything is done by hand, from feeding to catching, making it almost a labour of love, which is why you might find fishery manager Jim Beagan singing to these large grey-mottled fish at feeding time. He believes in respecting the fish; that if the fish are happy, content and well-fed, they will grow steadily.

The halibut (hippoglossus hippoglossus) is a deep-water, flat fish most associated with the Atlantic, although they are found in the Canadian Pacific and in Norwegian

waters. They are right-eyed (ie both eyes are on the top side of the head), can grow up to four metres in length and live to be over 50 years old in their natural habitat. But Atlantic halibut is now an endangered species due to intense over-fishing, and because they are slow to re-populate, halibut stocks cannot easily recover from the effects of over-fishing. Therefore a sustainable organic farm is the logical way forward to provide for a market that enjoys this mild, lean but fleshy fish.

Barge's farm is unique in that it operates not within cages in the sea, like salmon farming, but in land-based tanks where fresh seawater – 1400 litres per second – is continually pumped through the system. This aerates the water and produces a constant current which is crucial for stimulating and exercising the fish, keeping them happy and healthy – and their flesh firm and lean. In the wild, halibut like to congregate on the seabed, so it is vital that the tanks have solid flat floors where the fish can rest. Two full-time and three part-time workers monitor eight circular tanks which hold the halibut at various stages of the three-year farming process. The tanks are designed with platforms to make access, cleaning, feeding and observation of the fish easier. Naturally curious, the halibut enjoy tumbling and bobbing in the current and constantly break the surface with their gaping mouths to see what's going on. But they have to be protected from the sun's rays as their skin burns easily, which is why the cold, generally wet climate of Scotland's west coast is perfect for this cold-water breed.

Barge harvests three-and-a-half tonnes of halibut every week which is gutted and packed on the mainland and then transported throughout the UK, Europe and even America, where,

despite having access to its own doorstep stocks of Pacific halibut, has been wooed by Gigha's organic credentials and consistent, high-quality meat. For the future, Barge has plans to consolidate his operation, concentrating on developing the hatchery and continually improving the quality and price of his fish. In today's markets, halibut sells for around £23 per kilo in fishmongers.

Andy Race has delivered fish and shellfish to the Isle of Eriska for several decades, establishing himself as a supplier long before I joined the hotel in 1998. I first came across Andy's company as a trainee chef more than 26 years ago, so I feel that we go back a bit. Over the years, we've developed a great working relationship. My secret is to always make time for a chat and not just tick off a list of orders.

Running an established business out of Mallaig, Andy knows all the fishermen and is among the first to have access to their catch. It's a great advantage for us as it means that he'll often be able to offer us something a bit special such as wild seabass, red mullet or John Dory.

I'm happy to ask Andy what is available on any particular day and then create a menu accordingly – ensuring our guests taste the freshest fish and seafood the west coast has to offer.

Andy also offers some of the best traditionally smoked salmon you'll ever taste and he passed on some of his wisdom when he helped us set up our own smoker. He's just great to work with and I don't know what we'd do without him.

■ *Robert Macpherson is the head chef at the Isle of Eriska Hotel, Spa and Island's Restaurant by Benderloch, near Oban, 01631 720371, www.eriska-hotel.co.uk. Andy Race Fish Merchants are at the Harbour, Mallaig, 01687 462626, www.andyrace.co.uk*

Halibut should be allowed to 'age' for a couple of days before being eaten, and is best treated simply, such as pan-fried with lemon, lime and chive butter, as Libby Donaldson, chef at the Gigha Hotel, likes to cook it. Flaky and tender, it needs little fuss to bring out its sweet flavour.

The farm also produces smoked halibut to order to their own secret recipe, and the result is a light, dry, delicately smoky meat that is dark yellow in colour. Perfect with a crisp, cold Sauvignon, smoked halibut can more than match smoked salmon with its light taste, dry texture and lack of that filmy sensation often found with salmon. For palates dulled by the ubiquity of smoked salmon on restaurant menus, smoked halibut is a revelation and a refreshing change.

■ *www.gighahalibut.co.uk*

WHERE TO BUY

Outlets for buying fish and shellfish listed regionally then organised alphabetically.

EDINBURGH & LOTHIANS

■ George Armstrong Fishmonger

80 Raeburn Place, Edinburgh
0131 315 2033
www.armstrongsofstockbridge.co.uk
Tue–Fri 7am–5.30pm; Sat 7am–5pm.
Closed Sun/Mon.
This excellent fishmonger in Stockbridge sources local cold water fish direct from the coasts of Scotland, with live shellfish from the west coast as well as more exotic, equally fresh species from further afield. There's a smokery on the premises where salmon is prepared, smoked and packed. Always varied and colourful, you'll find varieties of snapper, grouper, and everything from mounds of spoots (razor clams) and crawling velvet crabs to increasingly rare wild halibut. If you're after a particular fish, owner Gavin Borthwick will find it and local delivery is free. The upbeat staff are genuinely friendly, helpful and knowledgeable.

■ Belhaven Smokehouse

Beltonford, Dunbar, East Lothian
01368 864025
Mon–Sun 10am–5pm.
Web/mail order.
Established in 1975, Belhaven is one of only a handful of independent fish farm processors in Scotland. Its Dunbar smoked salmon is made by smoking a fillet over oak chips from whisky barrels then preserving it using a traditional rum cure. Belhaven specialises in mail order but also has a shop open seven days a week – as well as its own fresh, marinated and smoked trout, it also stocks Lammermuir smoked cheese and Ballencrieff smoked bacon.

■ Clark Brothers Fish Merchant

220 New Street, Musselburgh
0131 665 6181
Mon–Sat 7am–5.30pm. Closed Sun.
The Clark Brothers' harbour-side shop has been selling fish in Musselburgh for well over 100 years. Crabs come dressed or whole, prawns range from small to jumbo and lobsters can be bought live or cooked. Cod, haddock and salmon are joined by more exotic fish sourced from international markets. The company smokes its own salmon and trout, and towards the end of July, you might just find bright green samphire nestling amid the fish and ice on marble slabs.

■ Eddie's Seafood Market

7 Roseneath Street, Edinburgh
0131 229 4207
www.eddies-seafood-market.com
Tue–Fri 7.30am–6pm; Sat 7.30am–5pm.
Closed Sun.
Eddie's Seafood Market has been trading in Marchmont since 1986 and true to its name, has the feel of a miniature market. Supplier to many of Edinburgh's restaurants, it overflows with sealife: Scotland's waters provide most of the fish and there's a particularly wide range of home-grown shellfish. Lobsters and langoustines meander around a large tank while exotic sea creatures packed into the ice-filled boxes on the floor might include snapper or even a whole shark. Everything is palpably fresh, from swordfish and tuna (sliced from the fillet in front of you) to haddock. Very busy at times, it's best to arrive early in the day in order not to miss out.

■ The Fisherman's Kitchen

96 High Street, North Berwick, East Lothian
See Delis & General Food Shops.

■ Something Fishy

16a Broughton Street, Edinburgh
0131 556 7614
Tue–Fri 7.30am–5.30pm; Sat
7.30am–5pm. Closed Sun.

A popular and well-established, traditional fishmongers set among the array of good food shops that now populate Broughton Street, this small shop caters to all fish tastes. From sustainable pollock to flashy monkfish, as well as a good selection of shellfish, Something Fishy has it all. The husband and wife team are happy to offer advice to guide you in your choice, and will also fillet the fish for you if required. Its in-house smokery also produces delicious smoked salmon, haddock and mackerel using traditional methods.

GREATER GLASGOW & CLYDESIDE

■ Alan Beveridge

1121 Pollokshaws Rd, Shawlands,
Glasgow, Lanarkshire
0141 649 5067
Tue–Sat 7.30am–6pm. Closed
Sun/Mon.

A fishmonger for more than 35 years, Alan Beveridge has an impressive selection of seafood. From his outlets on Glasgow's Pollokshaws, Fenwick and Byres Roads, choose from an array of fresh fish including glistening sardines, squid, skate, herring, meaty monkfish and tuna, and shellfish including prawns, crab, mussels, lobster and oysters when in season. Friendly and knowledgeable staff will guide you through the buying process and offer advice on preparation and recipes.

■ The Fish People

350 Scotland Street, Glasgow
0141 429 1609
Tue–Fri 7am–5.30pm; Sat 7am–1pm.
Closed Sun/Mon.

The Fish People is exactly the type of fishmonger everybody wishes they had on their street; luckily, being located directly outside the Shields Road Underground Station on the Southside of Glasgow, it isn't difficult to get to and you may even have sampled its wares without knowing it at one of the many quality restaurants and delis the Fish People supplies in Glasgow. As the name implies, this is the place to find a wide selection of the freshest quality fish and shellfish; you can also find pickled and smoked fish as well as wild smoked venison, rabbit, duck and pigeon. Competitive prices on sides of Loch Fyne smoked salmon make this place hard to resist, and it is willing to source products by request, even offering free delivery.

■ The Fish Plaice

1 St Andrews Street, Glasgow
0141 552 2337
Tue–Sat 8.30am–5.30pm. Closed
Sun/Mon.

Follow the fishy aroma up a narrow alley at the Saltmarket, and you will come across this old-style fishmonger installed in a railway arch, freshly hosed and glisteningly clean. Outside are boxes of whelks, oysters and rope-grown mussels; move inside next to the well-used gutting table to encounter a broad selection of fresh and frozen fish. Ham houghs and ribs along with rice and pulses emphasise the traditional side of the business while the presence of trendier ingredients such as seabass, bream and scallops suggest it is quick to respond to customer demand.

SOUTHERN SCOTLAND

■ Burns Country Smokehouse

Grange Mains Farmhouse,
School Road, Minishant, Ayrshire
01292 442773, www.burnsmoke.com
Mon–Sat 10am–5pm; Sun noon–5pm.
Café, Web/mail order.

Seeking to use the most traditional methods, Burns Country Smokehouse takes a week to produce its smoked salmon, from harvesting through to packing. It burns oak staves from malt whisky barrels to fuel the kiln and give the products their unique flavour, with all the processes being executed by hand. It also produces premium smoked bacon, utilising pork from a farm which has won a Freedom Food award from the RSPCA for the quality of its husbandry. Visit the award-winning farm shop and café to choose from an array of its own, and other locally sourced produce.

■ Dee Fish

146 King Street, Castle Douglas
1556 997199524, www.deefish.net
Tue–Fri 9.30am–4.30pm; Sat
9.30am–1pm. Closed Sun/Mon.

A family run business, Dee Fish has two trawlers – *Still Waters* and *Fulmar* – which between them keep its shops in Castle Douglas and Dalbeattie supplied with scallops, lobsters, prawns and a variety of white fish. Its smokehouse produces oak smoked salmon, trout and haddock, as well as smoking meat and game for a number of local butchers. It smokes only Grade A Scottish farmed salmon or wild salmon which has been caught by half-netters and stake nets on the rivers Nith, Cree and Dee. A variety of seafood is available to buy online.

Within minutes of leaving Edinburgh's city centre, you can find yourself in beautiful countryside, on amazing sandy beaches or in friendly little fishing towns that are especially great for me when I'm looking to source the best produce around. When it comes to fresh local food, I am particularly passionate about what the east coast of Scotland has to offer. One of my favourite places to source seafood is Eyemouth where DR Collin and Sons offer an unrivalled selection which never fails to deliver on quality.

The first thing that hits you on the arrival here is the harbour's distinct smell that brings back childhood memories of holidaying at the seaside. The fishermen in the area still boast Eyemouth's ethic of hard work and toil and they deliver some of the most wonderful shellfish and seafood. At the Old Smokehouse you can purchase fresh smoked salmon which is simply delicious. The staff are friendly and knowledgeable, offering advice whenever you need it. There is a traditional and old-fashioned sense of service here but they are always ahead of the competition when it comes to sourcing and serving unique artisan products.

■ *Roy Brett is chef partner at Dakota Forth Bridge, South Queensferry, www.dakotaforthbridge.co.uk DR Collin, 34 Harbour Road, Eyemouth, 018907 52018*

■ Fencebay Fisheries

Fencefoot Farm, Fairlie, Ayrshire
01475 568918, www.fencebay.co.uk
Mon–Sat 9am–5pm; Sun 10am–5pm.
Café, Web/mail order.

UKTV Local Food Hero Fencebay Fisheries is a food chain in its own right: there's a farm shop selling a range of foods produced by local Ayrshire farmers, fishermen and country folk and a small trout farm. Its smokehouse produces a number of smoked goods, and in addition to its rainbow trout, owners Jill and Bernard Thain smoke herring landed at Largs' pier. There's also a cookshop and Fins Restaurant, offering Scottish seafood platters fresh from the sea. On the last Sunday of every month, Fencebay plays host to an indoor farmers' market with a revolving group of local suppliers taking space in the whitewashed cowshed.

CENTRAL SCOTLAND & FIFE

■ Fish In Crieff

30 East High Street, Crieff, Perthshire
01764 654509
Tue–Sat 7am–5pm; Sat 7am–4pm.
Closed Sun/Mon.
Web/mail order.

Fish In Crieff moved along the street recently and now stocks not only a wide range of fish and shellfish bought direct from the boats in Scrabster, but also poultry, game and an expanding range of deli items such as olives, pastas, pesto and cheeses. Owner Willie Little, formerly of wholesalers Ocean Traders, still supplies Mhor Fish in Callander and helps to organise informative cooking demos there.

■ Mhor Fish

75/77 Main Street, Callander, Stirlingshire
01877 330213, www.mhor.net
Mon–Sun 10am–10pm.
Café.

Winner of the Best Newcomer in the prestigious Observer Food Monthly Awards 2008, this fishmonger-cum-café-cum-fish and chip shop features a huge counter piled high with oysters, mussels, prawns and fish caught fresh from the north coast of Scotland. Knowledgeable and enthusiastic staff will advise you on preparation, so don't be surprised to find a lemon nestling among your purchase of plump scallops. Alternatively, select your fish and ask for it to be grilled, seared, baked or fried: fish teas complete with freshly baked buttered bread and the proverbial mug of piping hot liquid are served in possibly the most stylish chippie café in Scotland.

LOCH FYNE OYSTERS John Noble and Andy Lane started Loch Fyne Oysters in the early 1980s with one clear idea: to grow oysters in the clear, fertile waters of Loch Fyne. Since then the business has developed on a national scale, but continues to abide by the environmental principles established at the outset. The impressive farm shop has grown too: from its beginnings in a garden shed beside the road, it has become a well-stocked store selling Loch Fyne seafood – oysters, mussels, scallops and langoustines – as well as an array of local meat and dairy produce, jams, wines, chocolates and organic dry goods.

NORTH EAST SCOTLAND

■ M&M Spink

10 Marketgate, Arbroath, Angus
07974 195654
www.arbroathsmokies.co.uk
Mon–Sat 8am–5pm; Sun 10am–4pm.
Web/mail order.

When Rick Stein waxes lyrical about your Arbroath Smokies you know they're going to be good. Bill Spink, a fish merchant based in Arbroath, has been producing these hot-smoked delicacies – among others – since 1965. Made with haddock caught in the North Sea, the smokies are salt cured and then hung to dry before being smoked over beech or oak hard wood chips. In addition to haddock the company smokes salmon, imbuing the fish with a special flavour thanks to the hot smoking process. It is able to ship both nationally and internationally. See the website or call into the shop for details.

■ Ugie Salmon Fishings

The Fish House, Crolf Road, Peterhead,
Aberdeenshire
01779 476209, www.ugie-salmon.co.uk
Mon–Fri 9am–5pm.
Web/mail order.
Located in Peterhead, Ugie Salmon
Fishings is based in a fish house built on
the River Ugie in 1585, the only building
in Peterhead to survive more than four
centuries. On the banks of one of north
east Scotland's most prolific fishing rivers,
it has been used by salmon fishermen for
over 100 years. Nowadays Ugie Salmon
Fishings operates this unique building as
a thriving business, curing, hanging and
smoking locally caught wild Atlantic
salmon (when in season) and top quality
farmed Scottish salmon on the premises.
A visit to the fish house gives a unique
opportunity to sample a taste of history.
Also available to order online direct from
its website.

HIGHLANDS, ISLANDS & ARGYLL

■ Gigha Halibut

Gigha Halibut Limited, Isle of Gigha,
Argyll
01700 821226, www.gighahalibut.co.uk
Based on the eponymous Hebridean
island, Gigha Halibut specialises in
production of sustainable Scottish
Atlantic halibut. Farming in a
replenishable and controlled way, it does
not deplete or endanger wild stocks of
halibut in the sea and is proud of the
provenance of its fish. The halibut are
grown over three years using a unique
land-based farming system that
harnesses the clean waters from the
Sound of Gigha, creating a natural and
protected environment in which they can
develop. Knowledgeable staff rear the
fish to organic standards and handle
them with the utmost care to ensure they
are healthy and happy. As well as
supplying some of the world's leading
restaurants, it produces smoked halibut,
using oak chips from the Craigallachie
distillery on Speyside.

■ Hand-Made Fish Co

Toll Clock Shopping Centre, Lerwick,
Shetland
01950 422214
Mon–Sat 10.30am–5pm. Closed Sun.
At Havra's Hand-Made Fish Company,
Dave and Tricia Parham produce
smoked haddock and smoked organic
salmon from the Skerries islands,
experimenting with the effects of various
woods such as beech, olive and juniper,
and they also have a supply of old oak
whisky barrels for general smoking
purposes. One of Rick Stein's food
heroes, the Parhams use ethically caught

haddock, cod, salmon, hake and ray,
fresh from the boat every day, and
smoke them over local fuel. All products
can be ordered over the phone with
next-day delivery the norm.

■ Inverawe Smokehouses

Inverawe Smokehouses, Taynuilt, Argyll
01866 822209
www.smokedsalmon.co.uk
Mon–Sun 8.30am–5.30pm. [Closed
Christmas Eve to mid Mar.]
Café, Web/mail order.
Inverawe, established in 1974 by Robert
and Rosie Campbell-Preston, is one of
Scotland's highest profile smokehouses.
Its salmon is smoked in a time honoured
traditional way (the process can take
around two days) that allows the fish
slowly to absorb the flavour giving it a
full-bodied and oak-smoked taste. One
of Rick Stein's food heroes, the award-
winning company has a royal warrant
and supplies its luxury goods to affluent
retailers such as Harvey Nichols. There's
a large mail order business, with various
gift hampers available, although if you're
nearby, the Argyll premises has a café
and shop selling the full product range –
this includes own-label mustards, jellies,
pickles and chutneys, as well as local
meat and cheese.

■ Jolly's of Orkney

Scott's Road, Hatston, Kirkwall, Orkney
01856 872417, www.jollyfish.co.uk
Mon–Fri 8.30am–5.30pm; Sat 9pm–2pm.
Founded by William Jolly over fifty years
ago, this thriving fishmonger sells a huge
range of local fish and shellfish. A
traditional kiln forms the centre of the
processing area and is used to smoke
salmon, kippers, mackerel and mussels
as well as a variety of meats. The
smoked salmon is traditionally brined
using salt and sugar then cold smoked
over an oak wood fire before being sliced
by hand, and kippers and mackerel are
smoked over oak dust in the kiln. Jolly's
also produce salted and marinated fish
using two different methods, both of
which have been used in the area for
thousands of years. Herring is salted in
layers in barrels, while other fish such as
ling is salted on a brining table then air
dried.

■ Loch Fyne Oysters

Clachan Farm, Cairndow, Argyll
01499 600264, www.lochfyne.com
Apr–Sep: Mon–Sun 9am–9pm. Oct–Mar
Mon–Sun 9am–6pm.
Café, Web/mail order.
See photo entry opposite

■ Loch Leven Shellfish

Loch Leven, Onich, Fort William, Argyll
01855 821444

www.lochlevenseafoodcafe.co.uk
Mon–Sat 9.30am–5pm.
Café.
On the shores of beautiful Loch Leven,
this enterprising shop and restaurant
developed in the last few years when
more and more customers started
asking the fishing company if they could
buy some shellfish to take home with
them. Now it has a successful shop
which, weather permitting, stocks live
lobster, langoustines, crab, mussels, surf
clams, razor clams, scallops and
oysters. It also sells frozen and cooked
fish, and if you want a lobster or crab
cooked while you wait they can do that
for you too. A range of pretty Spanish
cookware is for sale, and there are plans
to expand the food range into more
general deli items.

■ Andy Race Fish Merchants

The Harbour, Mallaig, Argyll
01687 462626, www.andyrace.co.uk
Mon–Fri 9.30am–3.15pm. Closed
Sat/Sun.
Based in the port of Mallaig in the
Highlands of Scotland, Andy Race fish
merchants is renowned for producing
the very best Scottish peat-smoked fish,
including kippers, organic salmon and
other high quality shellfish, all traditionally
smoked without using any dyes. Having
supplied to many of Scotland's most
prestigious hotels for over twenty-five
years, demand grew enough to merit
intruding a mail order service for us
mere mortals to benefit too. Taster
packs are available – with no charge for
delivery – to provide smaller quantities of
the most popular products such as
smoked trout, kippers, organic salmon
and mackerel to try.

■ Summer Isles Foods

The Smokehouse, Achiltibuie, Ullapool,
Ross-shire
01854 622 353
www.summerislesfoods.co.uk
Mon–Sun 9.30am–5pm (summer only).
A small, family-run smokehouse in
Achiltibuie, Summer Isles Foods was
founded in the 1970s when Keith
Dunbar and his wife Sheila fell in love
with the small community while on
holiday. They opened a smokehouse in
order to produce and sell local smoked
produce, and their subtly smoked
salmon is still created using the same
blend of rum, molasses and whisky
barrel chippings. The online shop
contains a wide selection of smoked fish
and cheese for home delivery, while
visitors to Achiltibuie can see the
smoking process in action and admire
the views enjoyed from this most
spectacular of locations.

FRUIT & VEG

Salad days

Claire Ritchie visits an Arran smallholding where a former chef makes a living from living the good life.

In these climate-conscious, eco-spirited – not to mention cash-strapped – times, it has become fashionable to talk of going back to basics, becoming self-sufficient and making do and mending, probably for the first time since post-war rationing threatened to dampen the country's spirits so thoroughly. Now these values have come to the fore once more, albeit with food miles, composting and eco credentials taking the place of rationing in the news, in businesses and in schools. It has again become popular to grow vegetables at home, even when space is at a premium. Herbs and lettuces can be grown in window boxes; carrots, beans and potatoes in patio containers – even the smallest plot of land can be used to provide sustenance for a family. And it doesn't take a huge leap to make commercial gains out of such a project.

Robin Gray, who farms a smallholding of approximately 20 acres with his partner by Whiting Bay on the Isle of Arran, is the living embodiment of this lifestyle trend.

Having trained as a chef under the great Raymond Blanc, and travelled the world both working and wandering, he returned to his native Scotland intent on taking a back-to-basics approach: living the good life, but making a living from it too.

Arran has a warmer climate than much of Scotland thanks to the Gulf Stream, and there's certainly no shortage of rain, but some of the produce Gray grows needs just a little extra help. Being by the sea has its benefits. 'We use the seaweed as fertiliser,' he says. 'We go down to the beach on our quad bikes every so often to collect it.'

He also has a polytunnel, under which he grows herbs such as lemon verbena, basil and the mixed salad leaves so popular with the chefs who make up the main customer group. At the end of the tunnel a white peach tree snoozes happily through autumn, ready to burst into flower again come spring. Wild, untended cherry tomatoes grow through the plant detritus in the tunnel doorway, the sweetest little gems. A

more serene setting would be hard to imagine.

So, with such quality soil and reasonable weather at his disposal, how does he decide what to grow? 'Ideas come from my organic suppliers,' he says. 'They show me what they're doing and I go from there. The elephant garlic, for example, happened that way.'

Crops of said elephant garlic, along with a rare type of beetroot called Ferrono, have been appropriated by Arran Fine Foods (part of Paterson-Arran), a local company specialising in preserves and pickles, who showcase some of Robin's produce in their latest Arran-specific range.

In 2008 Gray also grew a ton of pumpkins for the first time, as an experiment of sorts. Coming in all shapes and sizes, and with such evocative names as Turk's turban, sweet mama, crown prince and cha cha, the whole crop was a special order from one special customer: Andrew Fairlie at Gleneagles. 'People are intimidated by pumpkins,' says

Gray. 'We've only just got them onto making pumpkin soup – but where do we go after that?'

Well, Andrew Fairlie started with a dish of pumpkin gnocchi that he created in honour of the first crop of the strangely shaped gourds.

So far so profitable, but have there been any less successful ventures on these remote beach-side slopes? The answer is surprising for a Scottish smallholding. 'My least successful has to be the potatoes,' he says. 'I love them and I love growing them, but there's a lot of work involved for little return. It's been trial and error.'

And which crop would he call his

favourite? 'Probably the beetroot, but I do love the pumpkins.'

To Gray, there is no challenge in playing it safe, growing the same old fruit and veg that can be found in farmers' markets all over Scotland. But while it might not be a giant leap to get to Turk's turbans and ferrono beetroot, growing the rare jostaberry – a cross between a blackcurrant and a gooseberry – to satisfy demand from ever-choosier customers (such as Andrew Fairlie) who want to have new, innovative produce at their disposal, can come at a price.

'There are only a few people I can sell the more unusual produce to, because they're too specialist, too weird,' he says. 'The public might not know what to do with them!'

But with Robin Gray as such a thriving example of how this back-to-basics lifestyle can work, perhaps it's only a matter of time before the rest of us catch on.

■ *Robin Gray is one of the local food heroes profiled at www.taste-of-arran.co.uk*
For further Arran producers see www.thelarder.net

Pupkins, garlic and beetroot thrive on Robin Gray's smallholding, fertilised by seaweed

CHEF'S CHOICE

TOM KITCHIN ON EASSIE FARM'S ASPARAGUS

I rely almost fanatically on the seasons. My suppliers are invaluable and I trust them for their guidance on finding the best produce around – they are very much a part of the Kitchin team.

My trusted fish supplier Willie Little recommended I visit Eassie Farm near Glamis Castle to sample their asparagus when I first returned to Scotland and I've been using their quality produce ever since we opened. I always take time to visit the farm each year to see the asparagus – it's great to watch it grow so majestically.

The Eassie Farm asparagus is as good as I've tasted anywhere in the world; green, tender and with a thick skin holding all the juices together. Asparagus is only in season for a short time – six weeks to be precise, with a growing season lasting from the second week of May until late June. In recognition of this, I use asparagus in dishes on my à la carte menu, but also in the special celebration to the season menu.

Perthshire's unique combination of rich soil and cool climate means asparagus grows slowly. I am sure that the fantastic flavours of the Eassie Farm asparagus are down to this – alongside a well-developed drainage system – but I'm also convinced that what makes the asparagus superb is the farm owner's great knowledge and genuine passion.

■ *Tom Kitchin is owner and head chef at the Kitchin, 78 Commercial Quay, Leith, 0131 555 1755*
www.thekitchin.com
AH & HA Pattullo, Eassie Farm, by Glamis, Angus, 01307 840303

Keeping it REAL

Jo Ewart Mackenzie profiles an agenda-setting school project in which the pupils learn about the world of work while planting, growing and selling their own organic produce.

Iain Clyne knows his onions. So too do his volunteers. REAL Food is a social and community enterprise run by Clyne, a teacher and youth worker, that gives the pupils of Inverness High School the chance to grow, harvest and sell a diverse range of salads, vegetables and potatoes at community markets and from stalls in and around the city.

The scheme was dreamt up by a trio concerned about the aptitude of school leavers when it came to the world of work. Local businessman Dennis Overton and Inverness High School rector Ritchie Cunningham shared Clyne's desire to see pupils become better prepared for employment.

'Rather than moan from the sidelines, we decided to see if we could play a part in helping young people to understand and engage more with working life, so it would be less of a shock,' says Overton, managing director of Alness fish processor Aquascot.

The seeds for REAL (Real Education Active Lives) Food were sown. The three men envisaged an enterprise that would provide hands-on business experience and community involvement as well as something that would fit with the drive to promote healthy living at school.

When the project secured funding from the Schools of Ambition initiative and Highlands and Islands Enterprise in May 2006, the pupils began planting their first crop of root vegetables in the school grounds. They drew on the expertise of local farmer Donnie Macleod and learned how to cultivate the land using his organic principles.

Now they have three polytunnels on a plot of nearly one acre. From carrots, kale, leeks and cauliflower to rocket, mizuna, tomatoes and sprouting beans, REAL is a thriving market garden. Over 70 students are involved in the business and the produce is sold – by

the pupils themselves – through more than half a dozen outlets.

'Participation in a genuine business with the opportunity to develop employability skills, such as teamwork, selling, marketing, stock control, accounting and presentation, has proved so valuable to all the individuals involved,' says Clyne.

To complement its own produce, REAL has teamed up with local growers and producers in order to sell goods such as seasonal soft fruits, free range chicken and eggs, freshly baked bread and farmhouse cheeses.

Two years ago, REAL Food made do with a stand in the school hall and a stall at a monthly farmers' market. Now it has stalls at four weekly village markets and in three city locations. Its projected turnover for 2009 is £12,000. Thanks to demand from the community, the business recently started a ten-week training course on how to run an allotment.

With the Schools Social Enterprise Award from the cabinet secretary for education, Fiona Hyslop, and the Highlands and Islands Food Award for Innovation under its belt, what does the future hold for REAL Food?

'It's the same old story,' says Clyne. 'The future of REAL will depend on finding a sustainable niche for local food.'

■ *For more see real-ihs.blogspot.com*

The rise and fall of Scottish tomatoes

Unless there is a drastic change in its fortunes, the once mighty Clyde Valley tomato industry will soon pass into legend. Where once there were hundreds of Scots tomato growers, only a handful remain. Gordon Davidson speaks to one.

Unlikely as it might sound, with our supermarkets brimming with the pick of the Mediterranean, Scotland was once a tomato-growing force to be reckoned with. Until the mid-1960s, Scotland grew enough tomatoes to satisfy domestic demand, have some left over to send to markets in the south and occasionally go marauding on the continental export market. The Scots tomato industry was a product of the enthusiasm for technology that gripped the country at the start of the 20th century. The Clyde Valley had historically been the centre of Scottish apple growing, but that trade failed in the face of competition from overseas.

Bullishly, Scots growers sought higher value fruits to grow instead. Undeterred by such minor issues as climate, they constructed glasshouses, with state-of-the-art hot water heating systems, and stocked them with soon to be cherished varieties such as Ailsa Craig and moneymaker.

These hi-tech ventures were hugely successful and by the 1950s, the Clyde Valley had become synonymous with tomato production. 'There were hundreds of growers here once, and acres and acres under glass, a sea of glass it was,' says Jim Craig of Briarneuk Nursery, by Carluke, one of only four growers still commercially active in central Scotland.

So what happened? 'The problem was, the bulk of the greenhouses were built before the 1930s and were wooden-framed,' he says. 'By the 1960s, those houses were at the end of their useful lives and were ready to fall down – in fact, I remember quite a few that did.

'Everyone needed to re-invest if the industry was to keep its scale, but the Common Market was starting to take away the import tariffs that had protected us from Mediterranean competition. Many growers just decided to get out.'

Thereafter, competing with sun-grown Spanish tomatoes for supermarket shelfspace was a battle the more costly Scottish tomatoes were never going to win, however fresh they might be by comparison.

At the turn of this century, a coalition of Scots growers, including Craig, mounted a last assault on the multiple retailers, investing considerable cash in a 'Scotland's Tomatoes' brand. In the face of supermarket indifference, the initiative failed.

Nowadays, the remnants of the Scottish industry have forsaken the classic round red tomato in favour of specialist varieties – particularly plum tomatoes and yellow tomatoes. 'We're a niche business now, and hanging on, but I don't see any youngsters wanting to take up the reins once this generation retires,' says Craig. 'We will be the last of the line, unless something major happens to change the marketplace.

'At the farmers' markets, people are always delighted to get Scottish-grown stuff. But in the supermarkets, people always buy with an eye on the price. The fact is, heating those greenhouses is always going to put us at a cost disadvantage.

'Now if something was to happen to road transport, more attention to food miles perhaps, it could change things. Or if southern Europe was to have more water shortages . . . But that's looking decades ahead. If there's ever going to be a Scottish tomato revival, I doubt I'll be here to see it.'

■ *J&M Craig attends farmers' markets in Edinburgh, the Lothians and Fife*

CHEF'S CHOICE

TOM LEWIS ON FORAGING
FOR CHANTERELLES

It's normally around the second half of June – around Highland Show time – that I first find enough chanterelles for a single omelette for myself. Just some free-range eggs and a little bit of sage and the first mushrooms of the year. But after that we just go out into the glen by the hotel and pick them every day. I make sure everyone in the kitchen makes a habit of going out every afternoon for a bit of fresh air and to get some mushrooms in. It's even been known for someone to head out in the middle of service to pick a few to see us through – once or twice I've jumped on the motorbike at the back door and shot off in my whites down the glen with a basket on the back to collect what we need.

It's not just chanterelles but hedgehog, parasols, autumn chanterelles and even morelles, though they're transient and having found them in one site you might never see them again there. Once I was out with my brother-in-law and we collected 70kg in a day – if we've got excess we'll dry them or they're wonderful pickled. Like most seasonal food they're best with other food in season – maybe a bit of venison shot near the hotel, and a few garden veg, with some fresh chanterelles chucked on at the end.

■ *Tom Lewis is chef and co-director of Monachyle Mhor Hotel, Balqhidder, 01877 384622 www.mhor.net*

Home-grown in Scotland

Growing your own fruit and veg is remodelling its image from retirement hobby to environmental neccessity. Here Jo Whittingham explains how gardening is a cornerstone of our culinary heritage.

Gardens are one source of fresh seasonal Scottish produce that it's easy to take for granted. Our rich soils, cool, wet climate and long summer days suit cultivation so well that in the past, generations of Scots depended on home-grown produce for the only vegetables in their diet. The late-20th century's cheap imports and industrial-scale horticulture put an end to this self-reliance, but now, with spiralling allotment waiting lists and vegetable seed sales up by 40 per cent in the last two years, it's clear that home-grown veg is back on the menu.

We tend to assume that Scotland's food culture revolves around crops that thrive here, such as hearty neeps and tatties and luscious summer raspberries, so it's surprising to find that as late as the 17th century they were not widely grown in gardens. In fact, restrictive yearly tenancies meant ordinary folk had little incentive to improve their plots or money to buy new seed, so could cultivate only the toughest crops, such as kale, peas, broad beans and chard, from which they could collect seed for the following year.

Consequently change was slow and while wild raspberries were gathered from hedgerows, new foreign vegetables, such as the yellow Swedish turnip and the Andean potato, weren't commonly grown until later in the 18th century.

Instead, it was wealthy landowners who drove the development of Scotland's kitchen gardens. Keen to have a varied supply of fruit and vegetables, they employed small armies of skilled gardeners and constructed walled gardens – the must-have horticultural accessory between the 17th and 19th centuries. Built on a gentle, south-facing slope, often over several acres, high stone walls protected crops from the elements and provided support and shelter for trained fruit trees. In 1700 a laird, unlike his labourers, might have enjoyed a diversity of vegetables including lettuce, carrots, cauliflowers, celery, and even asparagus and artichokes.

With improving communication between estates in Scotland and England, progress was swift and gardeners succeeded in cultivating increasingly exotic crops. Extra warmth was essential for delicate plants and during the 18th century the addition of glazed frames to traditional hot-beds of rotting manure allowed melons and,

> GLORY OF THE GARDEN

Phantassie, East Linton
Organic vegetable growers who have expanded from a one-acre walled garden. Supply organic vegetable boxes, farmers markets and restaurants. www.phantassie.co.uk

Glendale Salads, Isle of Skye
Successful experiments in their own garden led Bridget and Kornelius Hagmann to start their business growing unusual organic salad leaves, herbs and soft fruit for their box scheme and local restaurants and hotels. glendalesalads@tiscali.co.uk

Raasay Walled Garden
One of Scotland's oldest walled gardens, until recently producing organic fruit, vegetables, herbs and flowers for the local market. However, a fire in early 2009 has thrown its future in doubt.

Argyll Hotel, Iona
Fabulous 20-year-old organic vegetable garden, maintained by three gardeners, supplying herbs and vegetables for the hotel restaurant.
www.argyllhoteliona.co.uk

Balfour Castle, Orkney
Full use is made of the Victorian walled kitchen garden to produce a daily harvest of fruit, vegetables and herbs for the hotel's kitchen.
www.balfourcastle.co.uk

from about 1750, pineapples to be successfully grown. But the real breakthrough came in the 19th century when glasshouses arrived, furnishing those who could afford them with peaches, grapes, figs, pineapples and even the occasional banana. Mertoun House in Roxburghshire has fine examples of these structures, still filled with immaculately trained white peaches and figs.

Gradually, innovations in cultivation and new crops filtered out of walled gardens and by the end of the 18th century the potato had finally become a

widely grown Scottish staple. To further encourage such progress and introduce competitiveness through annual shows, local gardening societies were set up during the 19th century, many of which, including Penicuik Horticultural Society (established 1842) and Killearn Cottagers' Horticultural Society (established 1850), still thrive.

While the ordinary man had no choice but to garden thriftily, running a grand Victorian kitchen garden was spectacularly expensive. Even though gardeners were poorly paid, many were required to keep large gardens running – the Duke of Buccleuch employed 42 on his Dalkeith estate in the mid-19th century – making their home-grown produce a pricey commodity. Inevitably then, with improved transport links, the importation of produce became possible, finally rendering pineapple pits and vineries outmoded and unnecessary expenses.

The end for many of Scotland's grandest kitchen gardens came when the First World War all but wiped out cheap labour and a generation of gardeners. Simultaneously, however, there was an explosion in domestic vegetable gardening, particularly in the cities, where any available land was turned into allotments (first created during the 1890s) to alleviate wartime food shortages and later economic difficulties. A corner of Edinburgh's Inverleith Park became allotments during the First World War, while the city's huge allotment site at Warriston Road was created for the unemployed during the depression of the late 1920s.

Ironically, as life became easier during the 1950s and 60s, vegetable growing on allotments and in back gardens suffered a similar fate to the Victorian walled garden. Commercial horticulture and cheap imports offered consumers affordable fruit and vegetables all year round. So allotments, perhaps associated with harder times, gradually fell out of fashion and many city sites were lost to development after years of neglect. Of course many old hands still grew their own in back gardens, but vegetable growing acquired a reputation as tricky, heavy work, which successfully deterred beginners for decades. Only a growing enthusiasm for local, organic food over the last few years has reawakened the passion for home-grown food in Scotland. A whole new generation of gardeners is discovering what our ancestors knew and relied upon; that surprisingly little effort can deliver the freshest, most delicious produce from our very own plots.

Road to the aisles

David Pollock goes by Glen Clova and Glen Ample
to discover why raspberries are Scotland's superberry.

The area around Fife, Angus and Perthshire may not be known internationally for its berries. In Scotland, however, the area is celebrated for its richness in red fruits, in particular strawberries, various currants, gooseberries and cherries. Of all of these, it is the raspberry that has forged the strongest reputation for itself.

'We have good soils here, Grade One and Grade Two, which are nice and fertile,' says John Laird, partner and farmer at Cairnie Fruit Farm in Fife. 'But it's mainly down to temperature and moisture that our raspberries are so good. We have sufficient rainfall without the searing heat you get down in England, but we also get less rain and frost than the west of Scotland; raspberries don't do well with wet feet, you see. They must be planted in well-drained soil, because they won't grow well if their roots are waterlogged. As far as temperatures go, somewhere in the 60s or low-70s is best. If they're up in the 80s or 90s the fruit ripens too quickly, so it doesn't have the same level of sugar or character of flavour.'

Another factor is the variety of raspberry being used, although the advantage to the producer of using different varietals is in extending the length of time they can harvest through the year. 'One of the earliest types we have is Glen Clova,' says Euan Cameron, partner and farmer at Fife's Pittormie Fruit Farm. 'It starts to show fruit around the first week in July and then we can go on until November with the likes of autumn bliss. I'm sure some of the tunnel boys have types which are ready even sooner, though.'

As a smaller producer who doesn't supply to supermarkets, Cameron prefers not to grow his raspberries under polytunnels, although to a larger operation such as Laird's they're essential, allowing as steady a stream of supply through as much of the year as possible. 'Gone are the days when you could call up a supermarket and say you've had rain this week, so you can't supply them,' he says, 'That just doesn't cut it.'

Laird also notes that the canes of longer established varieties such as Glen Clova can last for a decade and more, but that newer breeds such as Glen Ample and Glen Doll last for barely six or seven years, albeit with up to double the yield per cane.

As fruit juices and wines increase in popularity, as healthy breakfasters sprinkle berries on their muesli and as older customers seek out varieties by name to put in their jam, the Scottish

raspberry is wrestling back a lot of its market share from the strawberry. Quite simply, says Cameron, raspberries have benefitted from a health-conscious PR boost, although they're a more labour-intensive product.

They also face the same issues as the rest of the fruit farming industry, namely the increase in fertiliser costs in line with oil and the expectation that a workforce of overseas pickers will stay at home this year due to the declining value of the pound.

But for a supplier such as Laird with the means to extend his season back into spring, Fife is the best place to be when the price of raspberries is high. 'The rest of the UK isn't even online yet,' he says. 'So the supermarkets are dependent on importing from as far away as South America. Until June, the price of raspberries can be double what it is in late summer.'

> SCOTLAND'S PICK-YOUR-OWN FRUIT FARMS

Allanhill Fruit Farm and shop
St Andrews, www.allanhill.co.uk

Belhaven Fruit Farm
Dunbar, www.belhavenfruitfarm.co.uk

Boghall Farm, Thornhall, near Stirling

Blacketyside Farm, near Leven

Border Berries, Kelso,
www.borderberries.co.uk

Broadslap Fruit Farm, Dunning,
Perthshire,
www.broadslapfruitfarm.co.uk

Cairnie Fruit Farm, shop and maze,
by Cupar, www.cairniefruitfarm.co.uk

Charleton Fruit Farm and coffee shop, Montrose

Craigie's Fruit Farm and farm shop, South Queensferry,
www.craigies.co.uk

Lowe's Fruit Farm, Dalkeith

Newmill Farm, Blairgowrie,
www.newmillfarm.co.uk

Pittormie Fruit Farm and Nursery,
Dairsie, Fife,
www.pittormiefruitfarm.co.uk

Stenton Fruit Farm, near Dunbar,
East Lothian

Strawberry Grange Fruit Farm,
Peterculter

Wardmill Farm, Forfar

Wester Hardmuir Fruit Farm, by
Nairn, www.hardmuir.com

■ *For further details on these and other fruit specialists go to*
www.thelarder.net
www.pickyourown.org
www.berryscotland.com

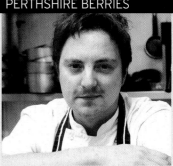

Nowhere else in the world encourages eclectic cookery more than Perthshire, and it's no more evident than during our berry fruit season. For decades now our local farms have reigned supreme producing the finest strawberries, rasps and blueberries. They're a staple not only on national menus but also healthy diets with edible skins full of antioxidants.

I have always had an association with berry time, having grown up here. My childhood was filled with seasonal work; when I wasn't pulling tatties I was scratching my hands at the rasps (eating more than I picked, of course), saving up for the next transformer toy. Nowadays I am just as excited to see and smell the big trays of berries being delivered to the restaurant in the morning ready for lunch. Sniff this, and if you don't smile it's time to seek advice on life!

As with most products from our local farmers, simplicity is the key in serving. More often than not their perfection can be dominated with balsamic ice creams and black pepper tuilles. Whether it's for my kids at home or if I'm serving berries up for lunch in the restaurant, whipped cream with a spoonful of home-made lemon curd on freshly hulled strawberries explodes my senses and I am left wondering if anything can demonstrate the taste of Scotland more.

■ *Graeme Pallister is chef at 63 Tay Street, Perth, 01738 441451,*
www.63taystreet.com

Forever fruit

Jo Ewart Mackenzie takes a look at the art of storing and preserving our glorious gluts of fruit.

For almost six months of the year, Scotland boasts a veritable bounty of fabulous, fresh seasonal fruits. From the delectable soft fruits of summer through to late variety apples and pears, the exciting and colourful feast of fruit available from June through November can keep us going year-round if properly stored and preserved.

The practice of storing apples, in particular, has been around since the first century AD with the same principles proving as pertinent today as they were back then. Using only unblemished fruits – one bad apple really can spoil the barrel – arranged in well ventilated boxes or crates so the apples, or indeed pears, are not touching each other (you can wrap individual fruits in tissue) and store in a cool, dry and dark place. Apples and pears stored in this way can last for months.

Another time honoured way of preserving windfall fruits is to make them into tangy chutneys to accompany thickly carved ham and ripe farmhouse cheeses. Peeled, cored and diced apples, or hard pears, combined with currants, peel, malt vinegar and brown sugar, scented with snapped cinnamon sticks and aromatic cloves simmered until sticky and golden, makes a full-bodied chutney, which will easily keep for a year or more in a cool, dry place. Or try domestic doyenne Elizabeth Beeton's recipe for peeled and cored apple quarters preserved in a simple sugar syrup infused with ginger.

Pre-dating the esteemed Mrs Beeton, as far back as the 17th century, fruit and sugar preserves, or *conserves*, were being made with gluts of soft fruits. More a fruit paste than a preserve as we know it, thickly pureed fruits mixed with sugar were poured into long

> SEASONAL FRUITS

Berries > June to October
Plums > August
Apples > August to October
(and from store until June)
Pears > August to November
(and from store until March)

moulds then sliced and served with cream for dessert, or with cheese, much like today's quince paste. It wasn't until sugar became more affordable towards the end of the 18th century that looser 'jams' were developed.

Based on traditional principles and recipes, Katrina Ashford of Rose Cottage Country Kitchen in Nairn started her 21st century preserves business with hand-made pots of old fashioned strawberry, gooseberry and apricot preserves. She now has 60 products in her range, which she sells at farmers' markets and through local farm shops.

'Not all products are available at the same time,' she says. 'It depends on the harvest – I have no plum jam this year as the crop has been poor and I only make rhubarb and elderflower jam in

the summer because elderflowers don't freeze well.'

Ashford freezes soft fruits such as raspberries and strawberries – gooseberries, brambles, black and redcurrants harvested on dry, sunny days all freeze successfully too – so she can produce jams year round. Using local produce in season, she sticks to age-old Scottish methods: preserves with a high fruit content hand-made in small, five pound batches in a traditional open pan. Some of her recipes date back to her granny's time, 'using the traditional 50:50 fruit to sugar ratio with no added sweeteners or water'.

Any tips? 'Patience! If your jam isn't setting, add a lemon per pound of fruit and leave it to sit for 15 minutes after boiling. You develop a sense for it.'
■ *You can find out more about Scottish producers of jams and chutneys at www.thelarder.net, including*

www.rosecountrycottagekitchen.co.uk
www.thejamkitchen.com
www.henshelwoodsfinefoods.co.uk
www.gallowaylodge.co.uk
www.isabellaspreserves.co.uk
www.scottish-preserves.co.uk
www.superjam.co.uk

Dealing with a year-round supply of fruit won't get you in a jam as long as you trust tradition

> IN THE PINK

A vegetable that acts like a fruit, rhubarb has proved remarkably well suited to the growing conditions of Scotland. It's no coincidence that it found its first UK foothold in Edinburgh.

Resilient, adaptable, versatile – in many ways *Rheum rhabarbarum* represents much of what Scotland does best, which is ironic given that it is in fact a vegetable originating in Asia, historically valued for its medicinal properties. The idea of using rhubarb in cooking is a relatively modern one, and in the UK at least seems to have coincided with sugar becoming more readily available. Introduced to Britain in the 18th century by Sir Alexander Dick of Prestonfield in Edinburgh – who was rewarded a Royal Society medal for his efforts – it has since become a staple of Scottish home cooking and a common feature of kitchen gardens, so easy is it to grow.

Technically a vegetable, but treated as a fruit – albeit requiring the addition of a sweetening agent – rhubarb is a good source of vitamin C and fibre and as such became crucial during the Second World War when home produce was all that could be relied upon. Rhubarb crumble, rhubarb fool, rhubarb tart are such key components of childhood meals that there is clearly some deep-rooted comfort connected with this plant. But that's not to say it can't break out from the nursery menu: the opulent restaurant at Prestonfield House – on the site of the plant's first introduction to Scotland's taste buds – is named after the plant, and serves up a dessert in honour of its tart pink charms. Simply titled Rhubarb, it includes a delicate rhubarb jam doughnut and a rhubarb and custard parfait.

In cooler climates such as that of Scotland, rhubarb's growing season begins in spring and continues throughout the summer, but it can also be forced (that is, grown under cover to raise the temperature), which produces a late-winter crop that is a sweeter, pinker, juicier version of its naturally grown sibling.
■ *www.rhubarb-restaurant.com*
Rhubarb is widely available from farm shops and local vegetable growers from late February onwards

TOP RHUBARB PHOTO: MEY SELECTIONS

Sour crabs and Scotch dumplings

Once every household had a repertoire of recipes to make the most of an annual glut. Now they are a year-round supermarket staple, yet rarely sourced from Britain, never mind Scotland. Catharina Day hunts for apples.

The native apple of Scotland was the sour crab, useful in a piquant chutney, although the largely temperate climate of Scotland meant the Romans bought their sweeter apples north. Later it was the monastic houses of the Benedictines and Cistercians that preserved the improved varieties during the Dark Ages.

As apples do not come true to seed, over the centuries many new local apple varieties have evolved. If worthwhile they were propagated, so we have the bitter sweet cookers such as Scotch dumpling, East Lothian pippin and beauty of Moray. One of the delicious eaters grown in Scotland is the bloody ploughman, said to have appeared as a seedling growing on a

midden in the Carse of Gowrie in 1880. The trees boast the brightest of ribbed red apples – splendid when full of fruit – and the flesh is spicy and sweet, especially if not stored long. The story goes that a ploughman stole some

apples and was hung for it, but this new variety gave him immortality.

The Oslin/Arbroath Pippin bred by the Cistercians is an exquisite tasting apple with a sharpness and spice that is sadly lacking in the imported Braeburn or Granny Smith. The orchard nursery run by John Butterworth in Ayrshire is a treasure of old and new Scottish varieties and he has had much experience in choosing varieties to suit each area of Scotland.

The United Kingdom imports about 75 per cent of its apples, which means that many Scots never taste local varieties. The Clyde valley and the Carse of Gowrie, once scattered with orchards, no longer grow fruit for the marketplace. Gradually, however, local varieties are finding outlets in farm shops, farmers' markets, direct from the orchard owner and local organic box schemes. The Children's Orchard, based in Glasgow, is helping to set up a network of orchards working with schools, communities, landowners and local authorities to provide places for children and others to experience the magic of orchards through the seasons, to play there, pick the fruit and eat or juice it.

■ *Butterworth's Organic Nursery is located on Auchinleck House Estate, Cumnock, Ayrshire, (www.butterworthsorganicnursery.co.uk). More on the Children's Orchard can be found at www.childrensorchard.co.uk*

Honey bunch

Honey is a special local food, requiring the cooperative efforts of thousands of bees and skilled keepers. *The Larder* puts half a dozen to the taste test.

Heather Hills Farm's Scottish Blossom Honey

From just north of Blairgowrie, Heather Hills' bees play a crucial role in pollinating the famous soft fruit from this part of Perthshire. Blossom honey is harvested in late June, and tastes milder, smoother and lighter than heather honey. This one is soft set and really quite sweet, though nice and creamy as well. www.heather-hills.com

Hood of Ormiston's Scottish Blossom Honey

A blossom honey from East Lothian with a paler colour and firmer set. Not so sweet, it's a soothing, mild flavour for the morning slice of toast. Small-scale beekeepers like Hood have attracted interest for the theory that hay fever sufferers can benefit from eating locally produced honey: a bit like seasickness remedies, however, it works for some but not others.

Nicoll's of Strathmore's Flower Honey

Nicoll's home base of Milton Haugh, between Dundee and Arbroath, is in prime position to benefit from lowland flowers in spring and heather from the upland slopes in summer. Although richer tasting and darker in colour than the blossom varieties tested, there were fewer of the nuances of flavour we found elsewhere. www.miltonhaugh.com

Honeyhill Bee Farm's Scottish Heather Honey

With its toffee consistency, dark colour and distinctive rich taste, heather honey is one of Scotland's unique foods. The St Cyrus bees who make this spend July and August in the Grampian foothills feeding on purple heather flowers. A bit too strong for some, a wee drop on a pancake and your heart will be in the Highlands.

Urr Valley Heath & Wildflower Honey

A clear, runny honey from a beekeeper near Castle Douglas. While it carries the perfume of the wildflower blossoms, it doesn't carry the same richness as the set honeys, but the style is a good choice for mixing into yoghurt or museli, or adding into a honey and wholegrain mustard salad dressing.

WS Robson's Tweedside Honey

This lovely mix of flower and heather honey comes from a farm that's actually in Northumberland, but inevitably the bees forage over the border. Honey, after all, takes pride in the food miles the bees clock to produce a single jar. This has a long, layered flavour and lots of body, without the oomph of full heather honey. www.chainbridgehoney.co.uk

WHERE TO BUY

Outlets for fruit and vegetables (including box schemes) listed regionally then organised alphabetically.

EDINBURGH & LOTHIANS

■ Craigie's Farm Shop and Jam Kitchen

West Craigie Farm, South Queensferry, Edinburgh, West Lothian
0131 319 1048, www.craigies.co.uk
Summer: Mon–Sun 9am–6pm.
Winter: Mon–Sun 9am–5pm.
Café.
Perched on a hillside with wonderful views down the River Forth, across Edinburgh and beyond, Craigie's is a family-run berry farm with an emphasis on seasonality of produce. With a farm shop selling seasonal, local foods, a deli/café serving light meals, activities for kids and farm trails as well as pick-your-own, this is a farm with a vision.

■ Crunchy Carrot

43 High Street, Dunbar, East Lothian
01368 860000, www.crunchycarrot.co.uk
Mon–Sat 7.30am–5.30pm.
Crunchy Carrot started off as a vegetable box scheme, but now the expansion into a well-stocked shop means that inside your veggie box you can now also request things such as local home-made bread (sourced from Pencaitland) or hand-made honey from Berwick. The boxes can be delivered weekly, fortnightly or whenever you need a vegetable top-up. Or you can pop into the friendly shop and pick up the goodies yourself.

■ Damhead Organic Foods

32a Damhead, Old Pentland Road, Lothianburn
0131 445 7425, www.damhead.co.uk
Mon–Sat 9am–5pm; Sun 10.30am–5pm.
Damhead was established by James and Sue Gerard in 1989, when organic food production was in its infancy. As well as their successful organic box scheme, they have an attractive farm shop selling fruit and vegetables from Damhead and local growers as much as possible. The shop also serves free coffee, and children can amuse themselves by feeding the pigs while adults browse the shop.

■ Dobbies

Melville Nursery, Melville Nurseries, Lasswade, Midlothian
See Delis & General Food

■ Earthy

33–41 Ratcliffe Terrace, Edinburgh
See Delis & General Food

■ East Coast Organics

24 Boggs Holdings, Pencaitland, East Lothian
01875 340227
www.eastcoastorganics.co.uk
Thu 2–7pm.
From a medium-sized farm just ten miles outside Edinburgh comes this highly efficient organic veg box delivery scheme. Various sizes of box are available depending on the size and needs of your household, with various combination options. What's in the box from week to week of course depends on what's in season, but the staples of potatoes, onions, carrot and salad leaves are always present.

■ Gosford Bothy Farm Shop

Gosford Estate, Aberlady, East Lothian
See Beef, Lamb & Other Meat.

■ Grow Wild

Unit 8 Block 3, Whiteside Industrial Estate, Bathgate, West Lothian
01506 656544, www.growwild.co.uk
Mon–Fri 9am–5pm. Closed Sat/Sun.
Grow Wild is based in Bathgate and delivers fruit and vegetable boxes to

Edinburgh, Glasgow and various places across central Scotland. The breadth of its service is impressive, as is the range of produce. You can customise your fruit and vegetables to suit yourself and it also offers organic meat, baking and wines. It even caters to your furry friends, with organic pet food.

■ Knowes Farm Shop
Knowes Farm, Dunbar, East Lothian
01620 860010
Mon–Sun 9.30am–5pm.
Knowes is a friendly and authentic farm shop located just outside East Linton. Local fruit, vegetables, meat and cheese. can be found on the shelves of Hilary Cochran's efficiently run operation, along with handy deli items. The eggs travel all of a few dozen yards from the hens pecking the grass beside the car park. Potato growing is a bit of a speciality of the farm, nurtured by its 'sun and dung' approach to natural growing. A number of heritage varietys of spud are normally available.

■ Oxenfoord Organics
The Gardens, Oxenfoord Castle, Pathhead, East Lothian
01875 320359,
www.oxenfoordorganics.com
Oxenfoord Organics' walled gardens are set within the picturesque grounds of Oxenfoord Castle; there couldn't be a more perfect setting for growing lovely organic vegetables. It has an online shop where you can stock up on ecological cleaning products and organic natural bodycare. And during the right season, you can also help out with fruit picking on the farm.

■ Phantassie Food
Phantassie, East Linton, East Lothian
01620 861531, www.phantassie.co.uk
Phantassie is one of a number of organic veg growers offering a box delivery scheme into Edinburgh. Working from a ten-acre farm near East Linton, which features a productive, 150-year-old walled garden, Phantassie owner Patricia Stephen is one of the forces behind Earthy Food Market, which provides a daily outlet for her veg, fruit, eggs and excellent salad leaves.

■ Real Foods
• **8 Brougham Street, Edinburgh**
• **37 Broughton Street, Edinburgh**
See Delis & General Food

■ Tattie Shaws
35 Elm Row, Edinburgh
0131 557 6720
Mon–Sat 9am–6pm. Closed Sun.
One of a dying breed of local independent greengrocer's shops, Tattie

Gosford Bothy Farm Shop

Shaw's remains steadfast in its competition with the bigger supermarkets. Always busy, this small shop is bursting with fresh produce, clearly labelled with point of origin for the food-mile conscious. It also stocks an admirable range of store cupboard basics and dried goods as well as fresh bread and dairy items, making this a potential one-stop venue for locally minded shoppers.

■ Your Local Farm
Balquhatstone Mains, Slamannan, Falkirk
01324 851750, www.yourlocalfarm.co.uk
Thu–Sun 9.30am–4.30pm.
For over eight years, Your Local Farm has been supplying vegetable boxes to central Scotland from its base at Balquhatstone farm in Slamannan, near Falkirk. Box prices are very reasonable, with a standard box priced at just £5. It's also worth enquiring about its seasonal meat produce. And don't forget to ask them to pop a jar of heather honey in with your box. Alternatively, just visit the shop and hand-pick your goods.

GREATER GLASGOW & CLYDESIDE

■ Ardardan Estate
Ardardan Estate, Farm Shop, Cardross
See Delis & General Food

■ Mollinsburn Organics
Cumbernauld Road, Mollinsburn, Glasgow
07847 181 063
www.mollinsburnorganics.com
Mon–Wed 10am–6pm; Thu 10am–7pm; Fri 10am–6pm; Sat 10am–5pm; Sun
noon–5pm.
Mollinsburn offers fruit and vegetable boxes, or a box with a mixed contents. It also offers pâtés, fresh hand-made coleslaw and gift hampers for special occasions – all prettily wrapped in recycled packaging. It's all very ethical indeed. And it's made easy for you, as you can simply order from home and have the goods delivered to your door.

■ Roots and Fruits
• **351 Byres Road, Glasgow**
0141 339 5164
Mon–Sun 8am–7pm.
• **455–457 Great Western Road, Glasgow**
0141 334 3530/339 3077
Greengrocer: Mon–Sun 8am–7pm
Deli: Mon–Sat 8am–7pm; Sun
10am–6pm.
With two branches in Glasgow – one on busy Byres Road and a newer branch on Great Western Road – this wholefood and organic delicatessen is perfect for stocking up on your five-a-day portions. There are plenty of fresh fruit and vegetables on offer, as well as everything else you could possibly need for a healthy diet. It also stocks a range of soya products, pulses and organic meats. If that all sounds a bit too saintly, you can always indulge yourself with a tub of organic ice-cream.

SOUTHERN SCOTLAND

■ Drumullan Organics
Drumullan, By Girvan, Ayrshire
01465 713080, www.drumullan.co.uk
Drumullan farm is situated just outside Ayrshire and it delivers veggie boxes to the surrounding area. Its produce is

Finzean Estate Farm Shop & Tea Room

grown on the farm and is strictly organic and you can pick and choose between different varieties of fruit and vegetables to make up your very own tailored box. It's a bit of an act of love, and the sweet strawberries it carefully nurtures each season are a real highlight.

■ Stair Organic Growers

11 The Yetts, Tarbolton, Mauchline
01292 541369, www.organicgrowing.com
Stair Organics provides a vegetable box scheme for areas across Ayrshire, Renfrewshire and Glasgow. It is particularly proud of its own apple orchard, which it planted in 1996 and is now starting to give a decent crop. Not everything is from Scotland, but it is all certified organic. It is also happy for customers to mix and match to their hearts' content, in order to find a box that suits them – don't forget to ask for some of those apples when they're in season.

CENTRAL SCOTLAND & FIFE

■ Ardross Farm Shop

Ardross Farm Shop, Elie, Fife
01333 330415, www.ardrossfarm.co.uk
Mon–Sat 9am–5.30pm; Sun 9am–4pm
Winter closed Mon/Tue.
Ardross Farm shop started off as a way of selling the select beef and fresh

vegetables grown in the surrounding fields. Since then its range has grown, but the basics continue to impress; with quality beef and fruit and vegetables of all colours and variety being the staple. Everything is guaranteed to be farm grown and/or produced. And the deal breaker? The delicious hand-made farm ice cream on sale in the shop.

■ Bee Organic

The Fens, Dronley Road, Burkhill
01382 581548, www.bee-organic.co.uk
The sweetly named Bee Organic company will hand deliver a range of farm grown organic fruit and vegetables to your door. You can control exactly what you want, by picking from its website. The vegetable boxes come in all sizes, starting with the 'mini' box. It also offers store cupboard essentials such as flour, pasta and grains. Its website has a recipe section to encourage you to be more adventurous with your five-a-day.

■ Bellfield Organic Nursery

Jamesfield Farm, Abernethy, By Newburgh, Fife
01738 850589
www.bellfieldorganics.com
Established in 1985, Bellfield Organics is a family business that grows everything from seed. It operates an organic vegetable box scheme, delivering to your door either weekly or fortnightly. It can also supply fruit, bread, eggs and milk.

Boxes are available in varying sizes, orders are placed either by email or over the phone and all produce is delivered the day after picking.

■ Blairgowrie Farm Shop

14–16 Reform Street, Blairgowrie, Perthshire
01250 876528
www.blairgowriefarmshop.co.uk
Mon–Sat 8am–6pm; Sun noon–4pm.
Blairgowrie Farm Shop sources its fruit and vegetables from local farms and claims to get the produce on the shelf much quicker than most supermarkets. It also offers many jams, chutneys and sauces made locally around Tayside. And if you need soft fruit for jam-making, it keeps some aside each day – it's all rather sweet and thoughtful.

■ Brig Farm Shop

Gateside Home Farm, Bridge Of Earn, Perth, Perthshire
01738 813571, www.brigfarmshop.co.uk
Mon–Sat 8am–6pm.
Café.
Brig Farm offers the best of both worlds; with fresh produce being sold in the shop and also served in the café. Recommended is its very own Highland beef made, of course, from the woolly haired cattle that roam the surrounding fields. And you must stop to admire its principles, as it is careful to keep food miles to a minimum by sourcing produce

from the neighbouring Perthshire farms, where possible, and never sourcing from outwith Scottish soil.

■ Dalchonzie Fruit Farm Shop

Dalchonzie, Comrie, Perthshire
01764 670416, www.dalchonzie.co.uk
Barbara and David Burberry began growing fruit on their farm in Perthshire back in 1989 and have worked hard to make sure their fruit is full of natural goodness. Initially supplying chain stores, they had a bit of an epiphany and decided to change to being small and local. Their farm shop now sells their lovely fruit as well as Barbara's home-made jams and preserves. She went a bit mad in the kitchen and they now offer a huge range of over 80 varieties.

■ Pillars of Hercules Organic Farm Shop & Café

Pillars of Hercules, Falkland, Fife
01337 857749, www.pillars.co.uk
Mon–Sun 9am–6pm.
Café
A pioneer of organic farming and a much loved farm, farm shop and vegetarian café on the edge of Falkland, Pillars of Hercules is one of Fife's landmark food venues. It sends out veggie boxes to most parts of the county, while its bags of salad leaves and other veg make it as far as Edinburgh. Farm trails allow you to see the crops close at hand. The small café punches well above its weight with a busy programme of talks, events and monthly evening dining. Look out for Pillars as a cornerstone of the Big Tent Festival held in the grounds of Falkland Palace each summer.

NORTH EAST SCOTLAND

■ Bridgefoot Organics

Bridgefoot, Newmachar, Aberdeenshire
01651 862041
www.bridgefootorganics.co.uk
This vast farm in the heart of Aberdeenshire offers fresh vegetables delivered weekly in a box. It also provides selected seasonal fruit, free-range eggs and some meat. And as part of its extended family ethos, several times a year there is the opportunity for volunteers to help out on the farm in exhange for home-made soup, bread and cheese. That way you'll learn exactly where your vegetables come from and see them from soil to plate.

■ Finzean Estate Farm Shop & Tea Room

Balnaboth, Finzean, Banchory,
Aberdeenshire
See Delis & General Food

■ Huntly Herbs

Whitestones, Gartly, Huntly,
Aberdeenshire
01466 720247
Call ahead for opening times.
Huntly Herbs specialises in making preserves from its own fruit, vegetables and herbs. Some are based on traditional jam and chutney recipes, but others are a little more experimental – such as the Strathbogie Sizzler chutney. Everything is hand-cooked in small batches so the flavour is rich and intense.

■ Lenshaw Organics

Upper Lenshaw Farm, by Rothienorman,
Inverurie, Aberdeenshire
01464 871243
Doorstep sales by arrangement only.
Since buying the farm almost two decades ago, Beryl and John Clarke have worked hard to grow and rear quality produce, devoting acres of land to vegetable patches and free-ranging animals. Upper Lenshaw is based in Inverurie, but they deliver organic vegetables and free-range pork and beef anywhere within a 40-mile radius.

■ Vital Veg

North Tillydaff, Midmar, Inverurie
01330 833823, www.vitalveg.co.uk
Vital Veg offers an organic vegetable box scheme, delivered weekly to your door. It is deeply passionate about home-grown produce, so much so that it offers vegetable starter plants to get you up-and-running wih your very own vegetable patch. All its produce is either grown on site or sourced locally. A choice of boxes allows you to specify 'detox' or 'smoothie and juicing' options.

HIGHLANDS, ISLANDS & ARGYLL

■ Brin Herb Nursery

Flichity, Farr, Inverness
See Delis & General Food

■ Macleod Organics

Kylerona Farm, Ardersier, Inverness
01667 462555
www.macleodorganics.com
Mon–Sun 9am–5pm.
Macleod Organics is working towards sourcing all its fruit and vegetables from Scottish soil. At the moment its target is 90 per cent fulfilled, which is pretty impressive. It is based in Ardersier and delivers to a widespread area across the Highlands. You can request that a whole host of other items, from organic farm haggis to totally degradable refuse sacks, be popped in your box.

■ Natural Vegetable Company

Clachandreggy, West Torbeck, Inverness
01463 250440, www.natural-vegetable-company.go1.cc
This is a six-acre organic farm supplying local hotels and restaurants as well as offering a local organic box scheme. It aims to supply only Highland produce, specialising in a natural range of seasonal varieties grown on the farm – from herbs and salad leaves in summer to root vegetables in winter. Both small (£10) and large (£15) boxes are delivered weekly or fortnightly to customers in the Inverness area.

Craigie's Farm Shop and Jam Kitchen

WHISKY, BEER & OTHER DRINKS

Something's brewing

Thanks to an explosion of micro brewers all over the country, Scotland is pushing back the boundaries of real ale innovation. Frank Park of the Scottish Real Ale Shop runs the rule over a selection of his favourite small breweries.

Valhalla Brewery

A feature of Scottish real ale is the use of local ingredients to add a unique flavour. The Valhalla Brewery on the island of Unst in Shetland has a strong Viking influence, including the name Valhalla, the hall in the celestial regions, home of the Norse god Odin, where slain Viking warriors were borne, to be revived by a horn full of ale. Valhalla brews six regular ales. The original is Auld Rock, Shetlanders' name for their island. Among the others is a very light bitter, Old Scatness, which is brewed from an ancient type of six row barley called bere. The beer takes its name from the Old Scatness archaeological dig at the south end of Shetland where evidence was found of beer making well over 2000 years ago. With an ABV of 4.0 per cent, this brew has heather honey added at the end of the boil to give a nice, refreshing, smoky aftertaste.

www.valhallabrewery.co.uk

Orkney Brewery

The famous Skullsplitter and Dark Island are two of the beers produced at the Orkney Brewery. Skullsplitter carries on the Viking influence, being named after Thorfinn Einarsson, the seventh Viking Earl of Orkney. It is a tawny red colour, with a fruity malty aroma and a spicy, fresh and dried fruit taste. Dark Island, twice CAMRA's Champion Beer of Scotland, is a very dark beer, deep ruby in colour, with a chocolate and mixed fruit aroma and a

coffee roast malt flavour. A connoisseur's version, Dark Island Reserve, is brewed twice a year and delivers ten per cent ABV by introducing whisky into the brewing process. www.orkneybrewery.co.uk

Colonsay Brewery

The brewing tradition on Colonsay and Oransay dates back to the monks who ruled the islands. Now the brewery is researching the processes used in those distant times. A five-barrel operation, Colonsay Brewery creates very traditional beers and lagers that strive to encapsulate the wild and rugged nature of the island in a bottle. It produces a lager, 80/- and IPA, the distinctive quality of each being attributed to the unhurried nature of brewing and the quality of the peaty water that adds to the flavour of the beers. www.colonsaybrewery.co.uk

Islay Ales

Islay Ales was founded in 2003 by Paul Hathaway, Paul Capper and Walter Schobert who decided that an island with seven (soon to be eight) distilleries, producing some of the most famous whiskies in the world, needed a brewery. The company specialises in cask and bottle-conditioned beer, which is the classic description of real ale. The beers are neither filtered nor pasteurised and so continue to ferment and mature in the cask and the bottle, which inevitably means a shorter shelf life. Islay Ales offers a superb selection including the very light Saligo lager-style beer, the tawny Ardnave and Finlaggan, the ruby red dark Nerabus and Black Rock and an excellent stout, Dun Hogs Head. www.islayales.com

Arran Brewery

A final stop on this island tour is the Arran Brewery, which has survived a period of administration to surface healthier, fitter and still with its superb selection of beers. Arran Blonde, Dark and Sunset have been joined by its latest, Arran Milestone, its first bottle-conditioned ale and winner of the Champion Bottle Conditioned Beer of Scotland at the 2008 Ayrshire and Galloway Beer Festival. Milestone is a dark, amber brew with a subtle balance of malt and floral hop character, giving a lingering fruity finish. www.arranbrewery.co.uk

The Isle of Skye Brewery

Established in 1995, the Uig-based Isle of Skye Brewery makes a good selection of ales including gems such as Red Cuillin, Black Cuillin and Cuillin Beast. Its Hebridean Gold is brewed with porridge oats, which creates an exceptional smoothness as well as a thick, creamy head. www.skyebrewery.co.uk

Heather Ale

The Williams brothers are leading innovators in brewing, having created the iconic Fraoch from an ancient Gaelic recipe for 'leann fraoich' (heather ale), which was revived and reintroduced to the Scottish culture. They add sweet gale and flowering heather into the boiling bree of malted barley then, after it cools slightly, they pour the hot ale into a vat of fresh heather flowers, where it infuses for an hour before being fermented. A light, amber ale with a floral, peaty aroma and full malt character, it has a spicy, herbal flavour and dry, wine-like finish. Heather Ales also pioneered the use of gooseberries in Grozet, pine and spruce shoots in Alba, elderberries in Ebulum and seaweed in Kelpie, all creating very interesting and uniquely Scottish ales. www.fraoch.com

Tryst Brewery

Centrally located in Larbert by Falkirk, Tryst was set up in 2004 by John McGarva. When John was young there was always home-made beer, wine and jam in the house. His dad was an enthusiastic maker of anything that could be grown and collected from his own garden, fruit farm or hedgerow. His beer style was a big Scottish 80/- usually made from a commercial bitter kit with extra hops for taste and sugar for strength (Electric Soup) and more than a few unsuspecting visitors were helped out the door worse for having a couple of pints. Tryst has concentrated on cask and bottle-conditioned beers offering a range of about ten real ales. Among these is Blathan (pronounced 'bla-han'), which translates from Gaelic as 'little blossom'. A single hop variety is enhanced with elderflower and pale malts to create a beer with a strong floral nose and refreshing taste. www.trystbrewery.co.uk

Traditional Scottish Ales

Stirling is the home of Traditional Scottish Ales which has an excellent range of beers including 1488 Whisky Ale, which is matured for up to 12 weeks in newly disgorged Tullibardine casks to give it a glorious rich, natural, malt whisky colour and a light Tullibardine aroma with a clean, fresh whisky aftertaste. www.traditionalscottishales.co.uk

■ *Frank Park is part of the family partnership that acquired the Lade Inn and Trossachs Microbrewery in 2005. Working with brewer Traditional Scottish Ales (TSA), they developed three real ales: Waylade, a creamy blonde bitter with a malty, fruity nose and lightly hopped aftertaste; Ladeback, a slightly sweeter amber ale with a dry, hop-dominated finish; and Ladeout, a dark ale with a complex flavour of dark chocolate and liquorice. When customers began asking for carry-outs and came prepared with their own jugs to be filled with the Lade beers, they decided to bottle the beers. The success of these gave them the idea to provide a wider selection of beers. This idea developed into the Scottish Real Ale Shop and they began sourcing real ales from microbrewers from Shetland to the Borders. The shop now has over 120 Scottish real ales from 26 microbreweries. The Scottish Real Ales shop and Lade Inn are at Kilmahog, by Callander (www.scottishrealales.com).*

Scotland's microbreweries

With some examples of their beers.

Arran Brewery,
www.arranbrewery.co.uk
Arran Blonde, Sunset and Milestone

Atlas Brewery, Kinlochleven,
www.sinclairbreweries.co.uk
Latitude Highland Pilsner, Nimbus
Blonde, Three Sisters

Black Isle Brewery, Ross-shire,
www.blackislebrewery.com
Blonde, Yellowhammer, Heather Honey
Beer

Brewdog, Fraserburgh,
www.brewdog.com
Punk IPA, Trashy Blonde and Paradox

Broughton Ales Ltd, Biggar,
www.broughtonales.co.uk
Old Jock, Black Douglas and
Greenmantle Ale

Cairngorm Brewery, Aviemore,
www.cairngormbrewery.com
Tradewinds, Wild Cat and Blessed
Thistle

Colonsay Brewery,
www.colonsaybrewery.co.uk
Lager, 80/- and IPA

Deeside Brewery, Lumphanan,
Aberdeenshire, www.hillside-
brewery.com
Macbeth, Brude and Broichan Ales

Fyne Ales, Cairndow, Loch Fyne,
www.fyneales.com
Avalanche, Highlander and Maverick

Harviestoun Brewery, Alva,
Clackmannanshire,
www.harviestoun-brewery.co.uk
Ptarmigan, Bitter & Twisted and
Schiehallion

Heather Ale, www.fraoch.com
Ebulum, Kelpie and Heather Ale

Hebridean Brewery, Isle of Lewis,
www.hebridean-brewery.co.uk
Clansman, Islander and Celtic Black

Innis & Gunn, Edinburgh,
www.innisandgunn.com
Oak-Aged Beer and new rum cask Oak
Aged Beer

Inveralmond Brewery, Perth,
www.inveralmond-brewery.co.uk
Independence, Ossian and
Thrappledouser

Islay Ales, Bridgend,
www.islayales.com
Nerabus, Black Rock and Dun Hogs
Head.

Isle of Skye Brewery, Uig,
www.skyebrewery.co.uk
Red Cuillin, Cuillin Beast and Hebridean
Gold

Kelburn Brewing Company,
Renfrewshire,
www.kelburnbrewery.com
Goldihops, Red Smiddy and Misty Law

Lade Inn House Ales, Kilmahog, by
Callander,

www.theladeinn.com/microbrewery
Waylade, Ladeback, Ladeout

Orkney Brewery, Stromness,
www.orkneybrewery.co.uk
Skullsplitter, Red Macgregor and Dark
Island

Stewart Brewing Ltd, Edinburgh,
www.stewartbrewing.co.uk
Pentland IPA, Edinburgh Gold and
Copper Cascade

Sulwath Brewers, Castle Douglas,
www.sulwathbrewers.co.uk
Criffel, Cuil Hill and Knockendoch

Traditional Scottish Ales, Stirling,
www.traditionalscottishales.co.uk
1488 Whisky Ale, William Wallace and
Lomond Gold

Traquair House Brewery,
Innerleithen, www.traquair.co.uk
Traquair House Ale, Bear Ale and
Jacobite Ale

Tryst Brewery, Larbert by Falkirk,
www.trystbrewery.co.uk
Drovers, Blathan and Antonine
Amber

Valhalla Brewery, Shetland,
www.valhallabrewery.co.uk
Auld Rock, Simmer Dim and Sjolmet
Stout

West Beer, Glasgow,
www.westbeer.com
St Mungo, Munich Red and Oktoberfest

Water everywhere

A combination of geography, climate and geology puts Scotland in an ideal position to exploit the modern taste for mineral water. David Pollock raises a glass to one of the country's smaller producers.

Mineral water is so named because it has absorbed minerals during its sometimes decades-long filtration through soil and rock to the spring. Yet the magic ingredients that differentiate it from spring water or ordinary tap water remain elusive.

Martin Simpson, managing director of the Ballater-based, family-owned Deeside Water, humbly describes his company as one of the 'smaller producers' in Scotland. But he talks about his product with all the hands-on enthusiasm of the small businessman.

'The thing about Deeside Water is that it has clinically proven health benefits,' he says. 'We've undertaken ten medical research studies to prove this, and also to prove that it has anti-ageing benefits for the skin. Ballater grew up as a spa town around 1760, so it's because of the water that the town is there – it has a long history of health-giving properties, but we've had this research done independently by hospitals and universities to prove that the water actually has anti-oxidant

properties. Otherwise, people are sceptical of these things.'

While not seeking to speak for the whole industry, Simpson does reckon that Scotland's relative remoteness and lack of industrialisation helps the perception that water sourced from springs and wells here is purer than almost anywhere else.

'The lack of people and pollution here does help, from our point of view,'

he says. 'The fact we're halfway up a hill in the middle of nowhere is certainly a contributory factor to water quality.'

Deeside, like Highland Spring, collects spring water through an automatic, enclosed system that pipes it straight to the bottling plant. This cuts down on human intervention and the possibility of contamination.

The quality of Scotland's water is also bolstered by the steady rainfall coming in from the Atlantic. Competition is fierce, however, and small producers in Scotland express their frustration at going into their local supermarket and seeing countless bottles of French water lining the shelves.

Simpson gets most of his materials – bottles, labels and gas for carbonation – from Scottish suppliers. What he needs is available right on his doorstep. He is pleased at the reduction in food miles this brings, and recognises that such practices are one way of diminishing the industry's environmental impact.
■ *www.deesidewater.co.uk*

All the fun of the fair

With a list of 70 different Fairtrade products, Edinburgh's Equal Exchange is at the forefront of the movement that has changed our attitudes to food shopping. Claire Ritchie meets the folk behind it

'**S**cottish people have always liked to support the underdog,' says Barry Murdoch of Equal Exchange, a Fairtrade organisation based in Edinburgh. 'That's why Scotland and Fairtrade seem to complement each other so well.'

Equal Exchange was founded in Edinburgh in 1979, when three voluntary workers returned to Scotland from aid projects in Africa. Back then the concept of trade being fair was barely on the global agenda, but since then fair trade has become a high profile issue and Equal Exchange has become Europe's biggest Fairtrade supplier. In the early days the company set up Café Direct – the biggest Fairtrade coffee brand in the UK today – and the first Café Direct sales were made in Edinburgh in 1981. Since 2005, the company has doubled in size and has over 70 Fairtrade and organic certified products – more than any in the UK.

The Fairtrade supply chain works in developing parts of the world by replacing the middleman and the exporter with a farmers' co-operative. The farmers are able to sell their goods directly to an importer – for example in Europe – which then sells on to the retailer. By shortening the supply chain, the farmers and their communites keep more of the profit.

So what is the secret behind all this success? Equal Exchange works with small co-operatives and producers in developing countries, particularly in Africa and South America. Equal Exchange pre-finances all of its producers by guaranteeing crops and prices, and it also helps with the organic certification process. As well as receiving a fair price for their crops, the farmers receive an additional 'premium' payment. This goes straight back to the farming organisation, which democratically decides how it should be spent – clean water supplies, education for the farmers' children, health care and so on.

The health benefits, such as the reduced risk of lung disease when crops are grown without the use of pesticides and fertilisers, means the farmers can put back the money into the community, building the business and building schools. Wherever possible, the products are packaged at source, too, which results in more of the profit staying within the community. Working with small producers means there is less pressure to produce huge quantities but more emphasis is given to ensuring they can grow high-quality produce that will attract a premium price.

Coffee, tea and cocoa are the products most closely associated with the Fairtrade concept, but they don't necessarily hold the key to future of companies such as Equal Exchange. 'These days the hot beverage market has become stagnant and heavily controlled by the supermarkets, so diversification into new products will be the key,' says Murdoch. Some beauty products are becoming Fairtrade, using for example cashew butter and coffee grounds in place of more traditional chemical products, and the first Fairtrade Palestinian olive oil has just been launched. Such diversification is not a new thing for Equal Exchange, a company that has been behind many Fairtrade firsts. It is responsible for the world's only Fairtrade wild rooibos tea, for example, and the first Fairtrade nuts.

If this sounds a million miles from the traditional notion of Scotland's larder, think again. Local produce and Fairtrade share an empathy with the source and quality of the food, along with a heightened awareness of the consequences of consumer purchases. More than half of Scottish towns are now labelled Fairtrade Towns, with whole islands, such as Arran, also on the case. 'Scotland is particularly disposed to the concept of Fairtrade because the people here are socially minded and, historically, are from a farming background,' says Murdoch.

Perhaps this underdog will win the day after all.

■ *www.equalexchange.co.uk*
www.chooseliberation.com
For more on Scotland's coffee specialists see listings starting on page 120 and www.thelarder.net

Blend not bland

The relatively recent focus on single-malt whiskies all but smothered the art and craft involved in blending but, as Josie Butchart explains, there's a new sophistication in the world of blended whisky.

If you are a whisky drinker who wants to cut a dash, the usual tactic is to order a single malt from a well-respected distillery. Bland blended whisky brands are simply for those who want to play safe and keep down the cost of a round. Well, perhaps that's how it used to be.

It was blended whisky that first took Scotland's national drink from rough raw spirit of Highland hillsides to an international market. The great boom in whisky in the late-19th and early-20th century was led by the famous brands – Ushers, Dewars, Cutty Sark, for example, blended whiskies all. It was the release of single malt whiskies in the last quarter of the 20th century that changed the status of blended whiskies. While some blends maintained their prestige, particularly in the export market – Johnnie Walker, Chivas and Dimple being classic examples – talking up single malts almost inevitably meant talking down blends. In recent years, however, another option has opened up for the adventurous whisky drinker.

Eight years ago, John Glaser left the security of a job with Johnnie Walker to set up his own boutique whisky blending company, Compass Box. 'I saw an opportunity to do things with whisky that other companies weren't doing: make it more approachable and create higher-quality blended whiskies,' he says. 'Our approach was seen as contemporary in a very staid business.'

If a blend is labelled a 'vatted malt' or 'blended malt Scotch whisky' it will be made entirely of single malt whisky; otherwise it's likely to include cheaper and less individual grain whisky, typically at a ratio of around 60 per cent grain whisky to 40 per cent single malts.

Central to Glaser's philosophy was the use of better quality and fresher oak barrels to mature his whiskies. 'It was about trying to make the liquid more interesting,' he says. 'Multinationals had been driving down the cost of making whisky, so many blends had lost character because the quality of the oak casks being used had gone down –

BENROMACH

ORANGERIE

A SCOTCH WHISKY INFUSION WITH FRESH ORANGE & EXOTIC SPICES

COMPASS BOX WHISKY COMPANY

Younger people are attracted to whisky blenders who take their drink seriously without getting snobby about it

they were being used and re-used to save money.'

Glaser explains that around 60 per cent of the flavour – or nose – of a whisky comes from the oak barrels in which it is matured. 'In a small way we have helped raise the profile of oak by using a much higher proportion of 'first-fill' barrels (those that have only been used once before) and experimenting with new oak.'

The result is a portfolio of unusual, high-end blended whiskies that range from the soft, fruity elegance of Asyla, which gets its sweetness from ageing a blend of lighter grain whiskies in first-fill American oak casks, to the big, bold flavours of Flaming Heart, a blend of malts aged in new French oak.

Quality blended whiskies are also at the heart of the Spencerfield Spirit Company, which was set up in 2005 by husband and wife team Alex Nicol and Jane Eastwood. They started by

purchasing the existing blended brands Sheep Dip and Pig's Nose from Whyte & Mackay. They then redesigned the packaging to give it a more contemporary look. Although they didn't tinker too much with the style of the blend they began using a higher percentage of older whiskies in the mix and more first-fill oak casks for maturation.

According to Nicol, the main consumers of this new style of blended whisky are younger (in their 20s and 30s) and tend to be more confident and adventurous than the average whisky drinker. 'You need a certain amount of confidence to ask for a whisky called Sheep Dip,' he laughs.

In another sign of the new wave that these blended whiskies represent, most of Spencerfield's marketing has been done through digital media or by simply giving people the chance to sample the whiskies at food and cultural events. 'The whisky business has tended to alienate younger people by being so serious,' he says. 'Not being so snobby about the whole thing helps.'

■ www.spencerfieldspirit.com
www.compassboxwhisky.com
www.ianmacleod.com
www.gordonandmacphail.com
www.lfw.co.uk

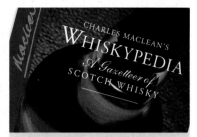

CHARLES MACLEAN'S
WHISKYPEDIA
A Gazetteer of
SCOTCH WHISKY

> LOADED BARRELS

The cask in which whisky matures can determine over 80 per cent of the flavour. In this entry from his new book, Charles MacLean sorts the wood from the trees.

By law, Scotch whisky must be matured in oak casks. Most of the casks (around 90 per cent) are made from American white oak (*Quercus alba*), the rest from European oak (*Quercus robur*).

The species of oakwood influences colour, aroma and taste (together, the last two are the 'flavour' of the whisky). American oak imparts a golden hue and sweet, vanilla or coconut flavours; European oak, being more tannic, makes for a richer, umbrageous colour, a drier taste and typically introduces dried fruits, nuts and spices to the flavour, and sometimes sulphury notes.

The casks are invariably second-hand: they will have been used previously to mature bourbon (for around three years; always American oak) or will have contained sherry (for one to two years, usually Oloroso sherry; mainly European oak, some American oak). Occasionally ex-wine barrels, or wine-treated casks are used (mainly European oak).

Casks come in a range of sizes. The commonest are 'barrels' (about 200 litres, also called 'American Standard Barrels' or ASBs), 'hogsheads' (250 litres, also called 'remade hogsheads' – they are made by combining staves from ASBs; four of the latter make three hogs-heads), 'butts' (500 litres, usually made from European oak and ex-sherry) and 'puncheons' (also 500 litres, dumpier than butts; made from both European and American oak).

Casks are used three or four times before they are deemed to be 'exhausted'. The first time they are filled with Scotch they are termed 'first-fill casks', thereafter they are 'refill casks'. Once exhausted, they may be 'rejuvenated' by being scraped out and retoasted or charred.

■ *Extract taken from* Charles MacLean's Whiskypedia: A Gazeteer of Scotch Whisky *by Charles MacLean, published by Birlinn Ltd, 2009. Reproduced with kind permission from Birlinn Ltd.*
www.birlinn.co.uk

Spirit of the age

The image of whisky is often wrapped in age-old traditions and lore. Now, for the first time in decades, new whiskies from brand new distilleries are beginning to appear. Josie Butchart seeks them out.

Artisan food and drink businesses run by passionate entrepreneurs are springing up all over Scotland. But what if your dream is make your own whisky? After all, small-scale distilling is illegal (the Excise Act of 1823 sets the minimum size of still at 40 gallons). Distilleries don't come cheap and even if you can afford the price tags you could wait years for one to come on the market.

In recent years a few adventurous souls have decided to build their own distilleries. These ventures are much smaller than the new distilleries planned by the big drinks companies – the most recent small project, Daftmill in Fife, produces just 20,000 litres of spirit a year compared with the 10 million litres that would typically be produced at a large distillery – but they can be many times more interesting for

the whisky drinker.

Harold Currie retired from a long career in the whisky industry in 1995 and became the main investor in the first modern distillery to be built on Arran. Over on Islay in 2005, Anthony Wills founded Kilchoman, the first distillery to be built on the island for 124 years. The same year the Cuthbert family, owners of Daftmill farm in Fife, transformed their old mill buildings into a distillery.

Even more distilleries are in the planning stages, including one at Port Charlotte on Islay which is to be built on the site of an abandoned distillery by the privately owned Bruichladdich distillery, and a carbon-neutral venture in Huntly, Aberdeenshire, being proposed by the independent bottler Duncan Taylor & Co.

Anthony Wills, managing director of Kilchoman, explains why so many

people are suddenly interested in creating their own whiskies by pointing to the surge in demand for premium and more unusual malts. 'There are now a huge number of collectors and enthusiasts looking for something a bit different,' he says.

Francis Cuthbert of Daftmill says distilling is an effective way of turning a low-priced commodity (barley) into something much more profitable. For a barley farmer there is also the opportunity to take whisky back to its traditional roots. That's because building new means the distillery can be designed to suit modern requirements and, ironically, that can mean a return to a more traditional way of doing things. Both Kilchoman and Daftmill are 'farm distilleries' where the barley used by the distillery is grown on site (100 per cent at Daftmill, 30 per cent at Kilchoman).

At Kilchoman they also practice floor malting, the traditional way of malting barley by hand. The distilleries planned at Port Charlotte and Huntly will be as green as possible, with the Huntly distillery using a woodchip-fuelled biomass plant to provide steam for the distilling process and a warehouse with a sedum or 'living' roof.

It's a move even the multinationals are making. Diageo's massive new distillery at Roseisle by the mouth of the Spey, with 14 stills and a price tag of £40 million, emits just 15 per cent of the carbon dioxide of an existing distillery of the same size, recycling water and generating power by burning its own waste.

There are, however, some disadvantages to starting from scratch. The most important is that whisky takes a long time to mature so it is a long time before money comes back into the business. The new spirit must be aged in oak barrels for at least three years before it can be sold as Scotch whisky and most single malt whisky isn't released until it is between eight and ten years old.

The Arran distillery released its first ten-year-old malt only in 2006. 'It was a big step for us to finally put an age statement on our whisky,' says managing director Euan Mitchell. 'It said: "We're here, we've arrived and we're not a baby distillery anymore."'

Kilchoman is poised to release its first three-year-old spirit in September 2009, but managing director Anthony Wills says he doesn't expect Kilchoman whisky to reach its peak until it is between seven and ten years old. 'Our intention is to do regular releases but only because we are targeting connoisseurs and they understand that a three-year-old whisky is not the finished article, that our whisky will get even better,' he says.

Daftmill, one the other hand, doesn't intend putting its whisky on sale at all until it is around ten years old. 'You only get one chance to make a first impression and we want that to be as good as it can be,' says Cuthbert.

The release of a brand-new whisky creates a buzz quite unlike the now-familiar rebranding and repackaging exercises from the well-known names. When these new whiskies are finally ready they offer the whisky drinker not just the chance to expand their whisky geography, but also taste the spirit of the age: a more traditional, greener, artisan product that harks back to the grassroots of whisky making.

■ *www.arranwhisky.com*
www.kilchomandistillery.com
www.daftmill.com

The berry beverage

David Pollock speaks to the makers of a distinctive soft drink made from Scottish raspberries.

Their first business was a product development consultancy in the food and drink industry. But a simple admiration for the Scottish berry was enough to convince husband and wife team Anne Thomson and John Gallagher to develop their own line. 'We always found it a bit sad that there weren't many products you could buy in shops that reflected the wonderful flavours of these berries,' says Thomson, from Alloa. 'Particularly raspberries, which Scotland is famous for.'

The pair focused on a raspberry juice drink, devising a recipe 'and a processing method that would maintain the fruit's flavour and aroma. Thomson's processing method is 'fast and cold,' moving quickly to the bottling phase. 'We decided to mix it with sparkling water, which gives the taste a bit of a lift, to create Bouvrage,' she says. 'It's a distinctive drink; it's not too sweet, and it has a very high fruit content.'

The creation process was harder than it sounds. 'Even after we had decided it would be a juice rather than, say, a dry product, it wasn't easy to find the methodology,' she says. 'What had been done before in this country had all been to do with apple processing, and the presses, the filtration, all the technical aspects are very different for each fruit. Plus other products on the market which use berries actually heat-treat the juice, which drives out flavour and aroma.

'We knew what the product was going to taste like, it was just a question of going down many blind avenues until it was a reality. There are many different ways of processing juice, from treating it with ultra-violet light to sending electric current through it and using high-pressure.'

Launched in 1998 at the Royal Highland Show, Bouvrage (old Scots for 'beverage') was a hit in delis, coffee shops and hotels. It was less profitable in supermarkets, so they focused on farm shops, farmers' markets and delicatessens.

Their company, Ella Drinks, has since introduced a line based on the blaeberry (the European cousin of the American blueberry) and they are seeking ways to carry their taste for the Scottish berry further into the sophisticated drinks market. 'There's a lot of rubbish out there,' she says. 'We aim Bouvrage at the discerning consumer, at those who find soft drinks are too sweet or lacking in nutritional value. And that *is* a very large group of people.'

■ *www.bouvrage.com*

WHERE TO BUY

Outlets for buying whisky, beer, tea, coffee and other drinks listed regionally then organised alphabetically.

EDINBURGH & LOTHIANS

■ Artisan Roast

57 Broughton St, Edinburgh
07590 590667, www.artisanroast.co.uk
Mon–Fri 8am–8pm; Sat 10am–8pm; Sun & bank holidays 10am–6pm.
Café.
Originally intended as a coffee bean shop with tasting samples, the Artisan Roast Café and Roastery relented to the pressure of devoted fans and started selling the real stuff in cups, such was the coffee's popularity. Supplier to cafés and restaurants across Scotland, it has a range of premium fresh coffees all roasted within days. Believing Fairtrade isn't the best model, it prefers to buy from growers who produce quality beans and pay them significantly more than the Fairtrade base rate, sourcing its beans from estates, co-operatives and collectives.

■ Cadenhead's Whisky Shop

172 Canongate, Edinburgh
0131 556 5864, www.wmcadenhead.com
Mon–Sat 10.30am–5.30pm; Closed Sun.
Web/mail order.
Scotland's oldest independent whisky bottler has been operating since 1842, bottling single cask whiskies and selling direct to the customer. It has a huge range of whiskies available, from the familiar big brands such as Glenlivet, Glenmorangie and Laphroaig to the smaller, less well known distilleries that can be found all over Scotland. Each of its cask whiskies spends a minimum of three years in the barrel, and all are non-chill-filtered and free of the artificial colourings that can detract from the character of the spirit. Depending on the size of the bottle, the age and strength of the individual whisky and the appeal of the distillery (those that have been closed for a while are the most sought after), there is a whisky to be found here for all budgets – from £1 to £14,000.

■ Demijohn

32 Victoria Street, Edinburgh
0131 225 3265, www.demijohn.co.uk
Mon–Sat 10am–6pm; Sun 12.30–5pm.
Billed as the world's first liquid deli, family-run Demijohn was first inspired by Southern Italian wineries. Purchase an empty bottle and choose from an array of predominantly British products

including liqueurs, spirits, oils and vinegars to fill it. Once empty, the bottle can be returned and refilled at a reduced price. This policy of re-using materials and reducing impact on the environment is central to the company's ethos. Supplies are sourced locally, predominantly from a network of small artisanal producers ranging from retired teachers to ex-bankers, all vetted to ensure they use clean, fair and sustainable methods of production in line with Slow Food UK principles.

■ Edinburgh Wine Merchants

30B Raeburn Place, Edinburgh, Scotland
0131 343 2347, www.edinburghwine.com
Mon–Thu 11am–7.30pm; Fri 10am–8pm; Sat 10am–9pm; Sun 12:30–6pm.
The Edinburgh branch of a successful chain of award-winning wine merchants based in Cambridge, this wine merchant stocks an impressive selection of boutique wines, beers and spirits. Completely independent, Cambridge Wine Merchants ships wines from cellars all over the world – from tiny family firms to huge co-operatives – straight to its branches. Browse an enormous range of products from cases of lager, Belgian beers and extensive range of malt whiskies right through to Cru Classés de Bordeaux. Online ordering is also available through the website.

■ Great Grog

161 Bonnington Road, Edinburgh
0131 555 0222, www.greatgrog.co.uk
Mon–Sat 10am–6pm. Closed Sun.
IWSC Scottish Wine Merchant of the Year 2008/2009, Great Grog offers the full wine experience. Visit the Causewayside shop above the warehouse, browse the monthly catalogue and website or attend tastings, courses and events at the company's Rose Street wine bar. There's off-street parking at the shop and free nationwide delivery; all it asks is you buy a minimum of twelve bottles. Take a ready-made case from £50 or create your own. Choose from hundreds of different wines, including occasional rarities such as D'Arenberg Dead Arm Shiraz, Noon, Molly Dooker, St Clair Wairau Sauvignon and Cloudy Bay etc – just sign up to the email database to be alerted of their arrival.

■ Green Mountain Coffee Roasters

Glenfinlas Ltd, 1 St Colme Street, Edinburgh
0131 220 8251
www.greenmountaincoffee.co.uk
Café, Web/mail order.
Based in Edinburgh's Colme Street,

Glenfinlas is the sole UK importer and distributor for Green Mountain, an ethical trading coffee company offering an astonishing number of organic and Fairtrade coffees by mail order (through the website or by telephone or fax – Edinburgh buyers can also collect their orders from the St Colme Street office). The quality-driven range includes one of the only truly organic and Fairtrade dark espresso roasts available – single estate La Minita Tarrazu from Costa Rica – and the rare, fabulously expensive, Jamaican Blue Mountain. It also has flavoured coffees, including organic hazelnut and decaffeinated beans in various styles.

■ Henderson Wines

109 Comiston Road, Edinburgh
0131 447 8580
www.hendersonwines.co.uk
Mon–Sat 10am–8pm; Sun 2–5pm.
Established in 2001, award-winning Henderson Wines combines specialist wine merchant and corner off-licence. With a wide selection of wines which reaches over 1200, as well as over 100 beers and 50 malts, it offers its services with proficiency, passion and energy. Expect quality and value and, with regular promotions, there's something here for everyone's wallet. The shop's staff are friendly and services include glass hire, ice, free delivery throughout Edinburgh and they're more than happy to help you track down that elusive bottle you've been looking for. They reimburse your parking costs when you spend over £25.

■ Howdah Tea and Coffee Company

42 High Street, North Berwick, East Lothian
01620 894 245, www.howdah.co.uk
Mon–Sat 9.30am–5pm. Closed Sun.
Established in 1992, Howdah Tea and Coffee draws you into this little emporium of aromatic beans and leaf with the smell of roasted coffee. The experience is a sheer joy thanks to the knowledge and enthusiasm of owners Pat and Mary Beales. Indulge in a demitasse of seriously rich espresso while enjoying the sight and smell of countless deliciously scented fruit and herbal teas. There are 50 teas to choose from, including breakfast blends, gunpowder, Assam and the evocatively-named Blue Lady.

■ Lockett Bros

133 High Street, North Berwick, East Lothian
01620 890799, www.lockettbros.co.uk
Inspired by a two-year journey harvesting grapes in Central Otago, New Zealand, Chris Lockett made the

Demijohn

decision to become a wine merchant and opened his North Berwick shop in 2004. Describing his business life as 'absolutely amazing', he has a clear passion for his subject. Together with his shop manager, Graham Kinniburgh, Lockett is dedicated to sourcing wines, selling a few New and Old World varieties exclusively through the shop. In addition, it stocks Scottish spirits, including Hendricks Gin and the obligatory malt whiskies, as well as a small selection of Cuban cigars. There is also an online ordering facility.

■ Royal Mile Whiskies
379 High Street, The Royal Mile, Edinburgh
0131 225 3383
www.royalmilewhiskies.com
Mon–Sat 10am–6pm; Sun 12.30–6pm.
Established in 1991, Royal Mile Whiskies has become something of an institution. Choose from 1000 malt whiskies and bourbons from around Scotland, Ireland and other parts of the globe including Japan and New Zealand. A selection of rare and collectors' items are available but don't come cheap – expect to pay £1,750 for a 1973 cask strength Talisker. However there are plenty of other single malts for around the £20–£40 mark with

rigorously trained and highly enthusiastic staff available to guide you through the buying process. They'll also direct you to their second venture just down the road, the Cigar Box, which offers a comprehensive range of Cuban cigars together with an extensive selection of rums.

■ Valvona & Crolla
19 Elm Row, Edinburgh
See Delis & General Food

■ Villeneuve Wines
• 49a Broughton Street, Edinburgh
0131 558 8441
www.villeneuvewines.com
Mon–Wed noon–10pm; Thu–Sat 10am–10pm; Sun 1–8pm.
• 82 High Street, Haddington
01620 822 224
www.villeneuvewines.com
Mon–Thu 10am–7pm; Fri 10am–8pm; Sat 9am–8pm. Closed Sun.
With more than 2000 wines on its list and up to 150 malt whiskies, outlets in Edinburgh, Haddington and Peebles and an online ordering facility, award-winning Villeneuve Wines can afford to be eclectic. Although it's not particularly traditional, you'll still find Old World favourites from France, Italy and Spain, and it has a penchant for smaller

producers, from the New World in particular. Glance along the shelves and find the likes of Concha y Torro, Penfolds and Montana, red and white wines from the Lebanon and a great selection of dessert wines. Along with these, it stocks an excellent selection of spirits, including those slightly more obscure brands not so readily available elsewhere.

■ Wood Winters
91 Newington Road, Edinburgh
0131 667 2760, www.woodwinters.com
Mon–Sat 10am–7pm; Sun 1pm–5pm.
Web/mail order.
See main entry in Central Scotland & Fife listings.

GREATER GLASGOW & CLYDESIDE

■ The Cave
421/423 Great Western Road, Glasgow
0141 357 5550, www.thecave.uk.com
Mon–Fri 9am–10pm; Sat 10am–10pm; Sun 12.30–10pm.
Located next to Glasgow's Kelvinbridge, the Cave lives ups to its name. Feast your eyes upon the impressive array of bottled beers from around the globe, the selection of intriguing world and organic wines

including some from Scotland and some excellent malt whiskies. The enthusiastic staff will go out of their way to source unusual varieties for you and a convenient chiller box will bring your white to a perfectly quaffable temperature in no time. Blackboards detail frequent deals on off-licence goods and a delicatessen area hosts a variety of speciality foods and chocolates.

■ Demijohn
382 Byres Road, Glasgow
0141 337 3600, www.demijohn.co.uk
Mon–Sat 10am–6pm; Sun 12.30–6pm.
See main entry in Edinburgh & Lothians listings.

■ Peckham & Rye
21 Clarence Drive, Glasgow
0141 334 4312, www.peckhams.co.uk
Mon–Sat 10am–10pm; Sun 12.30–10pm.
At nearly 30 years old, Peckham's is one of the most established groups of specialist wine and food shops in Scotland. One of Peckham's 11 outlets, the Glassford Street branch in Glasgow's Merchant City devotes its basement to wine, beer and spirits and is licensed until midnight. Other branches have more limited stocks of wine, although any item stocked in one branch can be quickly ordered into any other branch. The Peckham's range includes 1400 wines and some 140 world beers, including cervezas, pivos, birras, bakushas and many Scottish brews. Particularly strong on less common New World and Italian wines, it stocks the much-admired Brown Brothers range from Australia.

■ Robbie's Drams
3 Sandgate, Ayr, South Ayrshire
01292 262 135, www.robbiesdrams.com
Mon–Sat 9am–10pm;
Sun 12.30pm–10pm.
Web/mail order.
Based in Ayr's Sandgate, Robbie's Drams is a specialist whisky retailer specialising in single malts. In addition, you'll find an extensive range of blended and grain whiskies as well as Irish whiskey, bourbon whiskey and interesting ranges from other countries. Owner Robin Russell prides himself on the range and diversity of his whiskies. From the hundreds available in store, you'll find everything from special monthly offers to collectors' items and limited editions, from closed and silent distillery bottles to its own range of single cask bottles. It hosts in-store tastings, and helpful and experienced staff will try and source more obscure bottles for you.

Scottish Real Ale Shop

■ Tapa Bakehouse & Coffeehouse
• 21 Whitehill Street, Dennistoun, Glasgow
• 721 Pollokshaws Road, Glasgow
See Bread, Cakes & Chocolate.

■ Tchai Ovna
42 Otago Lane, Glasgow
0141 357 4524, www.tchaiovna.com
Mon–Sun 11am–11pm.
Café, Web/mail order.
Tchai Ovna Tea House opened its first shop in the west end of Glasgow in May 2000. Although never formally a cooperative, it has always sought to offer an alternative to more corporate bars and cafés. Filled with wooden benches and wicker chairs with ornate cushions, it boasts shelves lined with a dazzling array of teas in glass jars. In the summer the patio opens to a magical garden where vines creep and wrap around the railings. As well as selling speciality teas and infusions from around the world and a range of vegetarian meals, it hosts music nights and literary events. In 2004 it opened a second shop in Shawlands, on the south side of the city.

SOUTHERN SCOTLAND

■ Bairds
Glenrowan, Broughton, by Biggar
01899 220800, www.bairds-wines.co.uk
Phone ahead to check opening hours.
Web/mail order.
Melvyn and Isobel Baird's wine and spirit merchant sits two miles outside the Borders village of Broughton. It complements its selection of wines from Europe and the New World with various specialities, including organic and biodynamic wines. There are even vegan wines which do not use the conventional animal-based filters in the 'fining' process of removing sediment. Visitors are encouraged to taste the wines on offer; there's also provision for formal tastings at a dedicated venue. With the chance to sample wines while taking in the surrounding countryside, Bairds is a destination in itself.

■ Corney & Barrow
8 Academy Street, Ayr
01292 267 000
www.corneyandbarrow.com
Mon–Fri 9am–5.30pm; Sat 9.30am–5.30pm. Closed Sun.
With over 200 years experience, wine merchant Corney & Barrow has been increasing its hold over the last 20 years on the fine wine market in Scotland. This branch is attached to the company's main Scottish warehouse and customers can expect to find a dazzling range of wines and vintages. Extremely knowledgeable staff will offer assistance and can advise you on your purchases, while an informative website is set up to take orders online. Despite the enormous representation of top-end clarets, burgundies and New World gems, there are bottles to suit every pocket, with the French regional variety particularly good for bargains.

■ Villeneuve Wines
1 Venlaw Court, Peebles
01721 722500
www.villeneuvewines.com
Mon–Sat 9am–8pm; Sun 12.30–5.30pm.
Web/mail order.
See main entry in Edinburgh & Lothians listings.

CENTRAL SCOTLAND & FIFE

■ The Bean Shop

67 George Street, Perth, Perthshire
0173 844 9955, www.thebeanshop.com
Mon–Sat 9.30am–5.30pm. Closed Sun.
A haven for the coffee connoisseur, The Bean Shop in Perth has a wide selection of the best gourmet coffee beans from around the globe. Choose from exotic, organic and fair-trade coffee or try the famous Jamaica blue mountain coffee beans. A number of unique blends are designed to excite your palette – an Italian roasted gourmet blend is satisfyingly smooth, while the power of flavour behind the blend 67 will keep espresso drinkers very happy. It uses only Swiss water-processed decaffeinated coffee, and also offers a choice of organic and Fairtrade beans. Call into the shop for your daily dose or order beans online to keep at home.

■ J.L. Gill

26 West High Street, Crieff, Perthshire
See Delis & General Food

■ House of Menzies

Castle Menzies Farm, Aberfeldy, Perthshire 01887 829666
www.houseofmenzies.com
Summer: Mon–Sat 10am–5pm; Sun 11am–5pm. Winter: Wed–Sat 10am–4pm; Sun 11am–4pm. Closed Mon/Tue. Café.
House of Menzies, owned and run by various members of the McDairmid family, is a good example of what can happen when Scottish farmers decide to diversify. The doocot and cattle court at the home farm have been imaginatively converted into a lovely space selling new world wines and a small but well chosen range of deli food and treats. Majoring on wines from Australia and New Zealand, there is a wonderful selection from the smaller producers and wineries of the region. In the coffee shop, settle into one of the armchairs by the log fire and linger over the wine list.

■ The Scottish Real Ale Shop

The Lade Inn, Kilmahog, Callander
01877 330152
www.scottishrealales.com.
Mon–Sun 11am–6pm.
Café, Web/mail order.
Situated in the scenic Loch Lomond and Trossachs National Park, the Scottish Real Ale Shop near Callander opened in December 2006 and has been selling over 100 different Scottish beers, produced by breweries from the Shetlands to the Borders, ever since. A one-stop shop for Scottish beers, real ale festival and brewing information, the shop is a place where you can buy that elusive bottle from the Hebrides or delicious blonde from Islay. It holds a beer festival every year and has tastings throughout the summer weekend to enable you to try before you buy. Call into neighbouring Lade Inn – also part of the family operation – and enjoy a spot of lunch.

■ Spencerfield Spirit Company

Spencerfield Farmhouse, Inverkeithing
01383 412144
www.spencerfieldspirit.com
Established in 2005, the Spencerfield Spirit Company is owned by Alex and Jane Nicol and based in a 16th century farmhouse in Fife. His background with Glenmorangie, Laphroaig and Whyte and Mackay Distillers meant Alex was well placed to take on a couple of whisky brands on the verge of extinction. Sheep Dip and Pig's Nose may seem odd names for a whisky, but they have proved to be part of its appeal. One dates from the days when farmers would hide their home-distilled whisky from the taxman in vats labelled 'Sheep Dip', the other from the old country expression 'soft as a pig's nose', in reference to its smooth flavour.

■ Wood Winters

16 Henderson Street, Bridge of Allan
01786 834 894, www.woodwinters.com
Mon–Sat 10am–7pm; Sun 1pm–5pm.
Web/mail order.
Husband and wife team Cara and Douglas set up wine merchant Wood Winters in Bridge of Allan just over three years ago and have recently opened a second branch in Edinburgh. Believing that everyone should be able to enjoy wines that are a cut above those available in supermarkets – without the need to become a winebuff – they aim to make their service friendly and personable. Survey a selection of well chosen old and new world wines, as well as champagne and stickies, drink related gifts, cigars and chocolate. Tasting events take place every month in store, with seasonal food-matching themes. Check the website for dates a regularly updated section of bin ends.

NORTH EAST SCOTLAND

■ Gordon & MacPhail

George House, Boroughbriggs Road, Elgin 01343 545111
www.gordonandmacphail.com
Mon–Sat 9am–5.15pm. Closed Sun.
Gordon and MacPhail proudly claims to be the world's leading malt whisky specialist offering more than 450 presentations of own-bottled single malts, aged from 5 to 60 years old, and a stock holding of more than 700 whiskies, including its own G&M Benromach from what is officially Scotland's smallest distillery. As well as providing many tastings during the Spirit of Speyside Whisky Festival, private tastings can be arranged, tailored to your own specification. In addition, there are over 500 wines, a selection of champagnes, liqueurs and Scottish bottled beers to choose from, with specially trained staff on hand to offer advice.

HIGHLANDS, ISLANDS & ARGYLL

■ Arran Brewery Ltd

Cladach, Brodick, Isle of Arran
0177 030 2353, www.arranbrewery.co.uk
Easter–mid-Oct: Mon–Sat 10am–5pm, Sun 12.30–5pm. Mid–Oct–Easter Mon & Wed–Sat 10am–3.30pm.
Established in 1999, the award-winning Arran Brewery is set in the shadow of an imposing Brodick Castle. Naturally made and free from artificial additives and preservatives, the premium ales are produced in a high-tech microbrewery using traditional production methods. One of the most popular and recognisable brews is the clear and zesty Arran Blonde with its modern packaging and sleek club-friendly 330ml bottle. An excellent visitor centre allows you to watch the process from a viewing gallery, and included in the price of the tour is a complimentary tasting. From the shop or website you can buy various gift packs of the beer, as well as hampers including other Arran products.

■ Loch Fyne Whiskies

Inveraray, Argyll
01499 302219, www.lfw.co.uk
Mon–Sat 10am–5.30pm; Sun 12.30–5pm.
Regarded as one of the finest whisky retailers in the world by *Whisky Magazine*, award-winning Loch Fyne Whiskies has been distributing the water of life since 1993. It offers several hundred single malts as well as the Loch Fyne, a mellow, well-regarded blend. Visitors can call into the shop, which also offers tasting, hip flasks, quaiches, Loch Fyne marmalade, books and miniatures, while worldwide mail order can be arranged by phone or through the well-ordered website. 'The normal Loch Fyne Whiskies guarantee applies,' it explains. 'If you're not happy with it, send it back and we'll finish it off for you'.

DIRECTORY

WHERE TO EAT

A selection of restaurants serving Scottish produce listed regionally then organised alphabetically. Prices shown are for an average two-course evening meal, or the cost of a set-price menu, per person.

EDINBURGH & LOTHIANS

■ Amber

The Scotch Whisky Experience, 354 Castlehill, The Royal Mile, Edinburgh
0131 477 8477
www.amber-restaurant.co.uk
Mon–Sun noon–3.45pm; Tue–Sat 7–9pm.
£25
If whisky really is the 'water of life' then dining at Amber is an experience that should be tried at least once. Housed within the Scottish Whisky Experience at the top of Edinburgh's Royal Mile, the restaurant lives and breathes whisky, offering an awe-inspiring 330 varieties to sample – but fear not; it employs a resident whisky expert to guide you through to process. The food menu features an admirable range of Scottish produce, from estate-bred beef and lamb to seasonal game and wild salmon.

■ Atrium

10 Cambridge Street, Edinburgh
0131 228 8882
www.atriumrestaurant.co.uk
Mon–Fri noon–2pm, 6–10pm; Sat 6–10pm. Closed Sun.
£30
The Atrium is very much an Edinburgh institution, with owners Andrew and Lisa Radford having been at the helm since 1993. Chef Neil Forbes keeps things fresh in a kitchen where local produce is not just an ephemeral sales concept, but a real mission, even to the extent of listing local suppliers on the various menus. A lot of its own butchery is done on site, and Scottish seafood also features prominently on one of the city's most interesting tasting menus.

■ Blonde

75 St Leonard's Street, Edinburgh
0131 668 2917
www.blonderestaurant.co.uk
Mon 6–10pm; Tue–Sun noon–2.30pm, 6–10pm.
£17
Since opening in 2001, Blonde has established a reputation for relaxed dining with good-value food in bright, welcoming surroundings. An emphasis on Scottish produce goes hand in hand with a desire to use sustainable and seasonal foods, creating a menu packed with interesting choices for non-meat-eaters as well as those who might want to try the more standard venison, lamb or steak options.

■ Blue

10 Cambridge Street, Edinburgh
0131 221 1222, www.bluescotland.co.uk
Mon–Thu noon–2.30pm, 5.30–10.30pm; Fri/Sat noon–2.30pm, 5.30–11pm. Closed Sun.
£24
Occupying a floor in Edinburgh's esteemed Traverse Theatre building, blue has an elegant simplicty – all low lighting, minimalist furnishings and the natural feel of stone and wood – that subtly echoes the menu's Slow Food ethos. As befits the intimate ambience and discreet, courteous service, the menu modestly thanks a wealth of local suppliers shared with sister restaurant Atrium (see separate entry), one floor below.

■ The Boat House

22 High Street, South Queensferry
0131 331 5429
www.theboathouse-sq.co.uk
Mon–Sat noon–2pm; 5.30–10pm. Sun noon–2pm, 5.30–8pm.
£22
Since opening in 2003 on the shores of the Firth of Forth, the Boat House has established itself as a destination seafood restaurant. Chef-patron Paul Steward sources fish from all over Scotland. Delicate oak-smoked salmon is from a smokery just five miles down the road. Favourites such as lobster, langoustine and crab make frequent appearances on the menu, which changes every few days – although dishes such as the west coast scallops have been there since the beginning.

■ Champany Inn

Champany, Linlithgow, West Lothian
01506 834532, www.champany.com
Mon–Fri 12.30–2pm, 7–10pm; Sat 7–10pm. Closed Sun.
£50
Run for over 25 years by husband and wife team Clive and Anne Davidson, the Champany Inn was finally awarded a Michelin star in 2008. Scotch beef holds centre-stage here – and at the more informal Chop and Ale House next door – but there is also room for a plethora of seafood options on the menu, from Loch Gruinart oysters and lobsters to fillets of salmon hot-smoked to order over wood chips in the kitchen's own smokepot.

■ Creel Restaurant

The Harbour, 25 Lamer Street, Dunbar
01368 863 279
www.creelrestaurant.co.uk
Thu–Sat noon–2pm, 6.30–9pm; Sun noon–2pm. Closed Mon–Wed.
£18
Occupying a prime location just a stone's skip away from the harbour at Dunbar, the Creel is a sparsely decorated restaurant with low wooden ceilings, stripped floors and dark wooden furniture, making the food the star attraction. Owner-chef Logan Thorburn is a follower of Slow Food principles and endeavours to support local suppliers, using as much of East Lothian's native produce as possible. Elegant simplicity is at the forefront of the daily-changing menu on which, unsurprisingly, fish plays a starring role.

■ Creelers

3 Hunter Square, Edinburgh
0131 220 4447, www.creelers.co.uk
Mon–Thu noon–2pm, 5.30–10.30pm; Fri noon–2pm, 5.30–11pm; Sat noon–3pm, 5.30–11pm; Sun 1–3pm, 6–10.30pm.
£28
Sustainable seafood has always been at the heart of the Creelers concept – as anyone who has stopped by proprietor Tim James' Edinburgh farmers' market stall to snap up a scallop or fillets from the James family's own Arran smokehouse will know. In a prime spot, just metres from the Royal Mile, a relaxed, homely restaurant awaits, with terracotta floor tiles and chunky pine tables the backdrop to meals featuring some of Scotland's finest fish produce.

■ First Coast

97–101 Dalry Road, Edinburgh
0131 313 4404, www.first-coast.co.uk
Mon–Sat noon–2pm, 5–10.30pm. Closed Sun.
£16
First Coast opened in the west of Edinburgh in 2003 to instant acclaim, as the relaxed, neighbourhood bistro approach to dining was welcomed back into the capital's repertoire. Chef-proprietor Hector McRae might source local produce, but the cooking is far from parochial, with influences ranging from Scotland to Norway to the Far East. The inviting menu has no shortage of intriguing options, particularly for vegetarians, with provenance and sustainability the order of the day.

■ The Fruitmarket Gallery Café

Fruitmarket Gallery, 45 Market Street, Edinburgh
0131 226 1843, www.fruitmarket.co.uk
Mon–Sat 11.30am–4pm; Sun noon–4pm.
£10.50
Housed in a former Victorian fruit and vegetable market, as its name suggests, the Fruitmarket Gallery presents the very best in contemporary art just as its

ground-floor café serves some of the finest gallery food in town. An emphasis on carefully considered local and seasonal ingredients pays dividends when it comes to both the flavours and the menu ideas. Deli-filled rolls, salads, platters and specials are on offer throughout the year, the detail changing with each new exhibition.

The Grain Store

30 Victoria Street, Edinburgh
0131 225 7635
www.grainstore-restaurant.co.uk
Mon–Thu noon–2pm, 6–10pm; Fri noon–2pm, 6–11pm; Sat noon–3pm, 6–11pm; Sun noon–3pm, 6–10pm.
£26
Under the watchful eyes of owner Carlo Coxon and manager Paul MacPhail, the Grain Store has established itself as a stalwart of the Edinburgh dining scene since opening in 1991. This is an establishment known for its commitment to using the best of Scotland's produce – and the importance of highlighting its provenance – in a series of atmospheric stone-walled rooms above pretty Victoria Street. The menu reads like a who's who of Scotland's meat and fish, with oysters, duck, pigeon, lamb, beef and venison all vying for diners' attention.

The Grill at Dakota Forthbridge

Dakota Forthbridge, Ferrymuir Retail Park, South Queensferry
0870 423 4293
www.dakotaforthbridge.co.uk
Mon–Sat noon–2.30pm, 6–10pm, Sun noon–4pm, 6–10pm.
£22
The sleek, black, modern façade of Dakota at the Forth Road Bridge has an intriguing and slightly aloof quality. But once inside, this stylish hotel restaurant oozes class and sophistication. Chef Roy Brett's menu is dominated by the food of the sea – one highlight being a platter of oysters, lobster and crab served on a tower of ice – but there are a variety of land-based options on offer as well. Dakota has set its standards high, with its sustainable sourcing policies now endorsed by the Marine Stewardship Council (MSC) – the first restaurant in Scotland to receive such an award.

Iglu

2b Jamaica Street, Edinburgh
0131 476 5333, www.theiglu.com
Mon–Thu 6–10pm; Fri/Sun noon–2pm, 6–10pm.
£17
Since opening in late 2005, Iglu has been at the forefront of ethical sourcing in the Edinburgh restaurant scene. By specialising in organic, wild and local

First Coast

produce it is committed to finding the best Scottish ingredients available and working with small local boutique farms and producers to maintain high standards in meat, fish and seasonal vegetables. A cosy bar area downstairs serves home-made bar snacks while the main bistro is a slightly more formal and intimate affair.

The Kitchin

78 Commercial Quay, Edinburgh
0131 555 1755, www.thekitchin.com
Tue–Thu 12.30–1.45pm, 7–10pm; Fri/Sat 12.30–1.45pm, 6.45–10pm.
£38
Since opening in 2006 Tom Kitchin has brought a breath of fresh air to the Scottish culinary scene, scooping a Michelin star within his first year back home in Scotland. 'From nature to plate' is the philosophy here: all produce is seasonal and local, delivered daily to the restaurant by carefully selected suppliers, and is then transformed into inventive modern dishes with a French influence. An exceptionally good-value lunch menu is a key draw, as is the Kitchin's lively and easy-going approach to high-end dining.

The Mussel and Steak Bar

110 West Bow, Grassmarket, Edinburgh
0131 225 5028
www.musselandsteakbar.com
Mon–Fri noon–3pm, 6–10pm; Sat noon–10pm; Sun 12.30–10pm.
£26
If you're looking for a tender, char-grilled, farm-assured steak or generous pile of plump, steamed Scottish mussels then you've come to the right place. As well as the Buccleuch steaks of assorted cuts and sizes, and pots of mussels steamed in a choice of sauces, other seafood staples such as oysters and scallops make regular appearances, all served up in a relaxed environment where white-

washed walls, wooden tables and sea green banquettes complement the no-nonsense style of cooking.

Mussel Inn

61–65 Rose Street, Edinburgh
0131 225 5979, www.mussel-inn.com
Mon–Thu noon–3pm, 5.30–10pm; Fri–Sun noon–10pm.
£20
The Mussel Inn has a direct link to the farmers who cultivate the shellfish served in its Edinburgh and Glasgow restaurants. Its mussels and oysters are supplied by farms belonging to the Scottish Shellfish Marketing Group, formed in 1992 when a number of farmers combined as a co-operative to supply supermarkets, wholesalers and restaurants with the finest rope-grown mussels and oysters. The two informal bistro-style restaurants bring a casual dining approach to the best of Scottish seafood.

Number One

1 Princes Street, Edinburgh
0131 557 6727,
www.restaurantnumberone.com
Mon–Sun 6.30-10pm
£55 (set dinner)
The most opulent of Edinburgh's burgeoning set of Michelin-starred restaurants, with gold velour seating and deep burgundy panelled walls, Number One is set in the basement of the venerable Balmoral Hotel at the very heart of the capital. A fine array of top quality meat and fish are prepared with an eclectic twist in dishes such as slow cooked sirloin of Border beef with white onion purée and Perigord truffle jus, or wild halibut with turnip and saffron gratin. Executive chef Jeff Bland and head chef Craig Sandle also produce a seven-course tasting menu (£60), available with wines selected to match each dish (£50).

■ Oloroso

33 Castle Street, Edinburgh
0131 226 7614, www.oloroso.co.uk
Mon–Sat noon–2.30pm, 7–10pm; Sun
12.30–2.30pm, 7–10.30pm.
£33

Three floors up, with magnificent views from the heart of the New Town over the Edinburgh skyline, Tony Singh's flagship restaurant has been one of the capital's most glamorous dining venues of the decade. The wide terrace is surely one of the country's most compelling al fresco dining (or cocktail-sipping) locations. The à la carte menu is innovative and contemporary, with the selection of grills displaying an essential affinity with prime Scottish produce, including a range of Highland beef steaks.

■ Plumed Horse

50–54 Henderson Street, Edinburgh
0131 554 5556, www.plumedhorse.co.uk
Tue–Sat noon–1.30pm, 7–9pm. Closed
Sun/Mon.
£39 (set dinner)

Edinburgh's most recent Michelin-starred restaurant has gone from strength to strength since upping sticks from its previous Dumfriesshire home three years ago, with chef-proprietor Tony Borthwick continually showing that his business hunches are as sharp as his culinary instincts. From the small, intimate dining room to the eclectic works by local artists adorning the walls, his personality and vision are present in every aspect – and especially when it comes to the elegant, innovative food.

■ La Potinière

Main Street, Gullane
01620 843214, www.la-potiniere.co.uk
Wed–Sun 12.30–1.30pm, 7–8.30pm.
Closed Mon/Tue.
£20.50 (set dinner)

Award-winning food is often accompanied by a great deal of pomp, but this modest East Lothian restaurant is decorated simply and relies on the appreciative chatter of diners for atmosphere, letting the food do the talking much of the time. Being two of the founder members of the Scotch Beef Club, owners/chefs Mary Runciman and Keith Marley believe in using only the freshest and the finest ingredients available. The menu is brief – just two choices per course – and changes regularly according to availability and the seasons.

■ Restaurant Martin Wishart

54 The Shore, Edinburgh
0131 553 3557
www.martin-wishart.co.uk
Tue–Fri noon–2pm, 6.45–9.30pm; Sat
noon–1pm, 6.45–9.30pm. Closed
Sun/Mon.

£65 (six-course tasting menu)

Having won Edinburgh's first Michelin star back in 2001, Martin Wishart's kitchen is famed for its tasting menu, featuring six small but perfectly formed courses bursting with intriguing and delightful flavours, textures, colours and tasting sensations. There's now a cook school located a few streets away, allowing the capital's budding cooks access to some of the chefs' finely honed skills, and most recently a second Martin Wishart restaurant on the shores of Loch Lomond at Cameron House.

■ The Stockbridge Restaurant

54 St Stephen Street, Edinburgh
0131 226 6766
www.thestockbridgerestaurant.co.uk
Tue 7–9.30pm; Wed–Fri 12.30–2.30pm,
7–9.30pm; Sat 7–10pm; Sun 7–9.30pm.
Closed Mon.
£26

With twinkling fairy lights illuminating the entrance and crisp white linen and golden soft furnishings brightening the interior, the Stockbridge Restaurant is an elegant dining space that happily marries the neighbourhood's bohemian past and affluent present. Owner and head chef Jason Gallagher's enticing menu pays respect to the Scottish seasons and incorporates innovative takes on European classics, such as a wild rabbit carbonara and scallops with spring onion blinis.

■ Sweet Melindas

11 Roseneath Street, Edinburgh
0131 229 7953
www.sweetmelindas.co.uk
Mon 6–10pm; Tue–Sat noon–2pm,
6–10pm. Closed Sun.
£22.50 (set dinner)

Over the last ten years Sweet Melindas has developed a reputation for sourcing the best local and seasonal ingredients with a strong emphasis on seafood and game. Every morning chef-proprietor Kevin O'Connor hand-picks the best fish from Eddie's Seafood Market next door, and makes everything that is served in the restaurant from scratch – from the fresh bread and tapenade to the Valrhona truffles served with after-dinner coffee.

■ Tailend Restaurant and Fish Bar

14–15 Albert Place, Edinburgh
0131 555 3577
www.tailendrestaurant.com
Mon–Sun 11.30am–10pm.
£14

Co-owned by chief frier Colin Cromar (one-time proprietor of the renowned Anstruther Fish Bar) this cheerful venture prepares fresh fish and chips to order

throughout the day. The menu format is simple, with several types of fish primed and ready to be dipped in batter, rolled in breadcrumbs, or simply grilled with a drizzle of olive oil. Haddock, cod, langoustine and lemon sole all make it on to the main list, but take a peak at the specials board to see what else the day's catch has brought in.

■ Tony's Table

58a North Castle Street, Edinburgh
0131 226 6743, www.tonystable.co.uk
Tue–Sat noon–2.30pm, 6.30–10.30pm.
Closed Sun/Mon.
£20 (set dinner)

Following the success of Oloroso and Roti, Edinburgh restaurateur Tony Singh opened Tony's Table in early 2009 with the aim of serving quality uncomplicated food at reasonable prices in a relaxed environment. With a menu full of global influences, the kitchen always makes imaginative use of a range of Scottish produce. The new venture also houses an on-site bakery, baking fresh products throughout the day both for Tony's Table and to supply surrounding restaurants and hotel kitchens.

■ Tower Restaurant

Museum of Scotland, Chambers Street,
Edinburgh
0131 225 3003,
www.tower-restaurant.com
Mon–Sun noon–11pm.
£31

In the running for Edinburgh's best-located restaurant, the Tower is on the top floor of the Museum of Scotland and enjoys spectacular views of the castle – particularly after dark. One of three restaurants in the capital run by James Thomson's Witchery Group (The Witchery by the Castle and Rhubarb are the others), this is a popular and glamorous dining location, with its grill menu in particular commanding the attention with succulent steaks and tasty shellfish options.

■ Urban Angel

• 1 Forth Street, Edinburgh
0131 556 6323, www.urban-angel.co.uk
Mon–Sun 9.30am–10pm.
• 121 Hanover Street, Edinburgh
0131 225 6215, www.urban-angel.co.uk
Mon–Thur 10am–10pm; Fri/Sat
10am–11pm; Sun 10am–5pm.
£20

Urban Angel has become well known in Edinburgh for producing fresh, stylish food with a conscience since opening in 2004. It has two branches in the city centre and both are operations where uncluttered white walls, solid wooden tables and smooth-running service keep the focus on the carefully crafted food.

Esperante, Fairmont, St Andrews

Where to eat and drink in Scotland

Each business receives an annual visit by an assessor to ensure that they are maintaining high standards.

Businesses are assessed on • Hospitality and service • Quality and presentation of food and drink • Quality and freshness of ingredients • Housekeeping and hygiene.

So you can be assured of a great eating experience wherever you see the EatScotland logo. EatScotland Silver and Gold awards indicate excellent and outstanding places to dine.

Arbroath Smokies, Portsoy Boat Festival, Aberdeenshire

Discover EatScotland eating establishments throughout the country, as well as information on Scotland's fantastic produce and events, at **EatScotland.com**

Live it. Visit *Scotland.*
eatscotland.com   0845 22 55 121

Local, organic, Fairtrade and free-range are the watch words, and the menus boast a wide range of brunches, tapas and tempting mains, updated regularly to include the best seasonal produce.

■ The Vintners Rooms

The Vaults, 87 Giles Street, Leith, Edinburgh
0131 554 6767,
www.thevintnersrooms.com
Tue–Sat noon–2pm, 7–10pm. Closed Sun/Mon.

£34

Well-known Edinburgh restaurateur Silvio Praino presides over an impeccable 18th-century dining room, the historic destination of French wine for Scots merchants, its delicate plasterwork illuminated only by candles. Echoes of the Auld Alliance between France and Scotland are still very evident with dishes from chef Patrice Ginestière such as Aberdeen Angus fillet in an understated truffle sauce, served on a cushion of spinach. An approachable bar lunch menu puts this lovely location well within reach for more modest dining occasions.

■ Wedgwood the Restaurant

267 Canongate, Edinburgh
0131 558 8737
www.wedgwoodtherestaurant.co.uk
Mon–Sat noon–3pm, 6–10pm; Sun 12.30–3.30pm, 6–10pm.

£24

Behind a modest cream and brown exterior lies an elegant dining room producing imaginative Scottish dishes of the highest quality. The menu changes with the seasons and subtly combines elements of Asian cuisine with more traditional takes on carefully sourced local produce. An enthusiasm and love of food is obvious here, and the signature Salmon 3 Ways (poached with black pudding, smoked with wasabi and caviar, and cured with fennel and celeriac) showcases the restaurant's innovative approach perfectly.

GREATER GLASGOW & CLYDESIDE

■ An Lochan

340 Crow Road, Glasgow
0141 338 6606, www.anlochan.co.uk
Tue–Sat noon–3pm, 6–9.30pm; Sun noon–3pm. Closed Mon.

£25

An Lochan is run by the McKie family, who have hotels of the same name in Tighnabruaich, Argyll and Tormaukin, Perthshire. In this Glasgow outpost, the elegant but relaxed dining room features whitewashed walls bearing fish-centric modern art. Chef Claire McKie selects the freshest seafood from trusted suppliers in the Kyles of Bute while her meat and game come straight from Glendevon in Perthshire. How many big city restaurants can say they are on first-name terms with the people who catch their langoustines and stalk their venison?

■ Arisaig

Merchant Square, Glasgow
0141 553 1010
www.arisaigrestaurant.co.uk
Mon–Sun noon–3pm, 5–10pm.

£22

Having relocated to Glasgow's Merchant City after six years on St Vincent Street, co-owners Naveed Rashid and Stephen Bonomi continue to bring their passion for quality Scottish produce and relaxed dining to the Arisaig experience. The menu is packed with evidence of exhaustive ingredient sourcing – venison from the Argyll hills, Buccleuch beef, Isle of Shuna mussels, Shetland smoked salmon or Loch Etive oysters – showcasing some of the best the country has to offer.

■ Blas

1397 Argyle Street, Glasgow
0141 357 4328,
www.blasrestaurant.com
Tue–Sun noon–10pm.

£16

Blas (meaning 'taste' or 'flavour' in Gaelic) brings a touch of Hebridean sophistication to central Glasgow. Its passionate sourcing policy results in a menu featuring smoked salmon from an Ullapool smoke-house, goat's cheese from Ayrshire and of course Stornoway black pudding. Creel basket light fittings and modern Scottish paintings of island landscapes help to create an understated yet smart atmosphere, while the tapas-style system of ordering allows customers to sample a number of different dishes from the eclectic menu.

■ Cail Bruich

725 Great Western Road, Glasgow
0141 334 6265, www.cailbruich.co.uk
Tue–Fri noon–3pm, 5–10pm; Sat 10am–3pm, 5–10pm; Sun 10am–9pm. Closed Mon.

£24

Brothers Paul and Chris Charalambous opened the original Cail Bruich (meaning 'eat well' in Gaelic) in Quarriers Village by Bridge of Weir in 2006 and a couple of years later took on a second pitch in Glasgow's West End. Modern Scottish cooking is the order of the day on a menu showcasing Quothquan duck, Perthshire venison, Stornoway black pudding, North Sea monkfish and Kirkmichael pheasant – a sure sign that provenance is all important.

■ Fanny Trollopes

1066 Argyle Street, Glasgow
0141 564 6464, www.fannytrollopes.co.uk
Tue–Sat noon–2.30pm; 5.30–10pm. Closed Sun/Mon.

£18

The narrow dining room at Fanny Trollopes has only a handful of tables, so advance booking is essential. As you browse through the menu, staff may offer to tell you the story of Fanny, who arrived from Brazil over a hundred years ago and whose presence is felt in the neighbourhood. The menu is concise, and nods to the best of seasonal and Scottish produce, from Loch Fyne mussels and Bradan Rost salmon to Buccleuch Estate beef.

■ Gamba

225a West George Street, Glasgow
0141 572 0899, www.gamba.co.uk
Mon–Sat noon–2.30pm, 5–10.30pm. Sun 5–10.30pm.

£32

Gamba celebrated its tenth anniversary in 2008, the reward for being one of the most consistently excellent, top-end restaurants in Glasgow. Chef and co-owner Derek Marshall sources the freshest of seafood from the markets and displays a deft hand in the preparation of anything from bream to scallops. A broad range of global influences are evident in his cooking, which may feature curry spices, soya sauce or puy lentils in equal measure.

■ Gandolfi Fish

84 Albion Street, Glasgow
0141 552 9475, www.cafegandolfi.com
Tue–Sat noon–2.30pm, 5–10.30pm; Sun noon–9pm. Closed Mon.

£20

With its mirrored panels, polished furniture and huge glass front Gandolfi Fish is sleek – as is the cooking, where quality ingredients are served with a minimum of fuss. Conscious of his Gaelic heritage, owner Seumas MacInnes puts his faith in Scottish produce, believing it to be some of the best in the world. Barra crab, west coast oysters and sustainable pollack all feature on a menu unsurprisingly focussed on the fruits of the sea.

■ Heart Buchanan

380 Byres Road, Glasgow
0141 334 7626, heartbuchanan.co.uk
Mon–Fri 8.30am–9.30pm; Sat 9am–9pm; Sun 10am–6pm.

£8

Fiona Buchanan's bustling deli-café has a rustic authenticity, with shelves crammed full of goodies and well chosen wines. The stuffed head of a gargantuan Highland cow watches over the Byres Road crowd who line up at the counter for sandwiches, salads and sugar-glazed confections to takeaway or enjoy at the mezzanine bar. Here, emphasis is placed on the provenance of the ingredients stocked – from Scottish new potatoes to Uist langoustine and Ma Mackinnon's jams – based on the belief that a product's origin truly influences its quality and taste.

■ Martin Wishart at Loch Lomond

De Vere Cameron House Hotel, By Balloch
01389 722504,
www.martinwishartlochlomond.co.uk
Wed–Sat 6.30–10pm; Sun noon–2.30pm, 7–10pm
£50 (five-course tasting menu)
Martin Wishart opened this second branch of his burgeoning empire in December 2008, adding a further splash of sophistication to the already classy Cameron House Hotel. The famous five-course tasting menu is a feature here, and you can be sure that the meat and seafood on offer will be as fresh and beautiful as Scotland has to offer. Perhaps a Michelin star is on its way to the bonnie banks of Loch Lomond soon.

■ Michael Caines @ ABode

129 Bath Street, Glasgow
0141 221 6789, www.michaelcaines.com
Tue–Sat noon–2.30pm, 6–10pm. Closed Sun/Mon.
£34
With its pale green walls and immaculate table linen, Michael Caines is a refined backdrop for sophisticated food. Set in the ABode hotel, this is one of a number of dining venues around the UK overseen by Caines, yet the menu here is clearly tuned in to the ingredients available in Scotland, with shellfish, game and Mey Selection beef all in evidence. The imaginative Amazing Grazing menu offers three taster courses for less than the price of a starter, making it possible to sample the fine-dining experience in a refreshingly unintimidating way.

■ Mussel Inn

157 Hope Street, Glasgow
0141 572 1405, www.mussel-inn.com
Mon–Thu noon–2.30pm, 5–10pm; Fri/Sat noon–10pm; Sun 5–10pm.
£20
A branch of the restaurant of the same name in Edinburgh. See entry in Edinburgh & Lothians listings above.

■ Òran Mór

731–735 Great Western Road, Glasgow
0141 357 6200, www.oran-mor.co.uk
Mon–Sat noon–3pm, 5–10pm; Sun noon–4pm, 5–10pm.
£23

An Lochan

Situated in a former church at the heart of the West End, Òran Mór is a multi-purpose arts venue run by entrepreneur Colin Beattie. The brasserie decor is a mix of styles, a kind of updated Scottish spin on Art Nouveau, giving the room a slight Viennese atmosphere, with lush velvet curtains, church candles, wrought ironwork and tables set into comfy carved wooden booths. The brasserie serves contemporary cuisine with a French slant using Scottish produce.

■ The Sisters

• 1a Ashwood Gardens, 512 Crow Road, Glasgow
0141 434 1179, www.thesisters.co.uk
Tue–Thu noon–2.30pm, 5.30–9pm; Fri/Sat noon–2.30pm, 5–9.30pm; Sun noon–8pm. Closed Mon.
• 36 Kelvingrove Street, Glasgow
0141 564 1157, www.thesisters.co.uk
Tue–Thu noon–2.30pm, 5.30–9pm; Fri/Sat noon–2.30pm, 5–9.30pm; Sun noon–8pm. Closed Mon.
£23
Now with two restaurants in Glasgow – one at Jordanhill and a newer branch at Kelvingrove – The Sisters has established itself as a restaurant dedicated to providing excellent service and home cooking of the highest quality. The eponymous sisters are Jacqueline and Pauline O'Donnell, whose passion for sourcing shows in a menu brimming with the likes of Ullapool smoked salmon, Uist scallops, roast Arran pumpkin and wild Arisaig venison.

■ Storm

82 West Clyde Street, Helensburgh
01436 678318,
Wed–Sat noon–2.30pm, 6.30–10pm; Sun
11.30am–4.30pm. Closed Mon/Tue
£22
Opened in 2006 by veteran Glasgow chef
Hugh MacShannon (formerly of Rogano
and One Devonshire Gardens), Storm has
acquired itself a reputation for producing
some of the finest cuisine in the west of
Scotland. The interior is both calming and
plush, and exudes a sense of humour
entirely suited to the often inclement
Helensburgh weather. Scottish produce is
predictably to the fore, with comforting
yet modern bistro dishes ensuring the
locals keep weekends booked up far in
advance.

■ Stravaigin

• 28–30 Gibson Street, Glasgow
0141 334 2665, www.stravaigin.com
Mon–Thu 5–11pm; Fri–Sun 11am–11pm.
£25
• Stravaigin 2, 8 Ruthven Lane, Glasgow
0141 334 7165, www.stravaigin.com
Mon–Fri noon–11pm; Sat/Sun
11am–11pm.
£19
These glamorous yet informal west end
restaurants are two of Glasgow's
favourites. Stravaigin' is the old Scottish
word for roaming, reflected in innovative
and exciting food showing myriad
influences and local ingredients all put
together with flair, passion and
imagination. The daily menu
demonstrates a consistent desire to work
with new ingredients, combinations and
flavours, and the 'think global, eat local'
philosophy shines in everything from
Shetland crab cake to Carsphain fallow
deer.

■ Two Fat Ladies

• Two Fat Ladies @ The Buttery, 652
Argyle Street, Glasgow
0141 221 8188
www.twofatladiesrestaurant.com
Mon–Sat noon–3pm, 5–10.30pm; Sun
12.30–9pm.
• 118a Blythswood Street, Glasgow
0141 847 0088
Mon–Thu noon–3pm, 5.30–10pm; Fri/Sat
noon–3pm, 5.30–11pm; Sun noon–3pm,
5–9pm.
• 88 Dumbarton Road, Glasgow
0141 339 1944, Mon–Sat noon–3pm,
5.30–10.30pm; Sun 5.30–10.30pm.
£28
Boasting three distinctive venues around
Glasgow, owner Ryan James and his
impressive team have been recipients of
numerous awards over the years since
opening the original Dumbarton Road
branch in 1989, testament to the quality
of ingredients and cooking on show here.

Storm

The heavily fish-oriented menus are
almost the same across the branches,
even if the settings are slightly different.

■ Ubiquitous Chip

12 Ashton Lane, Glasgow
0141 334 5007
www.ubiquitouschip.co.uk
Mon–Sat noon–2.30pm, 5.30–11pm; Sun
12.30–3pm, 6.30–11pm.
£34.85 (set dinner)
One of Glasgow's most famous and well-
loved restaurants, The Chip consists of a
glass-roofed, cobbled courtyard liberally
supplied with leafy plants and a small fish
pond, giving it a pleasant outdoor/indoor
feel. A west-end institution since opening
back in 1971, the owners have
consistently sought to state the
provenance of the food they serve,
treating it in a simple, wholesome and
imaginative way without losing sight of
Scotland's food traditions.

SOUTHERN SCOTLAND

■ Braidwoods

Drumastle Mill Cottage, Saltcoats Road,
by Dalry
01294 833544, www.braidwoods.co.uk
Tue 7–9pm; Wed–Sat noon–1.45pm,
7–9pm; Sun noon–1.45pm. Closed Mon.
(May–Sep closed Sun).
£38 (set dinner)
Having won a Michelin star in 2000 – still
held to this day – Braidwoods exudes a
quiet confidence. The small dining room
boasts a handful of linen-clad tables, and
ostentation is limited to a few colourful
original paintings on the walls. Fourteen
years after Keith and Nicola Braidwood
took over the tatty Ayrshire but'n'ben that

previously occupied this site, their
frequently changing menu is a platform
for quality local produce presented with
expansive imagination and meticulous
care.

■ Fins Restaurant

Fencefoot, Fairlie
01475 568989, www.fencebay.co.uk
Tue–Sat noon–2.30pm, 7–9pm; Sun
noon–2.30pm. Closed Mon.
£27
It's a seafood restaurant, it's a farm shop,
it's a self-catering cottage – in short, it's
a little piece of foodie heaven on the
west coast, between Largs and
Ardrossan. The restaurant serves fish-
themed treats such as Cullen skink or
Thai fish cakes, and there are hot and
cold seafood platters available, with
seasonal catches from local waters
including langoustines, scallops and
squat lobster tails. Smoked salmon,
kippers, pates and more are also
available from the online shop.

■ Fouters Bistro

2a Academy Street, Ayr
01292 261391, www.fouters.co.uk
Tue–Thu noon–2pm, 6–9pm; Fri/Sat
noon–2pm, 6–9.30pm. Closed Sun/Mon.
£38
Since assuming ownership in late 2006,
chef George Ramage has put his stamp
on this Ayr landmark restaurant. The
basement premises were once 18th-
century bank vaults, but with space for
only about twenty covers the dining room
is cosy and intimate all the same. The
menu places a heavy emphasis on
Scottish ingredients – whether wood
pigeon, Stornoway black pudding or

Moray Firth seafood – all presented with trademark flair, passion and imagination.

◼ Knockinaam Lodge

Portpatrick, Dumfries
01776 810471
www.knockinaamlodge.com
Mon–Sun 12.30–2.30pm, 7–9.30pm.
£50 (set dinner)
Sitting at the waters edge, facing the Irish Sea, this hotel restaurant has a picture perfect location. Rich flavours and a good variety of dishes grace the Michelin star-rated menu, while white tablecloths and darkwood furniture giving it a slightly old-fashioned elegance. Bookings are essential if you wish to dine here.

◼ Smith's at Gretna Green

Gretna Green, Dumfries
01461 337007
www.smithsgretnagreen.com
Mon–Sun noon–9.30pm.
£18
A contemporary bespoke hotel in the heart of Gretna Green is revolutionary enough. But this one offers a good standard of smart comfort food at very reasonable prices, with interesting fish and game dishes, as well as lovely fresh vegetarian options also available. Menus change every three months to showcase seasonal ingredients.

◼ The Sorn Inn

35 Main Street, Sorn, Ayrshire
01290 551305, www.sorninn.com
Tue–Fri noon–2.30pm, 6–9pm; Sat noon–9pm; Sun 12.30–7pm. Closed Mon.
£17
The Sorn Inn has earned many plaudits for putting a quiet little Ayrshire village on the map, among them a much-prized Michelin Bib Gourmand for good food at moderate prices, which it has now held for four years. The old whitewashed inn houses a relaxed restaurant combining fine dining and brasserie-style elements, and owner-chef Craig Grant's menu also manages to balance the elaborate and the homely, using seasonal and local ingredients wherever possible.

◼ Windelstraw Lodge

Tweed Valley, Walkerburn
01896 870636, www.windlestraw.co.uk
£42 (set dinner)
Alan and Julie Reid's secluded but comfortable country house hotel by the banks of the Tweed near Innerleithen has six guest bedrooms and a dining room that makes more effort than most to show off the produce of the surrounding region. This includes fish from Eyemouth, meat from excellent local farms such as Peelham and leaves from its own garden.

CENTRAL SCOTLAND & FIFE

◼ An Lochan

Glendevon, Perthshire
01259 781252, www.anlochan.co.uk
Mon–Sun noon–3pm, 5.30–9pm.
£28
See An Lochan entries in the listings for Greater Glasgow & Clydeside and also Highlands, Islands & Argyll.

◼ Andrew Fairlie @ Gleneagles

Gleneagles Hotel, Auchterarder, Perthshire
01764 694267, www.andrewfairlie.com
Mon–Sat 6.30–10pm. Closed Sun.
£73 (set dinner)
Scotland's only Michelin two-star restaurant, a distinction it has held since 1996, this is one of the country's most sought-after upmarket dining experiences. It's not, however, an intimidatingly grand affair: set in a modestly sized room in the heart of Gleneagles hotel, it is stylish rather than stuffy, decorated with leaf motifs and framed contemporary artworks. Six-course dégustation and market menus are available (at £95 and £85 respectively), the dishes deceptively simple yet imbued with flavour and care. Famously, Fairlie's suppliers include his brother Jim, a sheep farmer, and Robin Gray, the salad leaf grower based on Arran.

■ Ardeonaig Hotel & Restaurant

South Road, Loch Tay, Ardeonaig, Perthshire
01567 820 400
www.ardeonaighhotel.co.uk
Mon–Sun noon–10pm.
£30

Set on the shores of Loch Tay, this traditional looking but contemporary styled small hotel is run by chef Pete Gottgens. A South African native, his enthusiasm for Scottish produce has seen him establish his own herd of black-face sheep, as well as ensure a supply of veg, herbs and salad from local gardens. The property itself boasts 14 acres of beautifully kept private gardens, while the recently refurbished kitchen and dining areas now include a seperate wine cellar and cosy 'study' eating areas.

■ Barley Bree

6 Willowbrae Street, Muthill, near Crieff, Perthshire
01764 681451, www.barleybree.com
Tue–Sun noon–2pm, 6–9pm. Closed Mon.
£23

Barley Bree Restaurant with Rooms keeps it interesting by changing the menu every week, to coincide with seasonal produce. For the meat-eaters, shooting season brings with it a banquet of fresh game. Adding a friendly feel to proceedings, Barley Bree also bake extra loaves of homemeade bread for customers to take a loaf home.

■ East Haugh Country House Hotel

by Pitlochry, Perth & Kinross
01796 473121, www.easthaugh.co.uk
Mon–Sun noon–2pm, 6–10pm.
£45 (set dinner)

This hotel offers ample offerings for those staying over or simply dropping by for a visit, with a bar menu comprising entirely of local produce, including vegetables from the hotel's own kitchen garden. Game is a speciality here, while the proximity of the hotel to Pitlochry allows it to offer an early dining option for theatregoers.

■ Huntingtower Hotel

Crieff Road, Perth, Perthshire
01738 583771,
www.huntingtowerhotel.co.uk
Mon–Sun noon–2.30pm; 6–9.30pm.
£26

Set beside a famous castle on the outskirts of Perth, Huntingtower Hotel is a traditional white stonewashed building with darkwood beams, set in six acres of landscaped gardens. There's a flavour of the upmarket country house hotel about the place, while chef Bill McNicoll's kitchen draws on the considerable array

of good food on his Perthshire doorstep for his French-influenced menu.

■ Mhor Fish

Main Street, Callander, Perthshire
01877 330213, www.mhor.net
Tue–Sun 10am–8.30pm. Closed Mon.
£12

This may well be the best fish and chip shop in the country. It combines the traditions of the familiar local chippie with the gourmet delights of a fishmonger's counter enabling you to pick and choose your own from catches fresh off the boats on the north east coast. Just ask for your selection to be grilled, seared, baked or fried and draw on the skilful kitchen team trained by the fine dining expertise of the Lewis family from Monachyle Mhor up the glen. You can sit in or takeaway.

■ Monachyle Mhor

Balquhidder, Lochearnhead, Perthshire
01877 384622
www.monachylemhor.com
Mon–Sun noon–1.45pm, 7–8.45pm.
£46 (set dinner)

This stylish gem of a hotel is the full stop at the end of a six mile single track road along Loch Voil, where the view from the dining-room window gladdens the heart even on the dreichest of days. Chef Tom Lewis has lived in the glen for more than 25 years and is the talent behind Monachyle Mhor restaurant's success story, which now stretches into nearby Callander with the family's Mhor Fish and Mhor Bread operations. Local, seasonal beef and game are the foundations of the lunch and dinner menus at the hotel, but with a gentle innovative twist here and there.

■ The Peat Inn

Peat Inn, by Cupar, Fife
01334 840206, www.thepeatinn.co.uk
Tue–Sat 12.30–2pm, 7–9.30pm. Closed Sun/Mon.
£29

The Peat Inn has existed on this spot since the 1700s and now, owned by award-winning chef Geoffrey Smeddle and his wife Katherine, it is one of Scotland's most cherished destination restaurants. Three small dining rooms make up the restaurant, where an atmosphere of refined elegance combines with friendly and attentive service. A French influence permeates the lunch and dinner menus, but the focus is firmly on Scottish produce, the availability of which was one of Smeddle's main draws when taking over the restaurant in 2006.

■ Sangster's

51 High Street, Elie
01333 331001, www.sangsters.co.uk

Tue 7–8.30pm; Wed–Fri 12.30–1.30pm, 7–8.30pm; Sat 7–8.30pm; Sun 12.30–1.30pm. Closed Mon.
£30 (set dinner)

Six years after opening this petite restaurant in Elie, chef Bruce Sangster won his first Michelin star in January 2009, having worked tirelessly at creating inventive, taste-driven dishes. The ever-changing menu features food sourced as locally as possible, and certainly from Scotland. From diver scallops from Ross-shire, crab from Kyle of Lochalsh, wild mushrooms from Speyside, venison from Glen Isla to pears, apples and fresh herbs from the back garden: local is best.

■ The Seafood Restaurant

• The Scores, St Andrews, Fife
01334 479475
www.theseafoodrestaurant.com
Mon–Sun noon–2pm, 6.30–10pm; Sun 12.30–2.30pm, 6.30–10pm.
£45 (set dinner)
• 16 West End, St Monans, Fife
01333 730327
www.theseafoodrestaurant.com
Mon–Sun noon–2.30pm, 6.30–9.30pm (winter hours: Tue–Sat noon–2.30pm, 6.30–9.30pm; Sun noon–2.30pm. Closed Mon.)
£35 (set dinner)

These sister restaurants in Fife have some of the best views going: the newer St Andrews branch is an extraordinary glass box perched next to the sea with panoramic views, while the original St Monans restaurant overlooks a pretty East Neuk harbour. Both restaurants, unsurprisingly, place a major emphasis on the fruits of Scotland's waters, and menus may feature Seil Island oysters, Isle of May lobsters, west coast scallops and locally smoked and kiln-roasted salmon.

■ 63 Tay Street

63 Tay Street, Perth
01738 441451, www.63taystreet.co.uk
Tue–Sat noon–2pm, 6.30–9.30pm.
£33.95 (set dinner)

As the name suggest, 63 Tay Street is situated in the heart of Perth, close to the River Tay. It is the first restaurant venture of local boy Graeme Pallister, who worked in various celebrated kitchens in the UK and in Jersey before realising his dream of going solo. The light, contemporary space makes for a sophisticated dining area, where locally sourced meat and seafood is showcased on a menu teeming with global influences.

■ The Wee Restaurant

17 Main Street, North Queensferry
01383 616263,
www.theweerestaurant.co.uk

Monachyle Mhor

Tue–Sat noon–2pm, 6.30–9pm; Sun noon–3pm. Closed Mon.

£22

As the name suggests, the Wee Restaurant is a cosy space, seating as it does only 24 covers. Established in early 2006, it is owned and run by Craig and Vikki Wood, whose ethos is to serve good seasonal food with fine wines in a relaxed atmosphere. The restaurant was presented with a Michelin Bib Gourmand (the award for good food at moderate prices) in 2008 and continues to prove that size isn't everything when it comes to quality restaurants.

NORTH EAST SCOTLAND

Castleton House Hotel

Castleton of Eassie, Glamis
01307 840340,
www.castletonglamis.co.uk
Mon–Sat noon–2pm, 6.30–9pm.

£30

Three miles from Glamis Castle in Angus, this small country house hotel offers elegant dining, while doing away with the formality of a dress code. Ingredients travel as little as possible before reaching the plate – take the Tamworth pork for example, where pigs are reared on the grounds, fed by windfall orchard apples and veg from the hotel garden. Free-range eggs and seasonal strawberries and raspberries from the garden can also be bought in the hotel shop.

Eat on the Green

Udny Green, Ellon
01651 842337,
www.eatonthegreen.co.uk
Sun & Wed/Thu noon–2pm,

6.30–8.30pm; Fri noon–2pm, 6–9pm; Sat 6–9pm. Closed Mon/Tue

£42 (set dinner)

Originally the village pub, and now a 70-cover restaurant which has expanded into the old post office, Craig Wilson's popular and well-respected restaurant is something of a flag-bearer for rural Aberdeenshire. A French style of cooking prevails in the upmarket style dishes, but with suppliers such as the respected Store, a near neighbour, this is a place with its roots in the local area.

The Milton

Milton of Crathes, North Deeside Road, Crathes, Banchory
01330 844566, www.themilton.co.uk
Sat–Fri 9.30am–9.30pm; Sun 10.30am–7pm.

£19.50 (set dinner)

Seasonal produce cherry-picked from local suppliers is on the menu here. On the outskirts of Aberdeen, this picturesque spot makes for a good pit-stop for coffee and home-baked scones, or a more filling lunch using ingredients sourced from within ten miles of the kitchen, such as free-range chicken, with creamed Scottish kale and Wark Farm's smoked pancetta. Check website for events, such as jazz evenings or Spanish dinner nights.

The Tolbooth

Old Pier, Stonehaven
01569 762287,
www.tolbooth-restaurant.co.uk
Tue–Sun noon–2pm, 6–9.30pm (Oct–Apr closed Sun).

£22

A location right beside the old stone

harbour in Stonehaven is about as ideal as you could ask for in a North East seafood restaurant. The catch from the creel boats based here often make their way up to the restaurant, set in a sixteenth-century building that has been a prison and excise house in former incarnations. Fish and shellfish dominate the menu in some finely designed dishes, though there are meat and vegetarian options here too.

HIGHLANDS, ISLANDS & ARGYLL

Airds Hotel & Restaurant

Port Appin
01631 730236, www.airds-hotel.com
Noon–1.45pm, 7.30–9pm.

This three AA rosette-winning establishment changes its menu daily and occasionally offers a seven-course Gourmet Menu accompanied by wines to suit. Lunch is described as informal although for evening service diners are requested to refrain from wearing trainers, T-shirts, shorts or jeans.

The Albannach

Baddidarroch, Lochinver
01571 844407, www.thealbannach.co.uk
Tue–Sun 7.30pm til late. Closed Mon.

£50 (set dinner)

Twenty years under the same ownership, the Albannach has been recognised with a Michelin star to accompany the host of other awards it has received over the years. A dark wood dining room in the hotel is the backdrop for a set five course menu described as a 'showcase for all things local, free range and wild'. Bookings are essential.

■ An Lochan

Shore Road, Tighnabruaich, Argyll
01700 811239, www.anlochan.co.uk
Mon–Sun noon–3pm, 5.30–9pm.
£28
Owned and run by the McKie family since
1997, the orginal branch of this award-
winning restaurant is nestled on the
shores of Loch Fyne, facing the Isle of
Bute – An Lochan meaning 'by the loch'
in Gaelic. An outpost in Glasgow and,
most recently, the conversion of a 17th-
century coaching inn at Tormauklin,
Perthshire, completes the trio. Loch Fyne
scallops, Perthshire venison, Stornoway
black pudding – all the usual suspects
are present on a modern, French-
influenced menu with a decidedly
inventive twist.

■ The Anderson

Union Street, Fortrose
01381 620236, www.theanderson.co.uk
Sun 1–3pm; Mon–Sun 6–11pm
£18
Scottish ingredients are given an
international makeover in this restaurant
and bar in the village of Fortrose, near
Inverness. A Manhattan seafood chowder
is loaded with queenie scallop and
Shetland mussels, or there is a decidedly
un-Highlands-style coconut shrimp
starter, served with a banana and sweet
chilli dipping sauce. For those who feel
like making a long weekend of it, there
are nine ensuite bedrooms above the
dining room.

■ Applecross Inn

Shore Street, Applecross, Wester Ross
01520 744262,
www.applecross.uk.com/inn
Mon–Sun noon–9pm
Prawns from Applecross Bay are a regular
favourite here, as is the fluffy haddock and
chips, but otherwise the menu changes
daily to showcase the best of local,
seasonal produce. Seafood is prominent
on the menu, with rollmop herring from
Orkney or salmon from Torridon sitting
alongside land-dwelling options like
venison sausage on bubble and squeak.
A lively bar and summer beer garden, not
to mention those gobsmacking views over
to Skye, are also large plus points.

■ Argyll Hotel

Isle of Iona, Argyll
01681 700334, www.argyllhoteliona.co.uk
Mon–Sun12.30–1.30pm, 7–8pm.
£18
The Argyll Hotel makes fine dining feel all
rather homely and unpretentious with
meat sourced from Mull, seafood from
the waters around the island and organic
vegetables from the restaurant's own
garden. A weekend brunch menu is also
available.

Ord Ban

■ The Boath House Hotel

Auldearn, Nairn
01667 454896, www.boath-house.com
Mon–Sun 12.30–1.30pm, 7pm til late.
Michelin-starred head chef Charles
Lockley is in charge of the cooking at this
Georgian mansion, which has been
operating as a luxurious country house
hotel since a large-scale refurbishment in
the 90s. Those popping in for a
champagne afternoon tea or upmarket
dinner are reminded of Boath House's
smart-casual dress code, and for those
looking to make a night of it, there are
eight opulently decorated rooms upstairs.
Booking is essential.

■ Busta House Hotel

Busta, Shetland
01806 522506, www.bustahouse.com
Mon–Sun noon–2.30pm, 7–9pm.
£35 (set dinner)
At Busta House Hotel, unsurprisingly,
Shetland produce plays a starring role in
the dining experience. Shetland hill lamb,
free-range pork and organic salmon from
Unst, Muckle Roe mussels, halibut from
Bressay, Yell Sound scallops and, most
recently (and a world first), organically
farmed cod from Vidlin. A nod to
neighbouring Orkney is also made with
beef and cheese on a menu heavily
influenced by island life.

■ The Captain's Galley

The Harbour, Scrabster
01847 894999, www.captainsgalley.co.uk
Tue–Sat 7–9pm.
£39.75 (set dinner)
A renovated old Scrabster ice house and
salmon bothy, this restaurant has a quirky
charm – with stone walls and low ceiling
beams. It serves up the freshest of fish
straight from the pier and due to the
unique freshness, sushi and sashimi (raw
fish) are also often on the menu. With
only eight tables, booking is very much
recommended.

Crannag Bistro

Dornoch Road, Bonar Bridge, Sutherland
01863 766111, www.crannag.com
Thu–Sat 6–9pm

Bonar Bridge lies at the confluence of four salmon rivers and the Crannag Bistro acts as a meeting point for various dining styles and inspirations. Run by Ian and Kathy Smith, this bistro serves easy-going food such as Dornoch Firth mussels or a Bonar Burger, all made with local ingredients. Takeaway pizzas and fish and chips are also available across the road at the Smith's other enterprise, the Curry Company, as are ready meals, including a range of 'Comforting Classics' and signature curries.

The Creel

Front Road, St Margaret's Hope, Orkney Islands
01856 831311, www.thecreel.co.uk
Mon–Sun 8–11pm.

The kitchen cupboards are stacked with local produce from the Orkney Islands at this northerly located restaurant with rooms. Strawberries are grown close by and served up with home-made ice cream, or there are Orkney Brewery beers and whiskies from the Scapa and Highland Park distilleries to try out. Vegetarians are advised to tell the chef in advance, and booking is recommended during the summer months.

Creelers

Brodick, Arran
01770 302810, www.creelers.co.uk
Tue–Sat 12.30–2.30pm, 6–9.30pm; Sun 1–3pm, 6–9.30pm. Closed Mon
£26

Edinburgh dwellers may be familiar with the central belt branch of Creelers, just off the High Street, but this bistro on Arran offers the added bonus of an adjoining shop, selling seafood from its smokehouse. An online shop and mail order service is available for those who can't make the trip to Brodick, although the island scenery does make a good excuse for a visit.

The Cross

Tweed Mill Brae, Ardbroilach Road, Kingussie
01540 661166, www.thecross.co.uk
Tue–Sat 7–8.45pm. Closed Sun/Mon.
£47 (set dinner)

This award-winning locations boasts only the finest fresh produce, locally sourced where possible. Organic chicken and eggs come from the Moray coast, Game from local estates, Highland beef, Shetland lamb and prime fish from Scrabster and Fraserburgh, and shellfish from Kyle of Lochalsh. Wild mushrooms are picked locally, with soft fruits coming courtesy of Alvie Estate.

Ee-usk

The North Pier, Oban
01631 565666, www.eeusk.com
Mon–Sun noon–3pm, 6–10pm.
£26

Gaelic speakers may pick up on the clue in the name – which translates as fish. Seafood is definitely the star attraction at this waterside bistro on Oban's North Pier. Taster platters of local mussels, fish cakes and salmon and prawn parcels make for a good diving in point, and there are monkfish, langoustine or scallop main course options to follow. Bag a window table to make the most of those spectacular bay views.

The Glass House Restaurant

Grant Road, Grantown-On-Spey
01479 872980
www.theglasshouse-grantown.co.uk
Wed–Sat noon–1.45pm, Sun 12.30-2pm, Tue–Sat 7–9pm. Closed Mon.
£27

Husband and wife team Karen and Steve Robertson opened this restaurant near Aviemore four years ago, and have been building a steady following ever since. The lunch menu is changed daily, offering two courses for £15 and, over and above the daily a la carte dinner menu, there is a fixed menu on Saturdays, with three courses and coffee for £35. Desserts such as lavender crème brulee or maple and coffee pannacotta round things off beautifully.

Glenelg Inn

01599 522273, www.glenelg-inn.com
Mon–Sun noon–2pm, 6–8.30pm (9pm summer)
£22

There is plenty to keep the foodie satisfied with the kitchen taking full advantage of local produce from langoustines, scallops, local venison and beef to monkfish and hill lamb. The bar boasts a selection of single malts, to accompany Glenelg's well-stocked wine cellar.

The Hamnavoe Restaurant

35 Graham Place, Stromness, Orkney
01856 850606
Apr-Oct Tue–Sun 7–10pm; Nov–Mar Fri/Sat 7–10pm; mid-May–Sep lunch Fri/Sat.
£24

Not the most glamorous, not the best known, of Orkney's eating spots, but one that is held dear by locals and regular visitors. Located up a cobbled street in the port of Stromness, it's a small place with an open fire and some intriguing art on the walls. Chef Neil Taylor keeps his menu and cooking simple but firmly based in local produce – much of it from the sea, though

the famous meat of Orkney is well represented and there's homely fare in the side dishes and puddings.

Hay's Dock

Lerwick, Shetland
01595 741569, www.haysdock.co.uk
Mon–Thu 11am–4pm; Fri/Sat 11am–4pm, 7–11pm; Sun noon–4pm.
£23

Located in the Shetland Museum and Archives, Hay's Dock specialises in using the best local produce, simply cooked and beautifully presented. With panoramic views of Lerwick Harbour, the restaurant offers a memorable dining experience, and is open for daytime snacks throughout the week, and dinner on Friday and Saturday. The bistro-style menu offers a range of modern dishes, all using the finest Shetland and Orkney produce.

Inver Cottage

Strathlachlan, Loch Fyne, Argyll
01369 860537, www.invercottage.co.uk
Wed–Sat 10.30am til late, Sun 10.30am–5pm. Closed Mon/Tue.
£15

Whether it's a cappuccino and some wickedly tempting home baking, a light and tasty lunch dish or something special from the dinner menu, Inver Cottage puts quality local ingredients to use in a fresh and imaginative way. With stunning views across the bay to ruined Old Castle Lachlan (home of the MacLachlan clan for over 1000 years), the dining room offers a relaxed and comfortable atmosphere whatever the occasion. Inver Cottage craft gallery and shop also sells an unusual selection of artwork and gifts.

Inverlochy Castle Hotel

Torlundy, Fort William
01397 702177,
www.inverlochycastlehotel.com
Mon–Sun 12.30–1.30pm, 6–9pm.
£64 (set dinner)

Enjoy Michelin star-winning food in one of the three period decorated dining rooms, showcasing furniture gifted to the castle by the King of Norway. Food is prepared in a modern British style, with Scottish staples such as crab, langoustines and black pudding regularly featuring on the menu. Booking is essential for dinner.

Isle of Eriska Hotel, Spa and Island

Benderloch, by Oban, Argyll
01631 720371, www.eriska-hotel.co.uk
Mon–Sun 7.45–9pm.
£40 (set dinner)

Now holding three AA rosettes, the Isle of Eriska's restaurant has recently been re-designed and completely refurbished and is open to non-residents for the first time.

Ee-usk

With longstanding chef Robert Macpherson in the kitchen, the large dining area enjoys stunnning views, while on the menu you'll be spoilt in terms of fish, with fresh boat deliveries daily.

■ Kilberry Inn
Kilberry, Argyll
01880 770223, www.kilberryinn.com
Tue–Sun 12.15–2.15pm, 6.30–10pm.
Closed Mon.
£20
The white-washed front, red tin roof and distinctive old-fashioned red telephone box are the first things you'll notice about Kilberry Inn but the food will soon grab your attention with simple, locally caught, seafood a forte.

■ Kilmartin House Café
Kilmartin, Argyll
01546 510278, www.kilmartin.org
Mon–Sun 10am–5pm, Thu–Sat 6–9pm.
This is a lovely setting, with hardwood beams, floors and tables and a green oak conservatory. There is also special exhibitions of local artwork. Open throughout the day for home-made snacks and lunches, it also serves evening meals Thursday to Saturday.

■ Kinloch Lodge
Sleat, Isle of Skye
01471 833333, www.kinloch-lodge.co.uk
Mon–Sun noon–2pm, 6.30–9.30pm.
£52 (set dinner)
'Authentic, charming and discreetly luxurious' is how author and cook Claire Macdonald justifiably describes her Highland hotel. The restaurant bears witness to her vision and attention to detail with all the ingredients carefully sourced from local suppliers wherever possible. The kitchen is now in the capable hands of Roux-brothers' trained chef Marcello Tully.

■ Kishorn Seafood Bar
Kishorn, Strathcarron, Ross-shire
01520 733240
www.kishornseafoodbar.co.uk
Mar–Nov Mon–Sat 10am–5pm, Sun noon–5pm; Jul–Sep Mon–Sat 10am–9pm, Sun noon–5pm.
£13
Anyone who still thinks Scottish cuisine is all deep-fried Mars bars and chip butties may be pleasantly surprised by a visit to this simple roadside café. Fresh lobster, home-made Cullen skink and whole dressed crab are among the highlights, and there are snacks of baked potatoes and venison burgers if fishy fare doesn't appeal. Customers can also purchase shellfish to take home: see website for details.

■ Loch Fyne Oyster Bar
Clachan, Cairndow, Argyll
01499 600236, www.lochfyne.com
Sun–Thu 9am–6pm; Fri/Sat 9am–7.30pm.
£24
In a beautiful setting overlooking the head of Loch Fyne, this is the original home of the famous oysters and the first of the restaurants which have now spun off into a nationwide chain. They serve their own shellfish, sustainably farmed on these very shores, and a variety of other locally sourced, high quality produce. You can eat in or, if it's booked up, buy from the well stocked counter and takeaway for a picnic.

■ Lochleven Seafood Café
Onich, by Fort William
01855 821048
www.lochlevenseafoodcafe.co.uk
Mon–Tue 6–8.30pm, Wed–Sun noon–2pm, 6–8.30pm.
£20
Sitting on the shores of Loch Leven, the Seafood Café grew from its roots as a

shellfish distribution centre. Public demand for the seafood arriving at its doors each day led to the creation of a relaxed and informal bistro led by head chef Barry Moran, formerly of Andrew Fairlie's kitchen at Gleneagles. Mussels, oysters, lobster, crab and razor clams make up the majority of the menu, though meat and vegetarian options are available.

■ Ord Ban
Rothiemurchus Centre, Inverdruie, Aviemore
01479 810005, www.ordban.com
Mon–Sun 9.30am–5.30pm, Fri/Sat 6.30–9pm.
£20
In the premises of a former schoolhouse, this smart café offers home baking or burgers, wraps and salads by day, and a cosy but upmarket dinner experience by night. If a full meal isn't needed, the bar serves coffees from an independent Perth roastery, and there is a selection of local malts for those who are partial to a wee dram. Outdoor tables are a summer addition, and kids are welcome year round.

■ Real Food Café
Tyndrum, Highlands
01838 400235 www.therealfoodcafe.com
Mon–Thu 10am–9pm; Fri–Sun 10am–10pm.
£8.50
The Real Food Café transformed an old Little Chef into a fish and chip (and more) stop that buys its produce from local farmers, artisan suppliers and sustainable fish sources. With its open-plan kitchen and eating area, as well as outdoor tables, this has become an important wayside stop for those travelling to and from the Highlands on the A82.

Seafood Cabin
Skipness Estate, Skipness, Tarbert, Argyll
01880 760207
www.theseafoodtrail.com/members/seafo
od-cabin.php
May–Sep Mon–Sun 11am–6pm. Closed
Sat.
Set in a beautiful estate with ducks
wandering around, the Seafood Cabin
invites guests to roam the grounds before
dining. Local produce is key, with tasty
crab always on the menu. The duck eggs
are also put to good use, in its renowned
home-made orange cake.

Seafood Temple
The Pier, Gallanch Road, Oban, Argyll
01631 566000, www.obanseafood.co.uk
£18
Pine wooden beams and rough stone
pillars give the Seafood Temple an instant
air of ramshackle beauty; indeed it is
affectionately referred to by locals as 'The
Shack'. The menu changes daily,
depending on the catch of the day, with
fresh seafood served simply with little
fuss.

Shorehouse Seafood Restaurant
Tarbet, by Scourie, Sutherland
01971 502251
www.seafoodrestaurant-tarbet.co.uk
Apr–May & Sep Mon–Sat noon–7pm;
Jun–Aug Mon–Sat noon–8pm, Jul/Aug
Sun 12–8pm.
Seafood lovers take note: this Tarbet
restaurant comes with the Rick Stein seal
of approval. Serving seafood caught by
local fisherman Julian Pierce and his son
Adam, it's a family-run operation that
Julian took over from his mother, Essie
nearly thirty years ago. Julian's wife,
Jackie, helps run the restaurant, with
daughters Lucy and Rebecca, and local
seals provide entertainment for diners as
they play in the bay below. Bookings must
be made over the phone.

Summer Isles Hotel
Summer Isles House, Achiltibuie
01854 622282
www.summerisleshotel.co.uk
Mon–Sun 12.30–2pm, 8pm prompt.
Nearly everything you eat here is home
produced or locally caught. From
scallops, lobsters, langoustines, crabs,
halibut and turbot to salmon, venison, big
brown eggs and wholesome brown bread
fresh from the oven, chef Chris Firth-
Bernard shows his Michelin star and
Scottish Chef of the Year worth,
producing local, delicious and healthy
food.

Sutor Creek
21 Bank Street, Cromarty
01381 600855, www.sutorcreek.co.uk
Noon–3pm, 6–9pm.
£15
Pizzas are the main draw at this Cromarty
harbourside restaurant on the Black Isle,
and fresh, local seafood makes for some
very memorable toppings. On Saturday
nights the wood fired pizza oven is also
put to good use roasting local meats in
preparation for Sunday lunch the
following day. Wine tastings, book clubs
and themed nights also appear on Sutor
Creek's social calendar. For more details
check its website.

The Three Chimneys
Colbost, Dunvegan, Isle of Skye
01470 511258
www.threechimneys.co.uk
Mon–Sun 6.30–9.30pm; mid-Mar–Oct
12.30–1.45pm.
£40
One of the greatest – and least expected
– success stories of Scotland's dining
scene in the last decade is Shirley and
Eddie Spear's 100 year-old former
crofter's cottage on the far north-west
coast of Skye. An inspiration to many,
Shirley has now stepped back from the
kitchen and Michael Smith now operates
as head chef, presiding over an intimate
but impressive dining experience
intimately connected to Skye's many
excellent food producers, from Sconser
scallops to Lusta shi-itakes. A tasting
menu entitled 'Seven Courses of Skye'
(£70) shows it all.

Tigh an Eilean Hotel
Strathcarron, Shieldaig
01520 755251
www.stevecarter.com/hotel/rest.htm
Mid-Mar to end-Oct 7–8.30pm.
£37.50 (set dinner)
Quite a formal and lavish dining
experience, with sea views and pre-set
tables, covered with obligatory pristine
white tablecloth. The food retains these
high standards, with quality ingredients
and carefully prepared dishes. Over the
winter of 2008, and additional upstairs
restaurant – the Coastal Kitchen – was
added, with a wood-fired pizza oven and
seafood options a speciality. Lunch is
available upstairs only.

The Torridon
Torridon
01445 791242, www.thetorridon.com
Mon–Sun 7–8.45pm.
£45 (set dinner)
One of the Highland's more dynamic
hotels and restaurants in recent years,
with Daniel and Rohaise Day Bristow at
the helm of an operation which combines
upmarket, relaxed luxury in the 19-
bedroom hotel with comfortable Highland
hospitality in the linked inn. In the hotel
dining room, head chef Kevin John

Broome clearly relishes the produce he
sources locally – some of it, in the case of
Loch Torridon langoustines, to be found
just out of the back door of the kitchen.

Two Quail Restaurant
Castle Street, Dornoch
01862 811811, www.2quail.com
Apr–Oct Tue–Sat; Nov–Mar Fri/Sat only.
£35 (set dinner)
With just 12 covers and three bedrooms,
Michael and Kerensa's Dornoch
restaurant is one of the smallest in the
Highlands – booking is, understandably,
recommended. The style of dining is
upmarket with classics from the Scottish
larder cooked using continental styles
and influences from around the world.

Ullinish Country Lodge
Struan, Isle of Skye
01470 572 214, www.theisleofskye.co.uk
Noon–3pm, 7–8.30pm.
£49.50 (set dinner)
Set in an idyllic white lodge, by the sea,
Ullinish Lodge serves contemporary and
interesting combinations of ingredients
that give your taste buds a proper
workout. Sometimes the dishes sound a
little weird, but the fun is in the tasting
and experimenting.

Walled Garden Café and Restaurant
Applecross, Wester Ross
01520 744440
www.eatinthewalledgarden.co.uk
The Potting Shed café and restaurant is
hidden away in the walled gardens of
Applecross House. The owners describe
themselves as a bunch of 'bumpkins'
who take nothing seriously, except when
it comes to food. Fruit and vegetables are
grown right there in the garden and
shellfish is brought back in their boat.
Free range eggs and wild mushrooms are
also locally sourced, making for an
altogether unpretentious, relaxing foodie
treat.

The Whitehouse Restaurant
Lochaline, Morven, Argyll
01967 421777
www.thewhitehouserestaurant.co.uk
Tue–Sat 12.30–2.30pm & from 6.30pm;
Sun 12.30–2.30pm.
£23
Before it sets off on a food-mile heavy
journey to Europe, local seafood is
bought up by this restaurant in the village
of Lochaline, which is a twenty minute
ferry ride from the Isle of Mull. If the
ingredients aren't from the sea, then the
hillsides of Morvern and Mull are the next
obvious source. A relaxed place but one
well worth the detour to get here.
Takeaway picnic lunches can be
arranged.

Scotland's food & drink attractions

It's not just restaurants, pubs and shops where the country's produce plays a central role - there are many attractions, visitor centres and other diversions too. Nell Nelson, the Woman Who Ate Scotland, offers this selected traveller's guide.

Distilleries

More than half of Scotland's malt whisky distilleries are concentrated in Speyside and most offer tours and tastings. One of the first to open its doors to the public, Glenfiddich Distillery offers a free tour of the main parts of this classic 19th-century building, with a tasting and, of course, an opportunity to shop included. As with many other distilleries, it's possible to learn more with an in-depth, two-and-half-hour Connoisseur Tour (£20; booking recommended) which includes a film, a longer tour and a tutored nosing and tasting session.
**Glenfiddich Distillery, Dufftown, Banffshire, 01340 820373
www.glenfiddich.com
Mon–Fri 9.30am–4.30pm.**

Find out about visiting other distilleries at:
www.scotlandwhisky.com;
www.scotch-whisky.org.uk;
www.maltwhiskytrail.com
www.whiskycoast.co.uk

Wineries

All the wine made at the quirky small Cairn o'Mohr Winery is made from berries, flowers and leaves that grow within a 20-mile radius of the farm on the rolling hills and woodland between Dundee and Perth. The assortment of oak leaves, elderberries, elderflowers, strawberries and raspberries are fermented with sugar, water and grape yeast then pressed by hand, filtered and bottled. There is an attractive shop where you can sample, as well as buy, the whole range which is stocked throughout Scotland.
**Cairn o'Mohr Winery, East Inchmichael, Errol, Perthshire
01821 642781
www.cairnomohr.homestead.com
Open: Mon–Fri 9am–6pm, Sat 10am–5pm, Sun 12.30–5pm. Regular tours take place every Thu and Sat in Jul and Aug. You can organise a group booking during the rest of the year**

Other Scottish wineries:
Moniack Castle Highland Wineries, www.moniackcastle. co.uk;
Orkney Wine Company, www.orkneywine.co.uk

Smokeries

The nature of brining and smoking meat, fish and cheese does not lend itself to lots of visitors donning white coats and slipping on plastic shoe covers, so if a smokery does offer tours it is usually from a viewing gallery. Inverawe Smokehouses, 80 miles north of Glasgow, has a visitor centre where

you can find all about the fish-smoking process, including a chance to see the gutting process, the brick smokehouses and the final packing through viewing galleries. There is also a tea room and shop selling the range of smoked goods – trout, salmon, eel, haddock, mackerel, pates and smoked meats, plus free entry to nature trails, picnic areas and a wildlife sanctuary.
Inverawe Smokehouses, Taynuilt, Argyll, 01866 822446, www.smokedsalmon.co.uk

Other good smokeries for visitors include: Marrbury Smokehouse, by Creetown, Wigtown, www.visitmarrbury.co.uk Summer Isles Foods, Achiltibuie, near Ullapool, www.summerislesfoods.com

Mills

In Blair Atholl there's a delightful traditional working water mill dating to the 1590s. Visitors can go on short tour and see the wooden wheel on the side of the restored stone building which is turned by the water gushing off the hills. This in turn drives a huge stone wheel that grinds the flour and oats. After your tour, enjoy the finished baked product in the charming wood-beamed tea room which used to be the original kiln drying floor. You can also buy oatmeal and bread flour should you be inspired to bake your own.
Blair Atholl Water Mill, Ford Road, Blair Atholl, 01796 481321 www.blairathollwatermill.co.uk Apr–Oct Mon–Sun, 10am–5.30pm.

Other mills: Preston Mill in East Linton (www.nts.org.uk) is one of the oldest meal mills in Scotland with its machinery still in working order and offers guided tours.

Fruit Farms

At Cairnie Farm near Cupar there are plenty of strawberries, blackcurrants, gooseberries, tayberries, brambles and cherries for you to pick yourself or buy ready-picked at this 120-acre fruit farm. There's also a Maize Maze – which can grow to 2.4m tall – for kids, along with go-cart tracks, giant straw bales, trampolines, swings and sand boxes. And when you're all exhausted head for the tearoom for freshly baked bread and Cairnie's jam.
Cairnie Farming Co, Cairnie, Cupar, Fife, 01334 655610 www.cairniefruitfarm.co.uk Farm shop May–Aug Mon–Sun 9.30am–6pm; Sep–Oct closed Mon.

Other pick-your-own farms: see panel on page 99.

> A COUPLE OF UNUSUAL PICNIC OPPORTUNITIES

**Vatersay > Outer Hebrides by sea kayak, www.clearwater paddling.com
Mountain picnic > Picnic in a mountain bothy in Perthshire, www.highlandadventure safaris.co.uk**

Dairies

Can't decide whether to have caramel shortbread or oatmeal, honey and whisky ice cream? Opt for Cream o' Galloway's Ice-Cream Experience, a twice-daily hour-long event that allows you to sample organic Fairtrade dairy ice cream, frozen yogurts and frozen smoothies at this family run farm. You can also make your own ice cream with milk, cream and sugar, then add your choice from the ingredients in the Ready Steady Freeze sessions that run mainly during the school holidays. There is also an ice cream parlour, tearoom and shop. To work it all off, check out the outdoor adventure playground, nature trails and cycle tracks.
Cream o' Galloway Dairy Co Ltd, Rainton, Gatehouse of Fleet, Castle Douglas, 01557 814040 www.creamogalloway.co.uk Visitor centre Apr–Oct Mon–Sun 10am–5pm (Jul/Aug 10am–6pm). Booking for all activities recommended.

Other interactive ice cream outlets include: Drummuir Farm, Collin, Dumfries, www.drummuirfarm.co.uk; Stewart Tower Dairy, Stanley, Perthshire, www.stewart-tower.co.uk

Trout farms

At Wellsfield Farm three former reservoirs have been turned into a very successful fish farm offering fly and bait fishing for the competent angler to the absolute beginner – and there is no shortage of fish – the fishery is stocked daily with rainbow, brown, blue, steelheads and tiger trout. If you want

to bag a trout or salmon, lessons are recommended and start at £25 per person, including instruction, fishing permit, rod or reel hire and a free booklet.
Wellsfield Farm Holiday Lodges, Trout Fishery and Equestrian Centre, Stirling Road, Denny, Stirlingshire, 01324 82280, www.wellsfield.co.uk Mon–Sun 8am–dusk (floodlit) all year

Other trout farms include: Rothiemurchus Estate, Inverdruie by Aviemore, www.rothiemurchus.net; Inverawe Smokehouse also offers fish feeding and lessons www.smokedsalmon.co.uk

Around Town

The problem with many foodie tours is that for health and safety reasons it is not possible to allow visitors to get too close and often a viewing gallery and well displayed information boards are the best you'll get. For a more direct approach, there are one or two places in Scotland where day-to-day life converges with a food and drink experience. A particularly good example is the small harbour town of Arbroath in Angus, the home of the Arbroath Smokie. Follow the 'smoke signals' round this picturesque harbour and you'll be able to track down several local smokeries where you can see the golden fish gently cooking in pairs over a smoking pit; even better you can buy and eat the succulent smoked fish straight from the source.

Picnics

There is no end to the picnic potential in Scotland – you are spoilt for choice with so many beaches, views, meandering rivers, woodlands and peaceful hillsides. To create your own – pick a good day, source a good deli or farmer's shop, then all you need is a setting which could be Arthur's Seat in the capital, Glasgow Botanic Gardens to see some open-air Shakespeare, beside the ruins of Linlithgow Palace, a sheltered beach on the west coast such as Arisaig or a burn in the Highlands such as Glen Muick. For something more unusual see the suggestions in the panel above.

■ *Nell Nelson is the presenter of the cycling and eating television programme* The Woman Who Ate Scotland *and is author of nutritional cookbook* Eat Well With Nell *(www.nellnelson.com).*

cooking up a storm

From chocolate fancies to seafood delights, Scotland has a great array of cooking schools where you can get to grip with the basics, hone your culinary skills or try something completely different - and still have fun doing it.

Bellini Cookery School

8b Abercromby Place, Edinburgh,
EH3 6LB, 0131 476 2602
www.bellinirestaurant.co.uk

Nestled in a cosy corner of Edinburgh's New Town is Bellini, a restaurant where a celebration of all things Italian is produced using the best in local, seasonal Scottish produce. The cookery school within the restaurant aims to teach people how to prepare delicious, healthy meals and show them that cooking doesn't always need lots of fuss or time. Classes are informal and hands-on, and can be arranged for groups or individuals. Course topics change all the time, but incorporate the best of Italian cookery, from lasagna to seafood, whether cooking a romantic meal for two or dinner for a big group of friends.

Coco of Bruntsfield

Unit A1, The Midlothian Innovation
Centre, Pentlandfield, Roslin
EH25 9RE, 0131 228 4526
www.cocochocolate.co.uk

Here, all your chocolate dreams are made solid – 70 per cent cocoa solid. Coco of Bruntsfield is what might be described as a little bit specialist. If it's not chocolate, it's not on the curriculum. The day starts with a brief overview of the history of chocolate and the journey from bean to bar,

before getting stuck into making the stuff yourself. Pupils have the chance to master the skills of tempering on marble and with a machine, making organic chocolate bars, molding fruit-filled, broken chocolate, producing rose creams and, just in time for bed, making some hand-flaked organic hot chocolate.

Cook School at Braehead Foods

7 Moorfields North Industrial Park,
Crosshouse, Kilmarnock KA2 0FE
01563 550008
www.braeheadfoods.co.uk

There is something for everyone at Braehead Cook School. Opened in late 2008, it offers classes as diverse as student cookbook, healthy eating, a Scottish red meat masterclass and Great British classics. To get youngsters enjoying and understanding food there is also the Saturday morning cookery school which is open for kids aged 5–12. The Braehead Cook School is run by renowned chef Steven Doherty who has worked, among other places, in the world-famous Le Gavroche.

Edinburgh School of Food and Wine

The Coach House, Newliston,
Edinburgh EH29 9EB, 0131 333 5001
www.esfw.com

Based in an 18th-century coach house within the grounds of Newliston House, ESFW has offered both formal and informal qualifications since 1987. Diplomas and certificate courses will equip the serious cook with the skills to work in a professional kitchen, while one-day courses on subjects such as panic-free entertaining are suitable for complete beginners and the more experienced home cook. If you enjoy consuming food more than producing it then the school's food and wine evenings could be for you. Courses are open to people of all ages and abilities.

Kinloch Cookery Courses by Claire Macdonald

Kinloch Lodge, Sleat, Isle of Skye
IV43 8QY, 01471 833333
www.claire-macdonald.com

Award-winning food writer, broadcaster and author Claire Macdonald offers keen foodies the chance to spend three nights at her home in a peaceful corner of the Isle of Skye. In a relaxed, informal atmosphere, students learn a variety of Claire's wholesome and hearty recipes. Based on Scottish seasonal produce, this cookery school caters for both the novice and the experienced cook and is paced so pupils can enjoy the beauty of Loch na Dal and the surrounding island.

Cooking Mania

75 Main Street, Davidsons Mains,
Edinburgh EH4 5AD, 0131 336 2012
www.cookingmania.co.uk

This is the only purpose-built kids cookery school in Edinburgh, where

vegetables are taken from the garden, eggs from the school's own hens and even salmon is smoked on site. Whether you book a lesson with the man himself or one of the other highly experienced staff, Nairn's Cook School is confident it can inspire both the beginner and the serious foodie.

Cook School by Martin Wishart

14 Bonnington Road, Edinburgh EH6 5JD, 0131 555 6655
www.cookschool.co.uk
Proud holder of a Michelin star since 2001, Martin Wishart has long been at the forefront of Scotland's fine dining scene. Now, keen to impart some of his knowledge and expertise to the public, he has opened his cook school in Edinburgh, just a few minutes' walk from the eponymous restaurant that made his name. He offers a range of courses to suit all levels, from fun evening demonstrations to professional practical classes in small groups, giving novice cooks the chance to build their kitchen confidence and more advanced cooks the space and techniques to perfect their skills.

Peckhams Cookery School

Peckhams Building, 65 Glassford St, Glasgow G1 1UB, 0141 552 5239
www.thecookeryschool.org
Based in the Peckhams building in Glasgow's Merchant City, this school offers over 40 courses on everything from fish and seafood to stocks, sauces and desserts, with themes as diverse as modern Scottish, Indian, pasta, home baking and classic Italian. One-day and evening classes are available, and there are also evening classes on wine and cocktail mixology. Most of the courses are aimed at adult cooks, but longer five-day courses – for both adults and kids – are held in the summertime. It also runs corporate and team-building courses, and hen parties are welcome too.

teaching staff with over 20 years cooking experience between them hope to foster and develop in children positive attitudes towards food. Courses run in school holidays and at weekends, on seasonal themes such as Easter and Christmas. It can also host kids'

birthday parties, which would make for an interesting talking point at school the next day. And if you think it's all just for kids, think again: Cooking Mania runs courses for adults too. Its dads in the kitchen nights have proven particularly popular for men who want to spend more quality time with their children by learning to cook with them.

Nick Nairn Cook School

Port of Menteith, Stirling FK8 3JZ 01877 389900
www.nicknairncookschool.com
More than ten years ago Nick Nairn had the idea to pass on some of his skills and food knowledge. He converted a piggery on his family's farm, and from these humble beginnings Nairn's has grown into one of Scotland's most famous cooking schools. Set in the beautiful scenery of the Trossachs, this is a school where local means really local. Herbs and

Scottish cookery books

A personal selection of inspiring books about Scottish food
and cooking by chef and author Christopher Trotter.

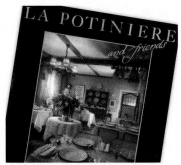

Theodora Fitzgibbon
A Taste of Scotland – Scottish Traditional Food *(Dent 1970)*

Having researched and written three books on Scottish food, there is only one person to whom I generally look if I need the final answer. Theodora Fitzgibbon has done the homework, discarded the inedible, re-written the unreadable and generally opened the door for Scottish food lovers the world over. From collops in the pan to stoved potatoes there are endless, delightful historical insights. My copy is battered and worn with use.

Catherine Brown
A Year in a Scots Kitchen *(Neil Wilson 2002)*

Catherine Brown's concern for tradition and a plea for honest food in her earlier *Broths to Bannocks* makes her perhaps the founder of today's back-to-basics, no-nonsense real food crusade. *A Year in a Scots Kitchen* couples her couthy storytelling style with a sense of seasonal eating and simple, earthy recipes reflecting those great Scots qualities of thrift and respect for the farmer. Recipes come with a brief homily on the associated traditions along with useful alternatives.

David and Hilary Brown
La Potiniere and Friends *(Century 1990)*

La Potinière and Friends is one of my favourite books. While I haven't cooked every recipe, Hilary Brown has influenced much of my cooking. In his own eclectic style, David Brown's story of the restaurant punctuated by Rolling Stones' song titles is a read in itself. It represents to me a time (the 1980s) when Scottish cooking in restaurants came of age – our gods were Betty Allen at the Airds, Gunn Erickson at the Altnaharrie Inn and David Wilson of the Peat Inn.

Clarissa Dickson Wright
The Haggis – a Little History *(Appletree press 1996)*

The smallest but by no means the least of all my choices is Clarissa Dickson Wright's little book on the haggis. In her own inimitable style she takes us from ancient Greece to the deserts of Arabia without once actually pretending that the haggis came from these places. Her point is that the haggis is such humble fair, the chances are that something like it would have been consumed the world over for as long as man has eaten beast.

Olive M Geddes
The Laird's Kitchen – Three Hundred Years of Food in Scotland *(HMSO 1994)*

Olive Geddes is still at the National Library of Scotland and her scholarly book was immensely useful to me. Her reference to much older books that are contained in the library provide a definitive view on Scottish food. Her skill lies in choosing just the right level of information to give you a well rounded picture over three centuries of cooking. There are some delightful plates of original recipes with simple translations by Ms Geddes.

Sue Lawrence
Scottish Kitchen *(Headline 2002)*

Sue Lawrence is a well-known contemporary food writer, winner of the BBC Masterchef award some years ago and holder of a coveted Glenfiddich Award for food writing. She has some great ideas using some of Scotland's fantastic produce and offers traditional recipes with a little twist such as her rediscovery of Robert Carrier's method of cooking salmon in the dishwashing machine. The book transcends the couthy image of Scottish food making, it contemporary and approachable.

Liz Ashworth
**Teach the Bairns to Cook –
Traditional Scottish Recipes
for Beginners
(Scottish Children's Press 1996)**
This book should be compulsory reading
for all primary school teachers. Liz takes
her young charges through Scottish
history from the food angle. From Cullen
skink to bridies, basic techniques are all
there as well as tips on safety and
hygiene in the kitchen. It is without
pretension and unpatronising. Never
mind teaching kids curries and pasta.
This will give them a great grounding.

Claire Macdonald (ed.)
**Scottish Highland Hospitality
(Black and White 2002)**
The Scottish culinary scene is constantly
changing with places coming and going as
fashions fluctuate. Claire Macdonald,
herself no mean cook and writer, has
assembled a varied but long serving bunch
of great cooks and chefs with some
excellent recipes truly reflecting
contemporary Scottish cooking. Names
and places still stand out, such as Becca
Henderson at The Cross and Alan Craigie
at the Creel in Orkney. Not just a cookery
book but a travel book as well.

Nichola Fletcher
**The Ultimate Venison Cookery
(Swanhill Press 2007)**
While many might say that to call a book
'the ultimate' is sheer arrogance, after
30 years of working with venison on her
hill farm above Auchtermuchty, Nichola
Fletcher has a point. Here is every
conceivable way with venison, including
preparation from hanging to boning and
explanations of what to do with all the
cuts including heart, liver and kidney. It's
an encyclopaedia, all infused with
Nichola's natural quirky humour and
sound knowledge.

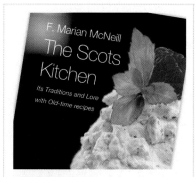

F Marian McNeill
**The Scots Kitchen
(Mercat Press 2006)**
This is a piece of history. Her 1929
introduction rings true today: 'in this age
of standardisation,' she says, rallying
cooks to the kitchen, 'let us follow in the
brave path of our ancestors'. Space
does not allow for specific recipes (look
to her 1946 publication *Recipes from
Scotland*, for those), but everything is
here, interspersed by an entertaining
narrative history. Recommended by
figures such as Derek Cooper, Elizabeth
Luard and Catherine Brown.

Nick Nairn
**New Scottish Cookery
(BBC Books 2004)**
This is Nick Nairn's coming-of-age book;
gone are the elaborate, overworked ideas
from his earlier days (I still cringe when I
look at the cover photo of *Wild Harvest*)
and although there is use of distinctly non-
Scottish ingredients, Nick does encourage
his readers at every turn to buy Scottish
wherever possible. What comes through in
this book is his imagination and deep
understanding of textures, flavours and
colour. Great photos which make you feel
that you could actually cook most of it.

Sue Lawrence
**A Cook's Tour of Scotland
(Headline 2006)**
Any book which has kale as a chapter
heading has to be applauded in my view.
Each chapter has its own little essay
about its subject, often based around
Sue's family history but also including
details of present-day producers, from
Ronnie Eunson's sheep on Shetland to
Richard Barclay's Rannoch venison and
Iain Spink's smokies. Sue's recipes are
imbued with a sense of the past but
always looking ahead, keeping things
fresh, simple and approachable.

Christopher Trotter is a Fife-based chef, hotelier, teacher and food inspector. He is a member of
the Guild of Food Writers and is the author of three books, including The *Scottish Cookery
Book* and *The Scottish Kitchen*. He now runs Momentum, a consultancy based around quality
and innovation.

SCOTTISH FOOD AND DRINK CALENDAR

APRIL

1–31 April

Appetite for Ayrshire and Arran

Various venues across Ayrshire and Arran, 08452 255121, www.ayrshire-arran.com
As if you needed another excuse to escape to the Highlands and Islands, this month-long festival will combine showcase events with a variety of food and drink offers. The idea is to get you enjoying local produce and, with special 'dine and duvet' offers, you can easily stay the weekend and really savour the flavours.

26 April

Celtic Food and Drink Festival

Scottish Crannog Centre, Kenmore, Perthshire, 01887 830583, www.crannog.co.uk
Step back in time with this Celtic food festival, designed to get you eating like a cave-man. The pre-historic cooking demonstrations will include spit-roasting, pit cooking and ancient bread making. All washed down with 'authentic' beverages, of course.

29 April–2 May

Paisley Beer Festival

Paisley Town Hall, Paisley, 0141 887 1010, www.paisleybeerfestival.org.uk
The buzz word at the moment is bespoke beers and this festival gives you the chance to sample fine local brews. It's a four-day event with over 130 cask conditioned ales and ciders to plough through in the time. It will also play host to acclaimed local Kelburn Brewing Company, which recently won the 'Best Bitter in Scotland' award for its Goldihops brew.

MAY

1–10 May

The Spirit of Speyside Whisky Festival

Various venues across Speyside, Aberdeenshire, www.spiritofspeyside.com
This ten-day festival will mark the opening of Homecoming Scotland's Whisky Month and Speyside, with its famous malts, is the ideal location. The jam packed schedule includes distillery open days, whisky trails and a Scottish Serenade musical event. This year will also mark the 10th anniversary of the festival – so expect the celebrations to reach new limits.

3–4 May

A Taste of Dumfries and Galloway

The World Famous Old Blacksmith's Shop Centre, Gretna Green, 01461 338441, www.savourtheflavours.co.uk
Dumfries and Galloway is an area rich in fresh local produce and this is the first of three Taste weekend events celebrating the area. This one is being held in the quirky Old Blacksmith's centre and over the two days, various food and drink producers from Scotland's south west will come together offering samples and items for sale.

10 May

Loch Fyne Food Fair

Loch Fyne Oyster Bar, Clachan, Cairndow, 01499 600264, www.lochfyne.com
This is a lively celebration of local food, with a farmers' market and various food stalls from local producers such as Winston Churchill Venison, Isabella's Preserves, Gillies Fine Foods and Fyne Organics. Drinks are supplied by Fyne Ales, with its bespoke range of bottled beers including 'Avalanche', with its lemony notes and 'Vital Spark', a rich malted beer.

16–17 May

Spirit Of The West

Inveraray Castle, Inveraray, Argyll, 08712 305580, www.spiritofthewest.co.uk
Another special event that ties in with Homecoming Scotland's Whisky month this May. The beautiful Inveraray Castle will use whisky as the excuse for a huge party taking in cookery demonstrations, fashion shows, live music, crafts, golfing and ceilidhs. It will also delve into the historic culture that lies behind each malt.

23–24 May

Traquair Medieval Fayre

Traquair House, Innerleithen, Peebleshire, 01896 830323, www.traquair.co.uk
Let Traquair House take you back to a time of battles, falconry and spit roasts with its Medieval Fayre. The house will be made to resemble what it looked and felt like hundreds of years ago and there will be food tastings as well as Fayre Ale beer, brewed specially for the event by the 18th-century brewery at the house.

The Spirit of Speyside Whisky Festival

23–31 May

Islay Malt and Music Festival

Various venues, Islay,
www.islayfestival.org
The Islay Malt and Music Festival is generally referred to as 'Feis Ile', its Gaelic translation. Founded in 1986 to celebrate the culture of Islay, it is a huge celebration focusing on the island's unique malts. The local distilleries fling open their doors for a week and welcome visitors to tasting events. There is also live music from local bands.

28–31 May

Taste of Edinburgh

Inverleith Park, Edinburgh,
www.channel4.com

This is regarded as an 'upmarket' food festival and they're not just blowing their own trumpet. Set in the lush green landscape of Inverleith Park, this outdoor event celebrates the best that Scottish restaurants, chefs and food and drink suppliers have to offer. Twenty of Edinburgh's top restaurants will showcase food, as well as demonstrations from Michelin-starred Martin Wishart and Andrew Fairlie. The Chef's Theatre is always a must see, as you can learn new tricks and then pass them off as your own.

JUNE

6 June

Taste of Grampian

Thainstone Centre, Inverurie, 01224 649604, www.tasteofgrampian.co.uk
Local Grampian producers put on a spread of fine smoked salmon, prime roast beef, sugary shortbread, ice-cream and creamy fudge (plenty for those with a sweet tooth, then) – all available to sample and buy. The programme also includes music, children's entertainment, cookery competitions and demonstrations from celebrity chefs Jean-Christophe Novelli and Phil Vickery.

Big Tent Festival

25–28 June

Royal Highland Show

The Highland Showgrounds, Ingliston, Edinburgh, 0131 335 5236,
www.royalhighlandshow.org
Top notch food and drink are always one of the highlights of the Royal Highland Show, with over 100 Scottish suppliers attending alongside gourmet suppliers from outside the UK. And as with any self-respecting Highland show, there will be produce competitions – so expect some huge carrots on display.

25–28 June

Flavour of Shetland

Victoria Pier, Lerwick, 01595 744944,
www.flavourofshetland.com
A huge outdoor event showcasing the very best food, drink, music, craft and culture Shetland has to offer. The cookery demonstrations always attract huge crowds, showing onlookers how to create delicious feasts using a range of the islands' produce. This year there will also be a special summer Up Helly Aa fire parade, which will likely add a few sparks to proceedings.

JULY

4-5 July

Tarbert Seafood Festival

Tarbert, Loch Fyne, www.seafood-festival.com
Scotland's seas are home to some of the finest fish in the world, and this annual festival of all things fishy is a celebration of that fact. The scenic harbour of Tarbert on Loch Fyne is the setting for the festivities and will include cookery demonstrations, street entertainment, exhibitions, craft stalls, live music, a carnival parade and, of course, seafood tasting galore.

2–5 July

Scottish Traditional Boat Festival and Food Fayre

Portsoy, Aberdeenshire, 01261 842951,
www.stbf.bizland.com
This festival celebrates the best of boats and food in Portsoy, but, if truth be told, the beautiful old boats take a bit of a backseat to all the food. The Food Fayre features the region's finest fish, meat, confectionary, cheese and drink. And if you wander round this beautiful harbour town you'll be able to sample some of their excellent specialties, including freshly prepared Arbroath smokies.

11–25 July

Classic Malts Cruise

West Coast of Scotland, 01983 296060,
www.worldcruising.com/classicmaltscruise
Sailing and malt whisky go hand-in-hand at this festival, as sailors from around the world gather on the west coast to take in the top distilleries. From Oban to Talisker, the sheltered sites of the distilleries are a welcoming haven and this cruising tour also allows participants to really explore all that is beautiful about the west coast.

25–26 July

Big Tent Festival

Falkland Centre for Stewardship, Falkland Estate, Fife,
www.bigtentfestival.co.uk
This is a food festival with a huge beating heart, in that its purpose is to promote suppliers who are trying to grow, market, process, package and distribute food in a more ecological way. So expect to find the best local, organic and seasonal produce at Scotland's largest eco festival.

AUGUST

2 August

A Taste of Dumfries and Galloway

Cream o' Galloway, Nr Gatehouse of Fleet, Castle Douglas, 01557 814040, www.savourtheflavours.co.uk

The second of a trio of events set around Dumfries and Galloway, and this one is perhaps the pick of the bunch in that it is being held at the Cream o' Galloway dairy, with its lovely green surrounds – not to mention the delicious ice cream that is churned out here. Enjoy samples and get involved with creating new flavours of the sinfully creamy stuff.

August (TBC)

Gourmet Glasgow Food and Drink Festival

Various venues, Glasgow, www.graonline.co.uk

This annual festival always creates a bit of a buzz around Glasgow, when every August the special 'Dine Around' offer gets people out and about enjoying a two course meal at top restaurants for only £15. There are also special events and demonstrations from some of Glasgow's top chefs.

8–9 August

Whisky Fringe

Mansfield Traquair, Edinburgh, www.royalmilewhiskies.com

Scheduled to take place during the Edinburgh Festival and Fringe, an impressive line-up of whisky distillers and bottlers will be offering information and tastings. Amongst them will be Bruichladdich, Morrison Bowmore, Moet Hennessey and Old Pulteney. Visitors are given a nosing glass and a whisky programme and left to explore some 200 whiskies.

Arbroath Sea Fest

8–9 August

Arbroath Sea Fest

Various venues, Arbroath, www.angusahead.com/VisitAngus/VisitEvents/SeaFestIntro.asp

The star attraction of the Arbroath festival is always going to be Arbroath Smokies; haddock hung up and smoked over a traditional hardwood barrel – you don't get fish much fresher or tastier. There will also be row upon row of harbour stalls offering trout, crackling pig and ostrich, as well as a host of other sea-themed fun – such as boat-dressing competitions and fishing displays.

22–23 August

Foodies At The Festival

Various venues, Edinburgh, 0131 226 7766, www.foodiesfestival.com

This is one of the most popular food events at the Edinburgh Festival, offering up food and drink master-classes and giving you the chance to seriously brush up your skills in anything from chocolate to cheese creations. This year there will also be a café seating area and a Chefs Theatre, with demonstrations from top Scottish chefs.

22-24 August

Orkney Beer Festival

Stromness Hotel, Stromness, www.stromnesshotel.com

There's something quite simplistic and comforting about hand-made beer and this festival offers the chance to take in Orkney's picturesque scenery while sampling the islands' very own fine ales. There will also be a wide range of guest beers and cask-conditioned ales on offer.

SEPTEMBER

Every weekend in September

Highland Feast

All across the Highlands and Islands, www.highlandfeast.co.uk

This is a unique event celebrating quality, fresh food that can be sourced locally across the Highlands. It may sound a simple premise, but so many people lose sight of this in their quest, for example, to find strawberries in deep mid winter. In a number of locations, events such as porridge-making and the Nairn Fresh Food Fun Day reinforce the importance of eating local produce.

5–20 September

Scottish Food Fortnight

Various venues across Scotland, 0131 335 0200, www.scottishfoodfortnight.co.uk

Scottish Food Fortnight takes place all across Scotland, from the tip of Shetland right down to the southernmost corner. It offers a varied programme of events that will include farmers' markets, exhibitions and samplings. And keep on the look-out for special food offers.

September (TBC)

Taste of Mull and Iona Food Festival

Iona Village Hall, Isle of Iona and Mull, www.wildisles.co.uk/food

Mull and Iona are two beautiful islands that share a rich cultural heritage and are home to some finely produced food and drink. This festival will offer farm tours, harvest feasts and seafood extravaganzas. Expect to find tasty local cheeses and dinky pots of home-made jam on sale.

4–6 September

Dundee Flower and Food Festival

Camperdown Country Park, Dundee, 01382 433815, www.dundeeflowerandfoodfestival.com
Camperdown is one of the prettiest parks in Dundee, and when you add to that some pretty flower displays and a selection of tasty treats it all becomes rather perfect indeed. Huge marquees will become home to some beautiful floral exhibits, not to mention free cookery demonstrations and samplings.

18–20 September

The Isle of Barra Whisky Galore Festival

01871 810088, www.whiskygalorefestival.com
The first ever Whisky Galore festival will take place this year, named after the famous comedy film that was shot on the Hebridean island 60 years ago. The event will include screenings of the film, re-enactments and visits to film sites – as well as placing heavy emphasis on whisky tasting, naturally.

September (TBC)

Organic Food Festival

Merchant City, Glasgow, 0131 666 2474, www.soilassociationscotland.org
We all know we should buy organic, but it can't do any harm to have a festival dedicated to organic produce – just to give us another gentle reminder. As well

as offering food and drink products that are better for you and the environment, there will also be tips on ethical fashion and household products along with some handy gardening advice.

20 September

East Renfrewshire Food Festival

Eastwood Park, Giffnock, www.dayvisitor.com or www.eastrenfrewshire.gov.uk
This festival takes the time to not only provide you with good quality local ingredients, but also in-depth knowledge on how to get the most from them. Well known chefs from the East Renfrewshire area will be on hand to offer demonstrations, cookery workshops and master-classes.

25-27 September

East Lothian Food and Drink Festival

Various venues across East Lothian, 01620 827282, www.foodanddrinkeastlothian.com
This is a real community-based event, with the stops being pulled out across the board. Restaurants, food outlets and visitor attractions will stage a variety of events and cook up a selection of dishes using only East Lothian produce. Included in the programme will be the renowned Glenkinchie Distillery ceilidh and a Food

and Fun day at the Scottish Seabird Centre.

26 September

Living Food at Cawdor Castle

Cawdor Castle, Nairn, 01667 404401, www.cawdorcastle.com
Held in huge marquees in the stunning grounds of Cawdor Castle, this is a rather superior celebration of organic and sustainable food. There will be over 50 stalls, as well as informative lectures and live music. Acclaimed head chef Charlie Lockley, from 4AA rosette Boath House, will also be providing a cookery demonstration at the event.

OCTOBER

23-25 October

Peebles Food Festival

Various locations across Peebles, 01721 729666, www.peeblesfoodfestival.com
This festival in the tranquil town of Peebles sounds like it might actually be a rather lively affair. There will be a Ready Steady Cook event, with cook-offs taking place in local primary schools, as well as wine and food guessing games. There will also be a large farmers' market selling tasty goods for you to take home with you.

NOVEMBER

1–7 November

Whisky Week

Glasgow, Edinburgh, Perth, Inverness, Dufftown, Fort William and Oban, www.whiskymag.com
This week-long celebration is likely to go down nicely, much like a good whisky should. In celebration of Homecoming and in recognition of one of Scotland's great contributions to the world, Whisky Week comprises a unique series of gala whisky dinners and whisky tastings held across Scotland. Any excuse, eh?

7–8 November

A Taste of Dumfries and Galloway

Kirroughtree Visitor Centre, Newton Stewart, www.savourtheflavours.co.uk
This is the last of a trio of events held throughout the year in Dumfries and Galloway, this one taking place at the Forestry Commission Scotland's pretty Kirroughtree Visitor Centre. Producers from across the south west gather to showcase their treats and share their foodie passions.

Dundee Flower and Food Festival

Farmers' markets around Scotland

Use the table below as a ready reckoner to find out where markets are held on any given weekend of the year, while fuller details about each market, including location, are given in the A to Z list opposite. For general news and updates, go to www.scottishfarmersmarkets.co.uk

FIRST WEEKEND OF EACH MONTH		SECOND WEEKEND OF EACH MONTH		THIRD WEEKEND OF EACH MONTH	
Ayr	Sat 9am-1pm	Ardrishaig	Sat 10am-1pm	Balloch	Sun 10am-4pm
Balloch	Sun 10am-4pm	Balerno	Sat 1am-1pm	Banchory	Sat 11am-3pm
Campbleton	Sat 10am-1pm	Dingwall	Sat 9am-2.30pm	Cupar	Sat 9am-1pm
Crossford	Sat 10am-3pm	Dumfries	Sat 10am-1pm	Dundee	Sat 9am-4pm
Glasgow (Queens Pk)	Sat 10am-2pm	Dunfermline	Sat 9am-1pm	Elgin	Sat 9am-4pm
Huntly	Sat 9am-1pm	Falkirk	Sun 11am-4pm	Glasgow (Queens Pk)	Sat 10am-2pm
Inverness	Sat 8.30am-3pm	Forfar	Sat 9am-1pm	Greenock	Sat 10am-2pm
Langholm	Sat 9am-1pm	Glasgow (Dowanhill)	Sat 10am-2pm	Hamilton	Sat 9am-1pm
Montrose	Sat 9am-1.30pm	Glasgow (Fort)	Sat & Sun 10am-4pm	Kilmarnock	Sat 9am-1pm
Perth	Sat 9am-2pm	Glenkens	Sat 10am-1pm	Tarbert	Sat 10am-1pm
Peterhead	Sat 10am-3pm	Inverurie	Sat 9am-1pm	Torlundy	Sat 10am-5pm
St Andrews	Sat 9am-1pm	Paisley	Sat 9am-1pm		
Stonehaven	Sat 9am-1pm	Peebles	Sat 9.30am-2.30pm		
		Stirling	Sat 9am-2pm		

FOURTH WEEKEND OF EACH MONTH		LAST WEEKEND OF EACH MONTH		EVERY WEEKEND	
Blairgowrie	Sat 9am-2pm	Aberdeen	Sat 9am-5pm	Edinburgh (Castle St)	Sat 9am-2pm
Cairndow	Sat 10am-1pm	Fencebay	Sun 9am-2pm	Ellon	Sat 8am-1pm
Clarkston	Sat 9am-1pm	Haddington	Sat 9am-1pm	Kinross	Sun 9.30am-4pm
Drumlanrig	Sun 11am-3pm	Kirkcaldy	Sat 9am-1pm	Stornoway	Sat 9am-1pm
Glasgow (Dowanhill)	Sat 10am-2pm	Largs	Sat 9am-2pm	Ullapool	Sat 9am-5pm
Kelso	Sat 9.30am-1.30pm	Macduff	Sat 9am-1pm	Wick	Sat 9am-4pm
Linlithgow	Sat 10am-2pm	Tain	Sat 10am-3pm	Wigtown	Sat 10am-4.30pm
Paisley	Sat 9am-1pm				

OTHERS

Applecross First Fri of each month 10am-1pm

Cairngorms Various venues and dates throughout summer

Edinburgh (Ocean Terminal) Second and foruth Fri of each month 10am-4pm

Hawick Third Fri of each month 9am-2pm

Jedburgh First Fri of each month 9.30am-1.30pm

Kirkintilloch Third Wed of each minth 10am-2pm

Lochcarron Last Fri of each month 11am-3pm

Milngavie First Wed of each month 10am-2pm

Oban First and third Thu 10am-3pm

FARMERS' MARKETS IN SCOTLAND: A-Z

■ **Aberdeen** Belmont Street, last Sat of each month, 9am–5pm, www.aberdeencountryfair.co.uk

■ **Applecross** Community Hall, first Fri of each month, 10am–1pm

■ **Ardrishaig** Chalmers Street, second Sat of each month, 10am–1pm

■ **Ayr** River Street, first Sat of each month, 9am–1pm, www.ayreshirefarmermarket.co.uk

■ **Balerno** Main Street, second Sat of each month, 10am–1pm

■ **Balloch** Old Luss Road, first and third Sun of each month, 10am–4pm, www.lochlomond shores.com

■ **Banchory** Scott Skinner's Square, third Sat of each month, 11am–3pm, www.aberdeenshire.gov.uk

■ **Blairgowrie** Community Market, fourth Sat of each month, 9am–2pm, www.strathmoreglens.org

■ **Cairndow** Loch Fyne Oyster Bar, fourth Sat of each month, 10am–1pm

■ **Cairngorms** Various venues and dates throughout Summer months, www.cairngorms-farmers-market.com

■ **Campbleton** Royal Hotel Yard, first Sat of each month, 10am–1pm

■ **Clarkston** Station Car Park, fourth Sat of each month, 9am–1pm, www.lanarkshirefarmersmarket.co.uk

■ **Crossford** Overton Road, first Sat of each month, 10am–3pm, www.lanarkshirefarmersmarket.co.uk

■ **Cupar** Bonnygate Car Park, third Sat of each month, 9am–1pm, www.fifefarmersmarket.co.uk

■ **Dingwall** High Street, second Sat of each month, 9am–2.30pm

■ **Drumlanrig** Drumlanrig Castle, fourth Sun of each month, 11am–3pm

■ **Dumfries** High Street, second Sat of each month, 10am–1pm

■ **Dundee** Reform Street, third Sat of each month, 9am–4pm, www.dundeecity.gov.uk/economicdev/farmersmarket/

■ **Dunfermline** Glen Gates, Bridge Street, second Sat of each month, 9am–1pm, www.fifefarmersmarket.co.uk

■ **Edinburgh** Castle Terrace, every Sat, 9am–2pm, www.edinburghfarmersmarket.co.uk; Ocean Terminal, second and fourth Fri of each month, 10am–4pm, www.oceanterminal.com

■ **Elgin** The Plainstones, third Sat of each month, 9am–4pm, www.aberdeenshire.gov.uk

■ **Ellon** Neil Ross Square, every Sat, 8am–1pm, www.aberdeenshire.gov.uk

■ **Falkirk** High Street, second Sun of each month, 11am–4pm

■ **Fencebay (Fairlie)**, last Sun of each month, 9am–2pm, www.fencebay.co.uk

■ **Forfar** Myre Park, second Sat of each month, 9am–1pm

■ **Glasgow** Dowanhill Primary School, second and fourth Sat of each month, 10am–2pm, www.scottishfarmersmarkets.co.uk; Queens Park, first and third Sat of each month, 10am–2pm; The Fort Shopping Centre, second Sat & Sun of each month, 10am–4pm

■ **Glenkens** Town Hall, St Johns town of Dalry, second Sat of each month, 10am–1pm

■ **Greenock** Clyde Square, third Sat of each month, 10am–2pm

■ **Haddington** Court Street, last Sat of each month, 9am–1pm, www.haddingtonfarmers market.co.uk

■ **Hamilton** New Cross, Quarry Street, third Sat of each month, 9am–1pm, www.lanarkshirefarmersmarket.co.uk

■ **Hawick** Town Centre, third Fri of each month, 9am–2pm, www.bordersfoodnetwork.co.uk/farmers_markets.html

■ **Huntly** Huntly Square, first Sat of each month, 9am–1pm, www.aberdeenshore.gov.uk

■ **Inverness** Eastgate Precinct, first Sat of each month, 8.30am–3pm, www.scottishfarmersmarkets.co.uk

■ **Inverurie** Market Place, second Sat of each month, 9am–1pm, www.aberdeenshire.gov.uk

■ **Jedburgh** Market Place, first Fri of each month, 9.30am–1.30pm, www.bordersfoodnetwork.co.uk/farmers_markets.html

■ **Kelso** Market Square, fourth Sat of each month, 9.30am–1.30pm, www.bordersfoodnetwork.co.uk/farmers_markets.html

■ **Kilmarnock** Foregate Square, third Sat of each month, 9am–1pm, www.ayreshirefarmersmarket.co.uk

■ **Kinross** Kinross Market, every Sun, 9.30am–4pm

■ **Kirkcaldy** Town Square, last Sat of each month, 9am–1pm, www.fifefarmersmarket.co.uk

■ **Kirkintilloch** Regent Centre Car Park, third Wed of each month, 10am–2pm

■ **Langholm** Scott Hay Gallery, first Sat of each month, 9am–1pm

■ **Largs** Vikingar Car Park, last Sat of each month, 9am–2pm

■ **Linlithgow** The Vennel, fourth Sat of each month, 10am–2pm

■ **Lochcarron** Lochcarron Hall, last Fri of each month, 11am–3pm

■ **Macduff** Fishmarket, last Sat of each month, 9am–1pm, www.aberdeenshire.gov.uk

■ **Milgavie** Douglas Street, first Wed of each month, 10am–2pm

■ **Montrose** Town House Car Park, first Sat of each month, 9am–1.30pm, www.gable-enders.co.uk

■ **Oban** Kintaline Farm Benderloch, first and third Thu of each month, 10am–3pm, www.lorn.org.uk

■ **Paisley** County Square, second and fourth Sat of each month, 9am–1pm, www.ayreshirefarmersmarket.co.uk

■ **Peebles** Eastgate Car Park, second Sat of each month, 9.30am–2.30pm, www.bordersfoodnetwork.co.uk/farmers_markets.html

■ **Perth** King Edward Street, first Sat of each month, 9am–2pm, www.perthfarmersmarket.co.uk

■ **Peterhead** Drummers Corner, first Sat of each month, 10am–3pm, www.aberdeenshire.gov.uk

■ **St Andrews** Argyle Street Car Park, first Sat of each month, 9am–1pm, www.fifefarmersmarket.co.uk

■ **Stirling** Maxwell Place, second Sat of each month, 9am–2pm, www.stirlingfarmersmarket.co.uk

■ **Stonehaven** Market Square, first Sat of each month, 9am–1pm, www.aberdeenshire.org.uk

■ **Stornoway** Point Street, every Sat, 9am–1pm, www.stornowayfarmersmarket.co.uk

■ **Tain** Duthac Centre, last Sat of each month, 10am–3pm

■ **Tarbert** Harbour Front, Harris, third Sat of each month, 10am–1pm

■ **Torlundy** Lochaber Rural Complex, Fort William, third Sat of each month, 10am–5pm

■ **Ullapool** Seaforth Car Park, every Sat, 9am–5pm

■ **Wick** Market Square, every Sat, 9am–4pm

■ **Wigtown** Mercat Cross, every Sat, 10am–4.30pm

Best in season

Buying fruit, vegetables and meat in season can make a world of difference to their quality and taste. Produced in conjunction with NFU Scotland's What's on Your Plate campaign, this is a handy at-a-glance guide to what's available and when in Scotland.

	JANUARY	FEBRUARY	MARCH	APRIL	MAY
VEGETABLES	Beetroot, Broccoli, Brussels sprouts, Cabbage, Carrots, Chicory, Leeks, Mushrooms, Parsnips, Potatoes, Turnips	Beetroot, Broccoli, Brussels sprouts, Cabbage, Carrots, Chicory, Leeks, Mushrooms, Potatoes	Broccoli, Brussels sprouts, Cabbage, Carrots, Chicory, Leeks, Mushrooms, Potatoes, Radishes	Cabbage, Carrots, Chicory, Leeks, Mushrooms, Potatoes, Spinach	Asparagus, Broccoli, Cabbage, Carrots, Chicory, Cauliflower, Lettuce, Mushrooms, Potatoes
FRUIT	Forced Rhubarb, Pears			Rhubarb	Rhubarb, Strawberries
FISH (* indicates best months for quality)	Langoustine*, Cod, Haddock, Monkfish*, Whiting*, Lobster*, Native Oyster	Langoustine, Cod, Crab, Haddock*, Monkfish*, Whiting*, Lobster*, Hake, Native Oyster	Langoustine, Cod, Crab*, Haddock*, Monkfish*, Whiting*, Scallops, Lobster*, Hake, Native Oyster	Langoustine, Cod, Crab*, Haddock*, Monkfish*, Whiting*, Scallops, Lobster*, Hake, Native Oyster	Langoustine, Cod, Crab*, Haddock, Mackerel*, Monkfish, Scallops, Lobster, Herring, Hake
MEAT	Beef, Lamb, Pork, Chicken	Beef, Lamb, Pork, Chicken	Beef, Lamb, Pork, Chicken	Beef, Lamb, Pork, Chicken	Beef, Lamb, Pork, Chicken
GAME	Red deer, Pheasant, Partridge, Duck, Goose, Woodcock, Common Snipe, Coot, Golden Plover, Hare	Red deer (hinds to 15 Feb), Hare			
HERBS			Mint, Parsley, Sorrel, Watercress, Wild Garlic	Rosemary, Watercress, Wild garlic	Mint, Parsley, Watercress, Garlic
OTHER	Milk, Eggs, Oats and other grains	Milk, Eggs, Oats and other grains	Milk, Eggs, Oats and other grains	Milk, Eggs, Oats and other grains	Milk, Eggs, Oats and other grains

It is legal to shoot a variety of birds, wildfowl and mammals in Scotland, but for many of these species, there is also a closed season during which time they must be left undisturbed to breed and disperse. As such, small game is generally unavailable during the spring and summer months.

compiled by

NFUScotland

JUNE	JULY	AUGUST	SEPTEMBER	OCTOBER	NOVEMBER	DECEMBER
Asparagus, Broad beans, Cauliflower, Cabbage, Carrots, Celery, Courgettes, Lettuce, Mushrooms, Onions, Potatoes, Runner beans	Beetroot, Broad beans, Broccoli, Cauliflower, Cabbage, Carrots, Celery, Courgettes, French beans, Lettuce, Mushrooms, Onions, Peas (shell), Peas (sugar snap), Potatoes, Runner beans, Shallots	Aubergines, Beetroot, Broccoli, Cauliflower, Cabbage, Carrots, Celery, Courgettes, French beans, Lettuce, Mushrooms, Onions, Peas (shell), Peas (sugar snap), Potatoes, Runner beans, Shallots	Beetroot, Broccoli, Cabbage, Carrots, Cauliflower, Celery, Chicory, French beans, Leeks, Lettuce, Mushrooms, Onions, Parsnips, Potatoes, Shallots, Summer squash, Turnips	Beetroot, Broccoli, Brussels sprouts, Cabbage, Carrots, Cauliflower, Celeriac, Celery, Chicory, Courgettes, Kale, Lettuce, Mushrooms, Onions, Parsnips, Potatoes	Beetroot, Brussels sprouts, Cabbage, Carrots, Celery, Chestnuts, Chicory, Leeks, Mushrooms, Parsnips, Potatoes, Pumpkin, Squash	Beetroot, Brussels sprouts, Cabbage, Carrots, Chicory, Leeks, Mushrooms, Onions, Parsnips, Potatoes, Squash, Turnips
Gooseberries, Raspberries, Strawberries, Tayberries, Rhubarb, Redcurrants	Blackcurrants, Gooseberries, Loganberries, Raspberries, Redcurrants, Strawberries, Tomatoes, Rhubarb, Blueberries	Blackberries, Blueberries, Gooseberries, Raspberries, Strawberries	Blackberries, Blueberries, Damsons, Plums, Pears, Raspberries, Strawberries	Apples, Elderberries Pears	Apples, Pears	Apples, Pears
Langoustine, Cod, Crab*, Haddock, Mackerel*, Monkfish, Scallops, Lobster, Herring*, Hake, Squid, Octopus	Langoustine, Cod*, Crab, Haddock, Mackerel*, Monkfish, Scallops, Lobster, Herring*, Hake, Squid, Octopus	Langoustine, Cod*, Crab, Haddock*, Mackerel*, Monkfish, Whiting, Scallops, Lobster, Herring, Hake, Squid, Octopus	Langoustine, Cod*, Crab*, Haddock*, Mackerel*, Monkfish, Whiting, Scallops*, Lobster, Herring, Hake, Native Oyster	Langoustine*, Cod*, Crab*, Haddock*, Mackerel, Monkfish*, Whiting, Scallops*, Lobster, Hake, Native Oyster	Langoustine*, Cod*, Crab*, Haddock, Monkfish*, Whiting*, Scallops, Lobster*, Hake, Native Oyster	Langoustine*, Cod, Crab*, Haddock, Monkfish*, Whiting*, Lobster*, Native Oyster
Beef, Lamb, Pork, Chicken	Beef, Lamb, Pork, Chicken	Beef, Lamb, Pork, Chicken	Beef, Lamb, Pork, Chicken	Beef, Lamb, Pork, Chicken	Beef, Lamb, Pork, Chicken	Beef, Lamb, Pork, Chicken
	Red deer (stags from 1 July)	Red deer, Grouse (from 12 Aug), Ptarmigan (from 12 Aug), Blackgame (from 20 Aug), Common Snipe (from 12 Aug), Hare	Red deer, Partridge, Grouse, Duck, Goose, Woodcock, Ptarmigan, Blackgame, Common Snipe, Coot, Golden Plover, Hare	Red deer (stags to 20 Oct; hinds from 21 Oct), Pheasant, Duck, Partridge, Grouse, Goose, Woodcock, Ptarmigan, Blackgame, Common Snipe, Coot, Golden Plover, Hare	Red deer, Pheasant, Partridge, Grouse, Duck, Goose, Woodcock, Ptarmigan, Blackgame, Common Snipe, Coot, Golden Plover, Hare	Red deer, Pheasant, Duck, Partridge, Grouse (to 10 Dec), Goose, Woodcock, Ptarmigan (to 10 Dec), Blackgame (to 10 Dec), Snipe, Coot, Golden Plover, Hare
Parsley, Watercress, Garlic	Fennel, Garlic, Sage, Watercress, Parsley	Basil, Garlic, Watercress, Parsley	Basil, Garlic, Watercress, Parsley	Parsley		
Milk, Eggs, Oats and other grains	Milk, Eggs, Oats and other grains	Milk, Eggs, Oats and other grains	Milk, Eggs, Oats and other grains	Milk, Eggs, Oats and other grains	Milk, Eggs, Oats and other grains	Milk, Eggs, Oats and other grains

Pigeon and rabbit are both technically regarded as pest species, so can be shot all year round. However, size and quality can be variable during the breeding season, and it is better to wait till autumn to take advantage of a well-fed crop of birds and bunnies. See: www.basc.org.uk/content/shootingseasons

Stamps of approval

There are many labels and terms applied to food in Scotland. Some are self-explanatory but a few common ones are significant enough to warrant some further information. The regulations covering labels such as these can be complex, but below is an brief interpretation of what's on the labels, and we've also listed websites where you can find out more.

ONLY ON SCOTTISH PRODUCE

LABEL/MARKS THAT YOU MAY SEE ON SCOTTISH FOOD AND DRINK IN SCOTLAND	APPLIES TO	EXPLANATION
Scotch Beef; Scotch Lamb	Beef, Lamb	It has to be born, reared and slaughtered in Scotland and it also has to be farm assured and have associated feed, transport, auction and abattoir assurance. Scotch Beef & Scotch Lamb are terms now 'owned' and policed by Quality Meat Scotland. The terms are approved and defined under a 'PGI' (Protected Geographical Indication, a European regional speciality food scheme) and it's all traceable back to farm. **Websites:** www.qmscotland.co.uk; www.scotchbeefandlamb.com; www.defra.gov.uk/ffodrin/foodname/pfn/products/documents/scotchbeef.pdf
Specially Selected Pork	Pork	The same as for Scotch Beef & Lamb but not covered by a PGI **Websites:** www.qmscotland.co.uk
Scottish Quality Wild Venison	Venison (wild, not farmed)	Wild venison from estates assessed annually against criteria for stalking, carcase handling and hygiene in larders **Websites:** www.sfqc.co.uk/processing/scottish_quality_wild_venison_sqwv
Scottish Beef, Lamb, Pork, Venison & any other meat or meat product	Meat	It's much less controlled than 'Scotch' with only occasional checks at point of sale by Trading Standards Officers (unless otherwise stated).
Orkney Beef, Orkney Lamb, Shetland Lamb	Beef, Lamb	Beef and lamb from these specific islands, recognised as distinctive because of the use of traditional breeds and the island's unique topography, geology and climate – defined and protected by PDO's (Protected Designation of Origin). Not necessarily farm assured or organic (see opposite). **Websites:** www.defra.gov.uk/foodrin/foodname/pfn/products/registered.htm#6
Quality Approved Scottish Salmon (Label Rouge in France) **& Quality Approved Shetland Salmon**	Farmed salmon	It's farm assured (see opposite) and processor inspected. Product is traceable & Scottish Farmed Salmon is PGI approved. **Websites:** www.scottishsalmon.co.uk; www.shetlandaquaculture.com; www.defra.gov.uk/foodrin/foodname/pfn/products/registered/salmon_scot.htm
Arbroath Smokies	Smoked haddock	Golden brown, cured and smoked haddock, attributed to the small fishing village of Auchmithie, near Arbroath, now defined and protected by a PGI. **Websites:** www.defra.gov.uk/foodrin/foodname/pfn/products/registered/arbsm.htm

ON SCOTTISH BUT ALSO ON FOOD & DRINK FROM OUTSIDE SCOTLAND

LABEL/MARKS THAT YOU MAY SEE ON SCOTTISH FOOD AND DRINK IN SCOTLAND	APPLIES TO	EXPLANATION
Farm Assured	Beef, lamb, pork, bacon, chicken, vegetables, fruit, milk, cereals, farmed salmon and trout	Farms are assessed (usually annually) by an independent 'certification body' to check animal welfare; staff competence; building safety/suitability; avoidance of environmental damage and safe use of medicines, pesticides and herbicides. It is difficult to sell to supermarkets without being farm assured. Most Farm Assured farms in Scotland will buy from and sell to other parts of what is called the 'assurance chain' (inspected feed, transport, auctions, abattoirs) so that product can eventually be sold as 'Scotch' (in the case of meat) or under some other brand that requires farm assurance as a pre-requisite. However, it is distinctly possible that much of what you buy may be farm assured but not labelled as such: labelling is largely up to the individual retailer. **Websites:** www.qmscotland.co.uk; www.sfqc.co.uk; www.ndfas.org.uk; www.assuredproduce.co.uk; www.assuredchicken.org.uk
Organic	Most food & drink except for anything 'wild' e.g. venison, fish (from non farmed sources)	Europe sets minimum organic standards for everything produced as organic in the EU. Organic certification bodies, in turn, set their own standards (substantial documents) which have to be approved by UK Government. There are 9 approved UK certification bodies, by far the biggest of which (in terms of farm numbers and land area covered) in Scotland is SOPA (look out for UK3 on packaging) and by far the best known (in terms of media coverage) is the Soil Association (UK5). However by no means all food labelled by a UK organic certification body has come from the UK. The certification body label is applied at the place of packing or processing and so could be different from the certification body that inspected the origin of the product. Around 700 Scottish farms and crofts are officially certified organic. **Websites:** www.defra.gov.uk/farm/organic; www.sopa.org.uk; www.soilassociationscotland.org
LEAF marque	Fruit and vegetables	An additional independent check, over and above Farm Assurance, on environmental care – such as crop rotation, wildlife habitats and soil management. Bear in mind that farms can be LEAF members (which involves self certification) but can choose not to participate in LEAF marque independent inspections. In other words not all LEAF farms qualify for the LEAF marque **Websites:** www.leafuk.org
Freedom Foods	Beef, lamb, pork, bacon, chicken, turkey, duck, eggs, milk and farmed fish	This is an RSPCA (Royal Society for Prevention of Cruelty to Animals) Scheme which uses certification bodies to independently inspect farms to RSPCA standards – so you can be pretty sure animal welfare is a fairly high priority. They (RSPCA) call it 'farm assurance with a difference' ie with a welfare accent. Interestingly it's not necessarily all 'free range' or 'outdoors'. Note also that in the 90s the Scottish SPCA (the Scottish equivalent of the RSPCA) decided not to establish its own scheme but to shadow a percentage of standard farm assurance inspections instead. **Websites:** www.rspca.org.uk; www.scottishspca.org
Lion Quality Mark	Eggs	This is the little red lion printed on lots of eggs (alongside the best before date) to say that it has all been produced safely and hygienically and that the eggs come from hens which have been vaccinated against salmonella. It's a British Scheme and is policed by an independent certification body, through the British Egg Industry Council (BEIC). The mark is on lots of eggs, including many Scottish ones. **Websites:** www.britegg.co.uk
Red Tractor	Beef, lamb, pork, bacon, vegetables, fruit, milk, cereals, farmed salmon or trout	Farm assured (as above) but British – possibly but not necessarily from Scotland. Strictly speaking food and drink from other parts of Europe could show the little red tractor too (if farm assured to the same or equivalent standards) but it would have to be shown alongside their own national flag. **Websites:** www.redtractor.org.uk

the Indexes

BY NAME: All shops, places to eat, producers and food personalities included in *The Larder*
BY LOCATION: (page 158-160): All shops and places to eat listed by region then town

BY NAME